Lighthouse of Tragedy

The Story of Bustard Head Lighthouse
Queensland's First Coast Light

by
STUART BUCHANAN

Best wishes from:
Stuart Buchanan

CORAL COAST PUBLICATIONS

By the same author:

THE LIGHTHOUSE KEEPERS

THE VIEW FROM PLUTO

LIGHT OF THEIR LIVES

TAXI

First published 1999 by Coral Coast Publications,
P.O. Box 90, Samford, Queensland 4520, Australia.
Telephone (07) 3289 1827

Reprinted 2000, 2004, 2006, 2009

National Library of Australia Card Number and
ISBN 0 9586433 0 X

Wholly produced in Australia.
Typeset and Designed by Sunset Digital Pty Ltd, Brisbane.
Printed by Fergies, Brisbane.

ACKNOWLEDGMENTS

First and foremost I thank my wife Shirley for her editorial work on *Lighthouse of Tragedy*; also for her tireless and enthusiastic research regarding Bustard Head lighthouse, which yielded results beyond our wildest expectations.

I also express my gratitude to the Lighthouse Historical Society of Queensland for the historical data and photographs they supplied and for their involvement in the preparation of this book.

Four people deserve special mention — Neville Murphy, Philip Shanahan, James 'Lofty' Hayes and Kevin Urban — who allowed me to include extracts from their personal writings about Bustard Head. Their stories are living history from an era that will never return.

Information on The "Turkey" Station Tragedy in Chapter 6 was provided by Desmond Gibney from his thoroughly researched manuscript of the same name. Desmond generously allowed me to precis his work for inclusion in this book. Permission was given by Tim Welch to reproduce his sketch, "Seconds before Tragedy", in Chapter 6.

Cheryl Nugent kindly permitted me to reproduce her delightful painting "Bustard Head Lightstation — After the Fire". As well, Cheryl provided many photographs taken by her father Allan Nugent while he was Lightkeeper at Bustard Head during 1934–35.

Most of our research was done at the National Archives of Australia, Brisbane, whose staff patiently guided us through the 'system'. In particular I thank Gregory Cope, Cheryl McNamara, Kay Campbell, Margaret Daly, Peter Capwell and Doug Potts.

Other major research was done at the Queensland State Archives, John Oxley Library, State Library of Queensland and Mitchell Library of New South Wales.

The Australian Maritime Safety Authority (AMSA) in Brisbane and Canberra were very helpful. My thanks go to John Sugarman, Jack Duvoisin, Dennis Conroy and Mark Oliver from the Brisbane office, and David Gray and Beth Tyerman from Canberra.

Important information was provided by: The United Kingdom Hydrographic Office, Taunton, Somerset; Mark Bolger from the Royal Australian Navy

Hydrographics, New South Wales; Ian Whillas from the Bureau of Meteorology, Brisbane; John Thorburn, B.A.; and Bill Kitson from the Surveying Museum, Department of Natural Resources, Brisbane, who supplied information on Bustard Head Astronomical Station.

Thanks also to the Department of Environment and Heritage, Brisbane; The Queensland Police Museum, Brisbane; Coroner's Section, Department of Justice, Brisbane; Queensland Maritime Museum, Brisbane; Miriam Vale Shire Council; Councillor Josie Meng; and Val Growcott, President of the Miriam Vale Historical Society.

Many people generously provided photographs and information. They are: Neville Murphy, Philip and Betty Shanahan, Win Fox, Jeannie and James 'Lofty' Hayes, Kevin and Irene Urban, Nell Thwaite, Audrey Anderson, John Christensen, Des and Betty Mergard, Malcolm Bradley, Norma Mills, Mavis Ord, Dorothy Buhl, Mavis Rowe, Aileen Cochrane, Jill West, Grace Dalziel, Joan Hutchison, Ron and Betty Kelley, Jack and Barbara 'Babs' Atherton, Rochelle Starr-Thomas, Roger Eason, Ben Betts, Jim Sue, Lyn Day, Kathy Mian, Boyd Rich, Sean Ulm, Bob Todkill, Lew Dickson, Malcolm Muir, Arnold Williams, Keith and Barbara Foster, Don Swanson, Mrs Birrell, Elma Leach, Jean Wright, Ian Oliver, and Nev Loxton.

CONTENTS

Location Maps
1 Discovery 1
2 A Mammoth Task 12
3 Keepers of the Light 32
4 A Cloud of Gloom 46
5 A Time of Learning 55
6 The "Turkey" Station Tragedy 76
7 Parting of the Ways 95
8 Fire! 105
9 A Southern Visitor 115
10 War and Peace 125
11 Rocks of Wrath 144
12 Fight for Life 158
13 The Pitiless Sea 170
14 Beginning of the End 190
15 What Now? 199
Head Lightkeepers of Bustard Head Lighthouse 1868–1986 209
Lightkeepers of Bustard Head Lighthouse 1868–1986 211
Staff List Bustard Head Lighthouse 1868–1986 213
Schoolteachers Bustard Head Provisional School 1882–1917 219
Endnotes 221
Appendices 230

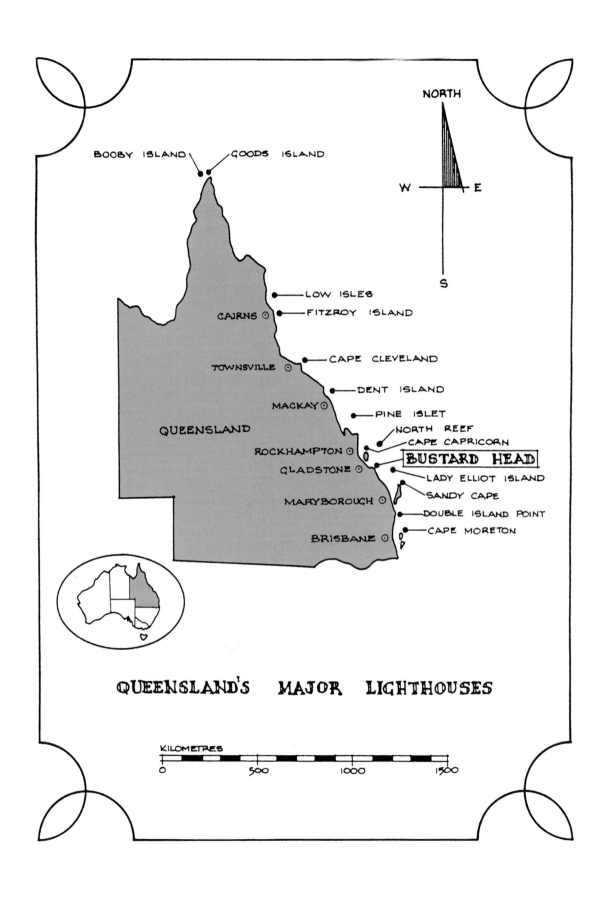

QUEENSLAND'S MAJOR LIGHTHOUSES

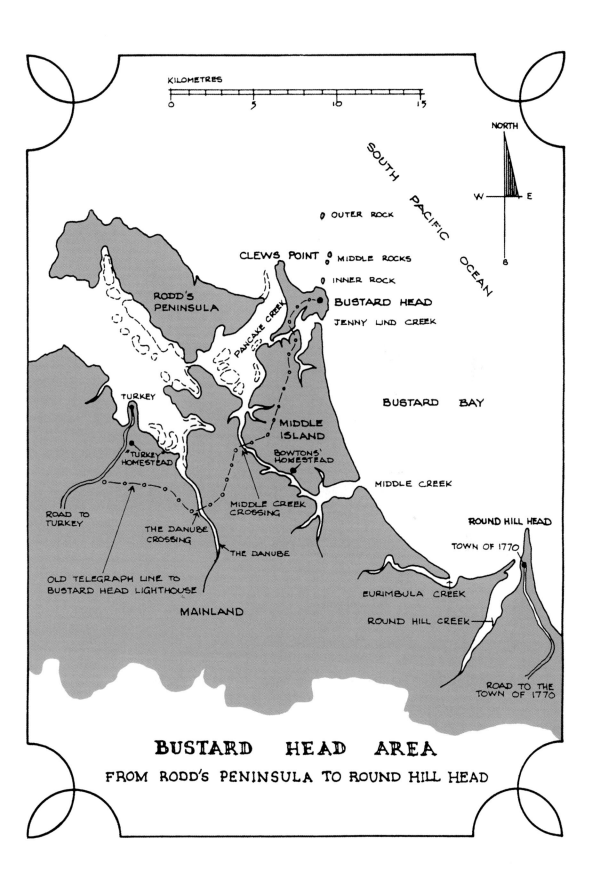

BUSTARD HEAD AREA
FROM RODD'S PENINSULA TO ROUND HILL HEAD

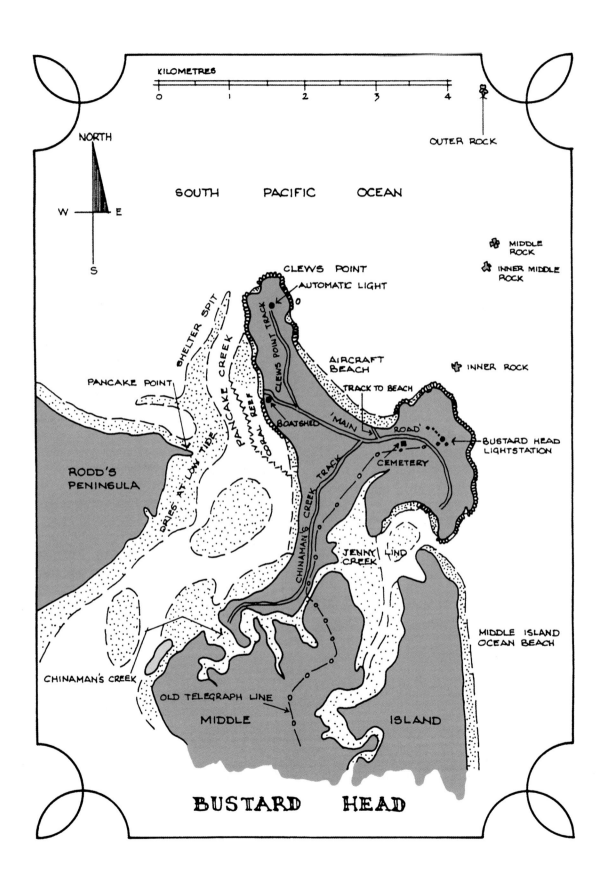

KILOMETRES

0   1   2   3   4

OUTER ROCK

NORTH

W   E

S

SOUTH   PACIFIC   OCEAN

MIDDLE ROCK

INNER MIDDLE ROCK

CLEWS POINT
AUTOMATIC LIGHT

INNER ROCK

SHELTER SPIT

PANCAKE CREEK

AIRCRAFT BEACH

PANCAKE POINT

TRACK TO BEACH

CLEWS POINT TRACK

CORAL REEF

BOATSHED

'MAIN

ROAD'

BUSTARD HEAD LIGHTSTATION

DRIES AT LOW TIDE

CHINAMAN'S CREEK TRACK

CEMETERY

RODD'S PENINSULA

JENNY LIND CREEK

MIDDLE ISLAND OCEAN BEACH

CHINAMAN'S CREEK

OLD TELEGRAPH LINE

MIDDLE   ISLAND

BUSTARD   HEAD

Chapter 1

DISCOVERY

Shrouded in darkness, the headland at the northern end of Bustard Bay appeared little more than a silhouette. But as the crisp clear dawn gave way to early morning sunshine, the greenness of the grassy slopes and pandanus palms intensified, contrasting dramatically with the russet cliffs and cobalt blue sea. However, Lieutenant James Cook on board the barque *Endeavour* was giving little thought to the beauty of the landscape, for dead ahead he saw rocks and white-capped breakers stretching well out from the headland. Cook recorded in his log:

> *At 4 in the AM we weighd [sic] with a gentle breeze at South and made sail out of the Bay. In standing out our soundings were from 5 to 15 fm, when in this last depth we were abreast of the north point and being day light we discoverd [sic] breakers stretching out from it about NNE 2 or 3 miles. At the outermost part of them is a rock just above water, in passing these rocks at the distance of half a mile we had from 15 to 20 fathom, being past them we hauld [sic] along shore WNW for the farthest land we had in sight.[1]*

It is a matter of conjecture whether earlier seafarers had visited these waters, but it is indisputable that those few words in Cook's log recorded for the first time the headland where Bustard Head lighthouse now stands and the dangerous rocks over which the light's powerful beams sweep each night to warn mariners.

Over the next 200 years this isolated section of coastline remained relatively unchanged. However, remote as it was, Bustard Head became the setting for an uncanny chain of events — shipwrecks, murder, abduction, suicide and drownings — all inextricably linked to the lighthouse and those who lived there, appropriately earning it the title "lighthouse of tragedy".

But back to Cook. On 22 May 1770, two days before he sighted the rocks off Bustard Head, Cook, on board the barque *Endeavour* during his voyage of discovery along Australia's east coast, came to a large open bay. Through the glasses he observed the land was covered with "palm-nut-trees" and saw two male Aborigines walking along the shore "who did not condescend to take the least notice of us". Wanting to shelter overnight in the bay, Cook tacked *Endeavour* inshore before anchoring at about 8.00 p.m.

Next morning, Cook, accompanied by Joseph Banks, Dr Solander and a party of men, went ashore, landing on Australian soil for the first time since leaving Botany Bay. They followed a channel into a large lagoon, now known as Round Hill Creek, found fresh water and collected many samples of flora. They also hunted their next evening's meal:

> *Upon the shore we saw a species of the bustard, one of which we shot, it was as large as a turkey, and weighed 17 pounds and an half. We all agreed that this was the best bird we had eaten since we left England; and in honour of it we called this inlet Bustard Bay.[2]*

Cook also named the northern and southern points of Bustard Bay — North Head and South Head, which were later to become Bustard Head and Round Hill Head respectively.

Lured by columns of smoke rising from the bush, Cook and his men ventured inland. They found an Aboriginal campsite with a few fires burning and some shells and fishbones lying nearby, but not a soul in sight. On returning to the ship, Cook was told that while they had been in the "woods", about twenty natives came down to the beach, looked at *Endeavour* for a while, then went away. Early next morning *Endeavour* weighed anchor, passed Bustard Head and its outlying rocks, and continued northwards, narrowly escaping disaster on the "insane labyrinth" of coral reefs, before reaching England the following year.

Cook's discovery of Australia's east coast unwittingly solved Britain's problem of what to do with her ever-increasing population of criminals sentenced to exile. The American War of Independence in 1775 resulted in the end of American colonies being used as dumping grounds for Britain's convicts. Soon, the British jails were overflowing. And so, on 26 January 1788 the First Fleet, comprising of eleven ships and carrying 717 convicts, arrived at Port Jackson to begin white settlement in Australia.

As private settlers and freed convicts took up land, exploration of the new colony followed. Little extensive coastal exploration was done to the north of Port Jackson until 1802, when Matthew Flinders aboard *Investigator* and in company with *Lady Nelson*, set out to circumnavigate Australia. On Monday 2 August 1802 Flinders arrived at Bustard Bay:

> *… we came to the south head of Bustard Bay; and the night being then at hand, we ran in and anchored on a sandy bottom, in 4½ fathoms, nearly in the same spot where the* Endeavour *had lain thirty-two years before.[3]*

Next day, Flinders had a close, but unintentional, look at the rocks off Bustard Head:

> *At daylight we proceeded along the coast; but the wind being very light, were no more than abreast of the north head of Bustard Bay at noon; and the ship being drifted by the tide toward some rocks lying off the head, a boat went to sound amongst them for a passage; in the mean time an air sprung up at north; and having got the ship's head to the eastward, we stretched off from the rocks. This north head lies in latitude 24° 0′, as laid down by Captain Cook, and bears from the south head N. 44° W., twelve miles; it is moderately high, and behind it is a mass of hummocky, barren hills, which extend far to the westward. A reef lies out as far as two miles from the north head; but within the outer rock above water our boat had 14 fathoms, and there was room for a ship to pass. Not being able to weather the reef before dark, we worked to windward during the night; bearing down frequently to the* Lady Nelson, *to prevent separation.*[4]

Thirty miles north-west of Bustard Head, Flinders sighted an opening between what are now known as Facing and Curtis Islands. A party of men landed on the southern end of Curtis Island:

> *The naturalist and his companions landed at the west side of the entrance, where some Indians had assembled to look at the ship; but they retired on the approach of our gentlemen, and afterwards taking the advantage of a hillock, began to throw stones at the party; nor would they desist until two or three muskets were fired over their heads, when they disappeared.*[5]

Realising that a large harbour existed behind Facing Island, Flinders spent four days exploring and sounding the area, naming the waterway Port Curtis. Fifty-two years later, Port Curtis was to become the harbour for Gladstone, a town whose existence would be greatly responsible for the establishment of Bustard Head lighthouse.

Sydney was still a shantytown when Lachlan Macquarie was appointed Governor of New South Wales in 1810. A practical as well as a visionary man, he instigated a program of fine quality public building works. In 1814 convict architect Francis Greenway, sentenced for forging an endorsement on a contract, arrived in the Colony. Macquarie put the designer to work, and was so impressed with his ability, appointed Greenway Civil Architect in 1816.

One of the buildings Greenway designed was the Macquarie lighthouse on South Head at the entrance to Port Jackson. Although a signal station had been built on South Head in 1790, and four years later a wood-fired light in an iron basket mounted on a tripod erected nearby, the Macquarie lighthouse, first lit

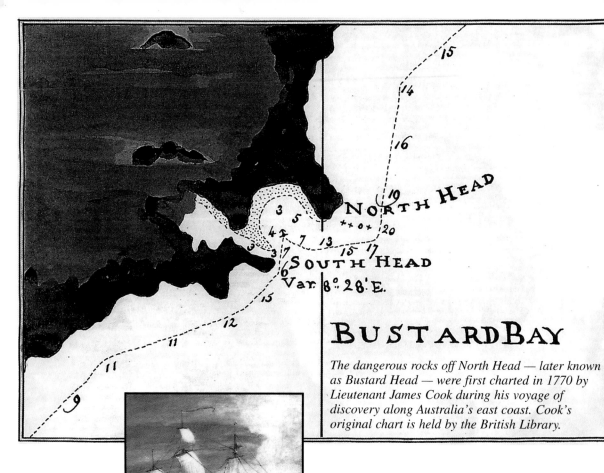

NORTH HEAD

SOUTH HEAD

Var. 8° 28' E.

BUSTARD BAY

The dangerous rocks off North Head — later known as Bustard Head — were first charted in 1770 by Lieutenant James Cook during his voyage of discovery along Australia's east coast. Cook's original chart is held by the British Library.

The barque Endeavour.

Bustard (Wild Turkey).

The supreme navigator, Captain James Cook.

"We all agreed that this was the best bird we had eaten since we left England; and in honour of it we called this inlet Bustard Bay."

on 30 November 1818, was Australia's first proper lighthouse. The lighting of the coastline had begun.

The need for additional garrison outposts and places to segregate the worst of the convicts resulted in Surveyor-General John Oxley's expedition northwards in 1823. Sailing in the *Mermaid*, Oxley investigated Moreton Bay and Port Curtis. Unimpressed with Port Curtis he returned south to Moreton Bay, discovering and naming the Brisbane River. Oxley's recommendation of a penal settlement at Moreton Bay was accepted, and so Brisbane Town was born.

As Brisbane developed and free settlement was eventually introduced, the amount of shipping traffic to the port increased rapidly. Most ships were from Sydney, and entered Moreton Bay across the dangerous South Passage bar between Moreton and Stradbroke Islands. Many vessels foundered there; but despite the dangers, this entrance continued to be used, because to use the safer Northern Entrance around Cape Moreton, added 50 miles to the trip. However, the South Passage bar began to deteriorate, and to encourage use of the Northern Entrance, the Works Department of New South Wales let out a contract by tender for the construction of a stone lighthouse at Cape Moreton.

The stone for the 20 metre high tower and lightkeepers' cottages was quarried from near the site. The revolving light was visible for 26½ nautical miles and consisted of twenty-one oil-wick lamps of the Catoptric system, that is, each lamp was placed in front of a highly polished metal reflector to increase the light's brilliancy — similar to a car's headlight. The light was officially exhibited for the first time on 14 February 1857.

Upon separation from New South Wales on 10 December 1859, the new colony of Queensland inherited Cape Moreton lighthouse, its only major light to guide mariners along 5,200 kilometres of coastline.

By the time the first Queensland Parliament assembled in 1860, development inland and along the coast was accelerating. With few, if any, roads to these far-flung settlements, ships were the main link to survival. Ports had been established at Maryborough, Gladstone and Rockhampton to service the unloading of machinery and supplies for those settlers producing exports of wool, cattle, timber and gold. During 1860, two hundred and ten vessels entered Queensland ports. With sparse navigational aids in the rivers and channels leading to the ports, and no coastal lights except for Cape Moreton, many a ship and those aboard them came to grief. Something had to be done.

At that time, Cape Moreton lighthouse was under the control of the Harbour Master's Department. In August 1860, a government select committee recommended that a Portmaster be appointed to take charge of the Department. The man chosen for the position was Lieutenant George Poynter Heath. Born in 1830 in Norfolk, England, Heath entered the Royal Navy as a fifteen year-old cadet. From 1846 to 1850 he served on board the H.M.S. *Rattlesnake* under the command of Captain Owen Stanley, engaged in a survey of New Guinea and Australia's north-east coast from the Palm Islands to Cape York. Then

Queensland's first Portmaster, Lieutenant George Poynter Heath. For twenty-eight years his diligence made safe the most dangerous coast of the continent.

until 1853 he served in *Fantome* and *Calliope* on the Royal Navy's Australian station, before returning to England to complete survey work for the Admiralty. He retired from active service in 1860 with the rank of Lieutenant, and a few months later sailed for Brisbane to take up the position of Marine Surveyor in the Department of the Surveyor-General.

Heath agreed to accept the combined positions of Portmaster and Marine Surveyor of Queensland for no increase in the salary he had been receiving, viz. £400 per annum. He was, however, paid an annual surveying equipment allowance of £280; also, as Lieutenant R.N., he received 5s. per diem half-pay. His appointment took place on 13 January 1862, and the Department became known as the Department of Ports and Harbors [sic].

The selection of Heath as Portmaster was a wise, perhaps lucky, decision; until his retirement twenty-eight years later, Heath, with enthusiasm, ingenuity and doggedness, laid the foundations, often in times of acute economic hardship within the Colony, to light and make safe the most dangerous coast of the Continent.

Only a few months after Heath's appointment, The Marine Board Act of 1862 was passed. It was:

> *An Act to Provide for the better Management of the Ports and Harbours of Queensland and for the better Regulation of Shipping and to Constitute a Board to be called the Marine Board of Queensland.*[6]

The Marine Board, as constituted in the Act, comprised of "the Portmaster of the Colony and four other members", and was subject to "the general supervision control and direction of the Treasurer of the Colony". The duties and powers of the Marine Board were set out in Clause 9 of the Act:

> *The Board shall be the Department to undertake the general superintendence within its jurisdiction of all matters relating to the preservation and improvement of the ports, harbours, havens, navigable creeks and rivers in the said Colony; and the regulation of shipping and seamen; the licensing, appointment and removal of pilots, the maintenance of pilots' establishments, the punishment of persons acting as pilots without a license, the amount save as herein provided of pilotage dues, <u>the superintendence of lights and other sea or harbour marks,</u> the placing or removing of moorings, the establishment of light and beacon dues ...*

Although the Act laid out the basic guidelines, with so much to do and with so few resources to do it, most new work over the next two years was connected with harbours, rivers and the pilot service; nothing was done to provide coast lights. No doubt as a result of pressure from ship owners, on 26 August 1863 The President of the Legislative Council, The Hon. M.C. O'Connell, moved in Parliament:

> *That a Select Committee be appointed ... to inquire into and report upon the requirements of this Colony, under its increasing Trade and Commerce, as to the provision of additional Lighthouses for its Coasts and Harbors [sic]; with power to send for persons and papers, and with leave to sit during any adjournment.*[7]

The first witness called to give evidence at the Committee was the Collector of Customs, W. Thornton, who recommended that a light be built at Sandy Cape on the northern end of "Fraser's Island" to warn shipping of Breaksea Spit which extended 20 miles north of the island. Thornton said: "A light there would be of great service to coasters from other colonies going to ports to the northward of Hervey's Bay, and to vessels taking the inside route through Torres' Strait to India."

Portmaster Lieutenant Heath was the next witness called; he agreed with Thornton's remarks, adding that many ships had left Brisbane heading north, never to be heard of again — possibly wrecked on Breaksea Spit. Heath rejected the Committee's suggestion of a lightship at the end of the spit, explaining that heavy seas together with limited elevation would reduce the range of the light, making it all but useless. He went on to say that if built, the Sandy Cape light should be of the first order[8] (the most powerful type), so the light could be seen by vessels well before approaching the vicinity of Breaksea Spit. When asked by the Committee where a second light should be built, Heath suggested either Cape Capricorn on the north-eastern end of Curtis Island or "Lady Elliott's Island", 28 miles north-west of Breaksea Spit.

A more extensive inquiry was held the following year. A new select committee was formed to examine the state of the rivers and harbours of the Colony, and later extended to cover "the necessity for additional Lighthouses on the coast of Australia, within the Colony of Queensland". Portmaster Lieutenant Heath was the first of eleven witnesses called to give evidence, beginning on 1 June 1864. Once again he recommended a light at Sandy Cape as first priority; Cape Capricorn and Lady Elliott's Island were also discussed. The Chairman of the Committee, Joshua Bell, went on to question Heath:

Bell: "Where is the next point you would take us to on the coast?"
Heath: "I think Bustard Head."
Bell: "How far north is that of Hervey's Bay?"
Heath: "About 100 miles."
Bell: "Is there anything connected with the position of Bustard Head that requires notice?"
Heath: "There are some very dangerous rocks near there."
Bell: "How far off are they?"
Heath: "About three or four miles, I think. It is a point at which many people who navigate the coast express a wish to have a lighthouse placed. If a coast light is to be exhibited between Sandy Cape and Cape Capricorn, no doubt Bustard Head would be the place for it."
Bell: "Is the land high at Bustard Head?"
Heath: "Yes; it is of considerable height."
Bell: "Would it require an expensive light?"
Heath: "I think that a second-class light would be sufficient."
Bell: "Is it from its distance between the other two lights that you recommend Bustard Head?"
Heath: "A light there would be useful to point out the entrance to Port Curtis, and to show the position of the rocks lying off Bustard Head. It would also be a useful light for vessels to make, after passing Breaksea Spit, previously to steering northward for any of the Northern Ports."

The Committee wasted no time in compiling their Report,[9] which was presented to Parliament on 31 August 1864, a mere week after the conclusion of the Inquiry. In reference to coast lights, the Committee recommended that four lighthouses were required between Queensland's southern border and Rockingham Bay (75 miles south of Cairns), viz. Cape Capricorn, Bustard Head, Sandy Cape and either Point Danger or Cape Byron. It also recommended that lighthouses should be erected on "Lady Elliott's Island and Double Island", but were not as such a "pressing nature" as the former four.

It was decided to proceed immediately with the erection of Bustard Head and Sandy Cape lighthouses. However, unlike Cape Moreton lighthouse which had been built of local stone, and at the time was the most economical method of constructing a lighthouse, Bustard Head and Sandy Cape had foundations of sand. This necessitated that both lighthouses be built of prefabricated cast-iron panels ordered from lighthouse manufacturers in England. The planning and construction of both lighthouses were intended to run concurrently. Requirements for the design of the Bustard Head lighthouse were formulated by Portmaster Lieutenant Heath in a letter to the Colonial Treasurer:[10]

> *The iron Light House for Bustard Head — 33 feet from foundation to Lantern floor. To be 18 feet diameter at base and 12 at top or the proper size for receiving a lantern for a second order light. These proportions of diameter may be altered if any benefit will be gained thereby. To contain three floors besides Lantern floor. The lower one 9 feet high and remaining space to be divided between the other two floors. Entrance to be the same as Light House for Sandy Cape.* (Author's note: i.e., The lower room to have a door opening outside, while the entrance to the lighthouse to be on the floor above, reached by a flight of steps and a small landing outside the tower). *Light to be Dioptric holophotal[11] fixed — varied by short eclipses — of the second order to illuminate an arc of 245° elevation 330 feet above sea level. Light required to be seen as far as horizon.*

Drawings for the two lighthouses were completed by the Crown Agents for the Colonies, London, in November 1865 and immediately put out to tender. In the meantime, Joseph Brady, the recently employed Engineer of Harbors [sic] and Rivers, had been directed to prepare plans for the foundations. In a report to the Colonial Treasurer 10 June 1865, Brady wrote:

> *During my recent visit to the north, I had under consideration plans for the foundations of the lights on Sandy Cape and Bustard Head, the lanterns and ironwork of which may be expected in the course of a few months. The lights in each case will be erected in iron towers on the summit of high sand ridges, somewhat difficult of access, and I think it will be desirable in a short time to commence the works at*

either or both of the above mentioned places, by the erection of huts for the workmen, also temporary buildings for stores and workshops. Tramways, with temporary landing stages and cranes, will also be required, all of which might be proceeded with at once. In the case of Bustard Head, which lies exposed to a heavy sea, I think it will be necessary to have moorings laid down at a sufficient distance from the shore, to prevent accident to vessels landing materials. It is also necessary to provide for the constant attendance of a small steamer of considerable power during the erection of these lights.[12]

Brady's comment of expecting the lanterns and ironwork in a few months was strangely premature, as at the date of his report the drawings in England were not even started. Almost a year later, on 25 April 1866, Brady reported to the Colonial Treasurer:

Contracts have been entered into with Messrs. Kitson and Co., of Leeds, and with Messrs. Hennet, Spink and Co., of Bridgwater, for the manufacture of the iron towers for Sandy Cape and Bustard Head (Author's note: respectively), *and with Messrs. Chance and Co., of Birmingham, for the lanterns. One of the towers may shortly be expected. Since the date of my last report, I have had the sites proposed for each of these lights surveyed and marked. The dwellings of the lightkeepers might now be proceeded with at any time, and would be available for the workmen employed in erecting the towers.*

The foundation at both places is sand; that at Sandy Cape of the finest drift sand, and in consequence I anticipate some difficulty and outlay in securing a foundation of sufficient stability for the tower. The amounts of the contracts are as follows:—

Sandy Cape tower	*£3,580*
Sandy Cape lighting apparatus	*£2,775*
Bustard Head tower	*£1,546*
Bustard Head lighting apparatus	*£2,109*
Total	*£10,010*

These were to be delivered in London for shipment during March and April. The gross estimate for these towers complete, is £25,000.[13]

Again, Brady's estimation of time was inaccurate. It wasn't until nearly a year later, on 22 April 1867, that the materials for only Bustard Head arrived in Brisbane. In May, Brady reported to the Colonial Treasurer explaining the delay:

Due provision was made in accordance with instructions for the erection of the lighthouses on Bustard Head and Sandy Cape; and the delay in this matter is owing solely to the non-arrival of the materials from England. These materials were contracted for in London by the Crown Agent for the Colonies, with the understanding that they were to be shipped during March and April, 1866. Owing, however, to a large demand from other Governments for lighthouse materials, it was only within the last month that the materials for Bustard Head light were received here. Tenders were immediately called for, receivable up to the 3rd proximo, for the erection; and there is every probability that the light will be in use early in November.

The amounts already paid in London on account of the Bustard Head lighthouse amount to nearly £4,000; and the further outlay on account of its erection, exclusive of dwellings for the lightkeepers, will be about £5,300.

My estimate for both lighthouses is £25,000; but as the Sandy Cape tower is a larger structure than that for Bustard Head, and the foundation being a very bad one, the outlay on Sandy Cape will be much in excess of that necessary for Bustard Head.[14]

Although the government had planned for Sandy Cape to be the top priority in regard to lighthouses, it was fate that only the materials for Bustard Head arrived, thereby giving it the privilege of becoming the first coast light erected in Queensland.

Chapter 2

A MAMMOTH TASK

Before the barque *Hermine* arrived in Brisbane from London with the materials for Bustard Head lighthouse, Portmaster George Heath arranged for them to be offloaded directly into the government steamer *Platypus* for shipment to Bustard Head. On 3 May 1867, a week after the *Hermine's* arrival, tenders were invited for the erection of the lighthouse, to be received no later than noon on 20 May. On 9 May a notice was issued extending the time for receiving tenders to the 3 June. However, it appears that the lightkeepers' cottages and outbuildings had not been included in the original tender. So, on 24 June new tenders were called, for the erection of the lighthouse, supply of materials and erection of the quarters and conveyance of all the materials from Brisbane to Bustard Head. Tenders closed on 22 July.

As the successful tenderer was now to be responsible for transporting the materials to the site, the lighthouse materials were offloaded from the *Hermine* onto the government's Queen's Wharf. An inspection by the Government Marine Surveyor's office found that eight of the cast-iron plates had been damaged by improper stowage, and neglect while unloading. One plate was broken in two places, while the others had broken lifting lugs or cracked flanges. The damaged plates were taken away for repairs to the value of £24. 4. 0, an amount recovered from the *Hermine's* agents, J & G Harris; the remaining materials, including the lens and lighting apparatus were stored in the leased premises of Lynch and Blick at Kangaroo Point.

Eight tenders were received ranging from £2,000 to £3,333. At an Executive Council meeting on 24 July, it was agreed to accept the tender of W.P. Clark from Brisbane for the amount of £2,508. Clark was advised of the acceptance of his tender on 3 August 1867 and was requested to "make the necessary arrangements for commencing the work forthwith". A condition of the contract required the work to be completed within six months; failure to do so, would attract a penalty of £10 per week.

Portmaster Heath wrote to the Port Curtis Harbour Master on 6 August informing him that the Colonial Architect Charles Tiffin would be visiting

After two false starts, a third and final tender notice appeared in the Queensland Government Gazette.

Gladstone for the purpose of going to Bustard Head with the contractor to point out the exact spot for the lighthouse and cottages. Heath requested that the Port Curtis pilot schooner *Enid* be made available for the trip, and that the Harbour Master accompany them to assist with the final selection of the lighthouse's position. Heath advised:

> *It should be as far to the south-eastward as possible and as near the shoreline, as any position can be obtained without losing any appreciable height of ground.[1]*

Although Engineer Brady had suggested that moorings be laid in the open sea close to the construction site, it was later decided by Heath to offload in Frying Pan Creek on the north-western side of Bustard Head. This creek was well protected from the south-east trade winds, but was just over 3 kilometres from the lighthouse site. However, contractor Clark chose to offload in Jenny Lind Creek on the south-eastern side of the headland where, although steep, it was only 600 metres to the site. Unlike Frying Pan Creek with its almost all-weather entrance, a treacherous bar at the mouth of Jenny Lind Creek made safe entry only possible in fine weather. In fact, the creek was named after the 130 ton schooner *Jenny Lind*, wrecked while trying to cross the bar on 2 February 1857. An extract from a letter, written shortly after the incident by the schooner's skipper, Captain Sherman, to the vessel's Sydney owners explains:

> *I am under the painful necessity of informing you of the loss of the* Jenny Lind *on the 2nd of February, in Bustard Bay, it blowing a heavy gale at the time. I run [sic] down to Lady Elliott's Island on the 1st, and hove-to under the fore-trysail, it being thick and rainy; at daylight the same. At 8 a.m. saw the land, distance two miles, it still blowing heavy, with squalls. Finding the vessel driving in shore, I run [sic] her into a little creek to save the lives of the people; trusting she might go inside the bar, and come to anchor, and get her out again. The first sounding I got was seven fathoms. The vessel struck in four feet water, the sea making a breach all over her; as soon as she breached to, I cut away the main-mast to keep her from going on her beam-ends. That night I succeeded in getting all hands on shore, with a great deal of trouble; for as the tide rose, the sea came in frightful. That night the vessel beat up about a quarter of a mile in the sand. We got all the spars and sails sent down, and pitched our tents on shore; but as soon as the vessel beat in far enough we moved on board, for fear of the blacks. The wind still continued to blow a gale, without any cessation until the 10th February; then we took the boats and started for Port Curtis, which place we reached on the 12th safe.[2]*

Although Captain Sherman considered the ship a total loss, the *Jenny Lind* was sold to a Gladstone resident, refloated, refitted, and began trading again between Sydney and Port Curtis. The 10 ton cutter *Lady Darling* wasn't so fortunate; on 26 March 1866 while at anchor off the mouth of Jenny Lind Creek, her anchor cable broke. *Lady Darling* drifted onto the bar and was broken up by the swell within a few days.

Despite those incidents, it was Clark's choice to offload in Jenny Lind Creek. For this purpose he obtained the services of the Brisbane registered 48 ton paddle-wheel steamer *Gneering*. On 17 August, only a fortnight after Clark was notified of being the successful tenderer, the *Gneering* cleared Brisbane for Bustard Head. Under the command of Captain J. Watson, the *Gneering*, with sixteen passengers aboard, was carrying 65 tons of ironwork, 3 tons of flour, 10 cwt. of potatoes, 10 cwt. of sugar, 7 tons of salt, 1 chest of tea, 40 lbs. of tobacco and 50 lbs. of coffee.

On her arrival at Bustard Head, a strong south-east gale prevented the *Gneering* from entering Jenny Lind Creek. For seven days she took shelter in Frying Pan Creek. Then, on 29 August, she weighed anchor, crossed the Jenny Lind bar, and at high tide intentionally ran aground beside a flat grassy area at the bottom of a spur which led to the lighthouse site. A temporary tramway was erected from the ship to above high water mark, and a trolley pulled by horses quickly transferred the cargo from ship to shore. By nightfall the *Gneering* was empty.

Also delayed by the south-east gale was the government's Inspector of Works Robert Ferguson, who was to remain on site during the construction of the buildings. He had been detained in Gladstone for seven days, and arrived at Bustard Head by the Port Curtis pilot schooner *Enid* on the same day as the *Gneering* discharged her cargo in Jenny Lind.

Contrary to Engineer Brady's original suggestion of erecting the three light-keepers' cottages and storage shed first to accommodate the workmen, for the first three months the men were mainly employed constructing a tramway from the creek to the building site and breaking down granite for use in the concrete footing of the lighthouse. Granite of the size required — 25 and 50 millimetre diameter — was found near the top of the ridge, but was rotten and crumbly; so large blocks of sound granite had to be quarried and crushed manually, a slow and tedious job, taking a day for one man to produce half a yard. By the end of the first month 30 yards were on hand. The stone was found to be excellent for the cottages' chimney footings and inside piers, but not suitable for the outside piers. In his monthly report to the Colonial Architect, Inspector of Works Ferguson wrote he had recommended to the contractor "to fetch as many bricks (sound and hard) as will build all outside piers from ground level, as the material (granite) is so hard and difficult to work with the facilities here that it would be impossible for him to get it to my satisfaction".

Delayed by headwinds, the *Gneering* returned to Jenny Lind Creek on 30 September with more ironwork for the lighthouse. On the way she had called at Maryborough to load timber for two of the cottages. A few days later a vessel hit the rocks off Bustard Head. Ferguson advised of this in a report to the Colonial Architect:

> The Lady Young *steamer struck on the Outer Rock of [sic] Bustard Head on the morning of the fifth of October. On being made aware of the circumstance I proceeded to Pancake Creek (as I thought she would run for it on getting of [sic]) and rendered every assistance as the vessel came in to pilot her up and point out a proper bank for to lay her on. I also visited the steamer days afterwards to know if I could render any assistance.[3]*

The *Lady Young* was repaired and continued her voyage. In the above report, Ferguson refers to Pancake Creek, meaning Frying Pan Creek. This is the first recorded mention of Pancake Creek, the name that remains to this day. Extensive research has failed to categorically explain the change, although it is known the cutter *Pancake* traded along the coast in that era, skippered by a man called "Pancake Dick".[4]

Again detained in Pancake Creek for eight days while a strong south-easterly blew, the *Gneering*, by 4 November, had landed her final load of materials in Jenny Lind Creek. By this time the tramway from the creek had been built to the top of the ridge, 50 yards of granite crushed, the shed and store erected (except for the doors and windows), the piers of the cottages were being put in and the carpenters were preparing the timbers. Ferguson complained that progress was slow, caused by having only two carpenters and ten labourers on site. Over the next month the tramway from the creek reached the lighthouse site and all the cottage materials were delivered. The framework of the Superintendent's cottage was erected, and the piers to the two smaller cottages completed.

Now the hard work of transporting the cast-iron lighthouse panels from the creek began. The larger panels — nearly 2 metres square and 30 millimetres thick — weighed over three-quarters of a tonne. Little work was done in breaking up the granite during this time, and a slight conflict arose between Ferguson and the contractor over this matter. In a chasm at sea-level below the lighthouse site, the contractor had found a deposit of shingle of suitable size for the concrete. Ferguson did not want to use it, claiming it was "a salt water deposit thrown up by the surf" and not in accordance with the specification. The matter was referred to the Colonial Architect who agreed to let the shingle be used if it lay above spring high tide.

Trouble was also being experienced with the quality of cement. Ferguson poured some samples of French cement only to find that, when set, it was little better than mortar. Further experiments showed that if the concrete with the French cement was buried in the ground, it set as hard as the British cement and therefore no problem for the lighthouse footings, but of no use for external work.

All materials were delivered to the lighthouse site by the end of December. Since the men's arrival at Bustard Head, no mention had been made of Aborigines in the area. It wasn't uncommon in situations such as this for building materials to be pilfered by local Aborigines. Perhaps not three-quarter tonne cast-iron panels, but certainly smaller metal objects that could be converted into useful tools. However, Ferguson made no note of such an incident occurring in his monthly reports to the Colonial Architect. Even back in 1857 when the schooner *Jenny Lind* was wrecked crossing the bar into Jenny Lind Creek, Captain Sherman wrote " . . . as soon as the vessel beat in far enough we moved on board for fear of the blacks"; he did not say he saw any "blacks". Unlike some future lightstations, no mention was ever made during Bustard Head lighthouse's history of any communication with Aborigines.

There is no doubt Aborigines had inhabited the Bustard Bay area. They were the Meerooni clan from the Gooreng-Gooreng tribe, sighted by Lieutenant James Cook in 1770. Early explorers observed that the tribe frequented the coastal areas while fresh water was available, but moved inland following the game to the rivers' headwaters during the dry times. In the 1830s a smallpox epidemic, carried by the Waka-Waka tribe from the south, caused scores of Gooreng-Gooreng deaths. Later, a second epidemic, this time of dropsy, reduced numbers even further. Conflict with white settlers and the introduction to Gladstone in the 1850s of the Native Police Force, which recruited Aborigines to enforce the law on other Aborigines, almost annihilated the tribe. Little wonder none were seen at the lighthouse.

At the end of December 1867, Ferguson applied to the Colonial Architect for a period of leave:

> *Being here now for a period of four months, and at our rate of progress it will take four months yet to finish the contract; living for that period on salt provisions and likely to do so for the remainder of my stay here. I would respectfully ask you to grant me leave of absence for a period of 10 ten days as that would about suit me to return by steamer.*[5]

Leave was granted to take place from the end of January. On the second day of the new year another wreck occurred in Jenny Lind Creek, this time with loss of life. Ferguson reported:

> *I regret to inform you that a casualty occurred in Jenny Lind Creek on Jan 2ⁿᵈ by which one man lost his life. On this day the Master of the cutter* Live Yankee, *a vessel of about ten 10 tons from Rockhampton, with Lime, came to me and made the following*

statement: when attempting to take the Bar, this morning, my mate, named Peter — was carried overboard when putting a sweep forward; I immediately dropped my anchor, and hove overboard, planks, water casks, and sweeps, the current was very strong, and he was carried away from the vessel, and was unable to reach them, he struggled for ten minutes, or more, and then disappeared. The vessel was driven ashore, and has since been abandoned, the body has not been recovered up to this date.[6]

Little was done during January. Only two men were employed on the cottages, while the rest were taking up the tramway from the creek and laying it down to the shingle on the opposite side of the headland. While in Brisbane on leave, Ferguson wrote to the Colonial Architect informing him that progress was so slow, entirely due to the "non employment of sufficient labour that there is literally nothing to report". The cottages had come to a standstill for fourteen days because the two carpenters were employed at building a boat. Then one carpenter and three labourers left on the schooner for Brisbane, leaving only seven men on site.

Further conflict had developed between Ferguson and the contractor. Ferguson had been advised by Clark that he would be ready to pour the footing for the lighthouse about 4 February — while Ferguson was on leave — and that "he would not wait for inspection one hour after he was ready".

Ferguson's leave must have mellowed him a little. When he returned to Bustard Head he appeared happy with the work that had been done. In his monthly report to the Colonial Architect he wrote:

I have the honor [sic] to inform you that I arrived here on the 22nd March being detained at Gladstone, and afterwards in Rodd's Bay, for a period of 16 sixteen days; by head winds and bad weather. During that time we made repeated attempts to reach the Head, and in two instances had to run back from the mouth of the creek (Author's note: Ferguson is referring to Pancake Creek), *the sea was so heavy and the schooner taking so much water.*

Upon my arrival here I found that considerable progress had been made during my absence, the concrete having been completed, the base plates laid, and three 3 courses of shell plates erected, these plates are very readily put together, and with the appliances here, take but little time. This portion that is the Iron Work, is being carefully and well done. I also believe the concrete to have been faithfully done, there being more cement than I thought would have been from the measurements, that is 150 one hundred and fifty casks. Of stone there was not enough, so I believe there is more concrete in the foundation than specified.[7]

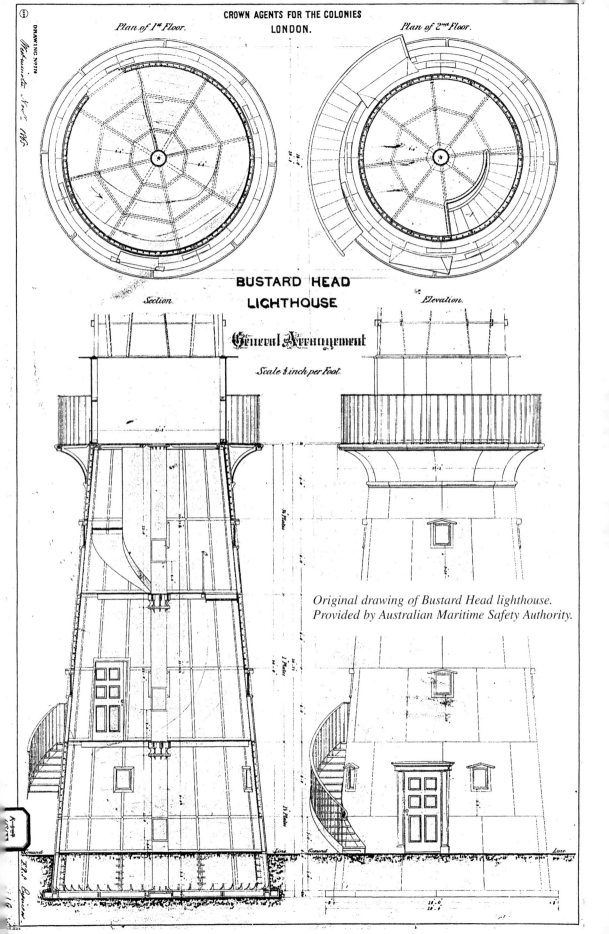

Original drawing of Bustard Head lighthouse.
Provided by Australian Maritime Safety Authority.

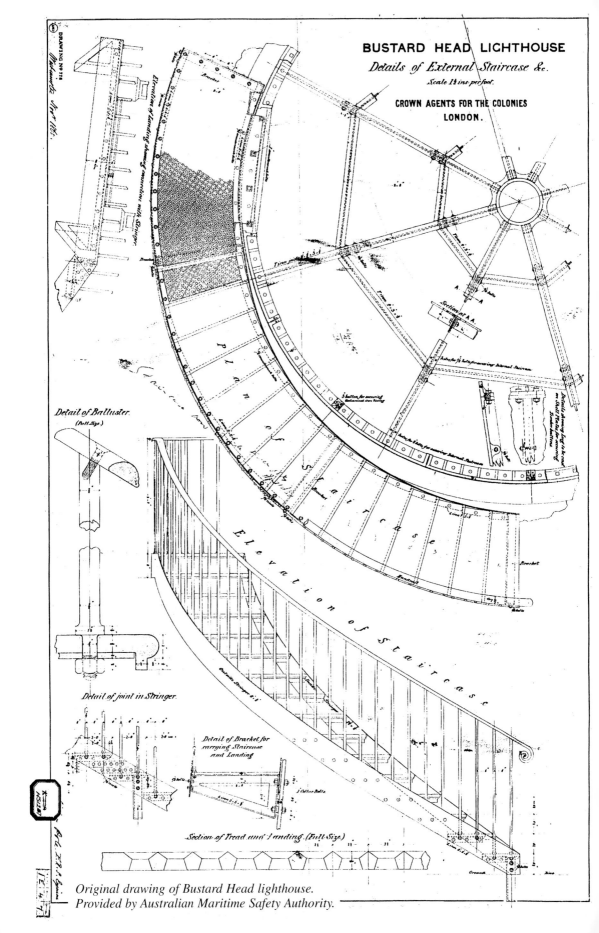

Original drawing of Bustard Head lighthouse.
Provided by Australian Maritime Safety Authority.

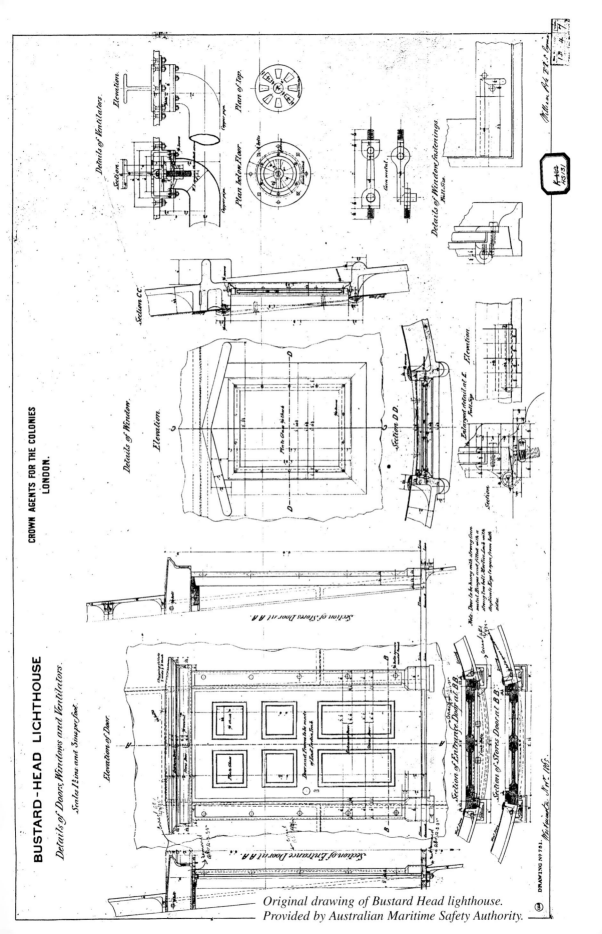

Original drawing of Bustard Head lighthouse.
Provided by Australian Maritime Safety Authority.

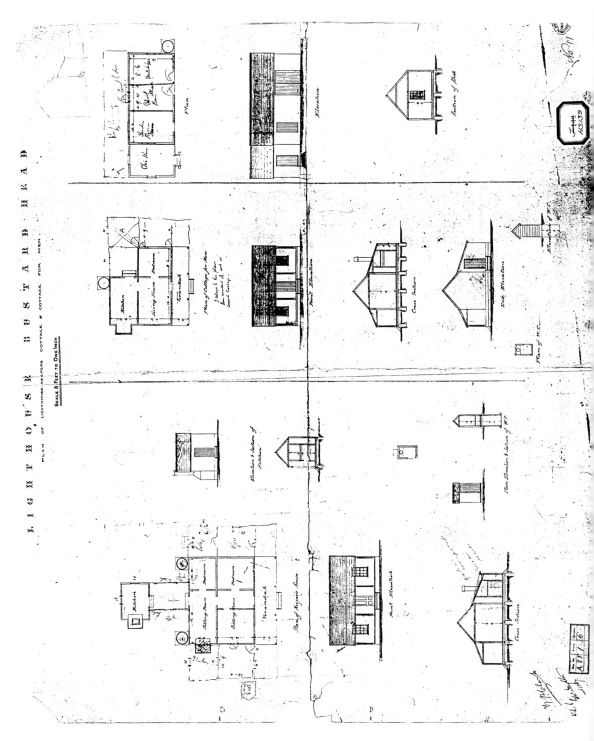

Original drawing of Bustard Head lightkeepers' cottages. The Superintendent's cottage is at the left. Two identical cottages (centre) were built for the lightkeepers. The storeroom/workshop building is at the right. Proposed alterations and extensions to the buildings were roughly pencilled in at each stage of development.

Provided by Australian Maritime Safety Authority.

GENERAL ELEVATION

Original drawing of the Bustard Head lens done in 1865. This huge Chance Brothers Second Order lens weighed 5 tonnes and stood just under 3 metres high. Its beam was visible 23 miles out to sea.

Provided by Australian Maritime Safety Authority.

The clockwork machinery used for rotating the lens was driven by heavy weights hung on a chain that descended through the centre of the tower. Once every two hours throughout the night, a lightkeeper, by means of a crank-handle, wound the weights back up to the underside of the lantern room floor.

Photograph provided by Neville Murphy.

The cast-iron door head to the ground floor entrance of the lighthouse. A similar one was at the first floor entrance until its removal in 1935.

KENNET & SPINK, MANUFACTURERS, BRIDGWATER. 1866.

Copper oil cans used for refuelling the light. The can at the left was used with the original wick burner in 1868. The other two were sent to the station in 1917 when the wick burner was replaced with a kerosene vapour lamp.

From Lighthouse Historical Society of Queensland collection.

Although the remaining carpenter had left during Ferguson's absence, two new carpenters had been employed and were hard at work on the cottages. Ferguson concluded his report:

> *I am sorry to inform you that a Death has taken place here during my absence. The deceased was one of the last employed, and was in delicate Health and subject to Fever and Ague, he received a blow on the Head when in the foundation through the jib giving way. He was carried up and put to bed and everything that was possible, was done for him but of no avail, as he died on the following day and was buried.*
>
> *Another wreck has taken place in Jenny Lind Creek, the vessel being a cutter of about five tons; in taking the Bar she was driven ashore and was broken up; I am happy to say no lives were lost.[7]*

By March, the six-month contract completion date had passed. Perhaps because of this, Portmaster Heath dispatched a small temporary light to the Port Curtis Harbour Master for delivery to Bustard Head. This was to be erected and maintained by Ferguson. However, Heath had second thoughts about the light, thinking it may be mistaken for the recently erected harbour light on Gatcombe Head, at the southern entrance to Port Curtis. It is doubtful whether this temporary light was ever erected. During April and the beginning of May, progress on the tower was good. The shell plates were all fixed, the first, second and lantern room floors put in, as well as the balcony cornice and railing, external stairs and internal sheet steel lining. The lantern room was all but finished; only the copper sheeting remained to be fixed to the dome rafters. A fair bit of work still had to be done to the cottages, and the carpenters were working "from daylight to dark".

The relationship between Ferguson and Clark began to deteriorate again. Ferguson wrote to the Colonial Architect, asking if he could spare the time to visit Bustard Head for the final inspection while Ferguson went to Brisbane to prepare the specification for the lighthouse at Sandy Cape:

> . . . as I want to detail fully the way in which work is to be performed as I now fully understand it, which will save a great amount of argument especially with contractors like the present.[8]

Very bad weather had delayed the fitting of the copper sheeting to the dome for eight weeks. This was completed on 28 May. The internal stairs to the tower were fixed and the whole lot painted inside and out. Only the plate glass panes remained to be fitted to the lantern room, before the lens and clockwork mechanism used for rotating it were installed. The third cottage was weather-boarded, battened and ready for the roof shingles.

During June, Ferguson rendezvoused with Portmaster Heath off Woody Island in the "Great Sandy Island Strait" for an inspection of the Sandy Cape lighthouse site. Heath had sailed from Brisbane on board the Port Curtis pilot schooner *Enid*, which had been in Brisbane for repairs and alterations. As the cattle trade in Gladstone had ceased for some months, there was little need for such a large pilot vessel in the port. Its retention was solely due to the approaching completion of Bustard Head lighthouse, when it could be used for the conveyance of oil and provisions. In Brisbane, Heath had taken on nearly a year's supply of oil, oil tanks and "as many stores as the vessel would contain". After visiting Sandy Cape, Heath and Ferguson sailed north, arriving at Pancake Creek on 22 June. Ferguson found that the lens and clockwork mechanism had been installed satisfactorily, but other work associated with the cottages, including tank stands and water closets, done in his absence, was not. As well, Clark had "totally disregarded" instructions from Ferguson, written before he left for Sandy Cape. In his last report from Bustard Head to the Colonial Architect, Ferguson wrote:

> . . . Contractor has declined to do any of these alterations. But says that he will leave when he finishes to his own satisfaction . . . [9]

It seemed a convenient time for the parting of the ways. In Heath's yearly report to the Colonial Treasurer, he describes his visit to Bustard Head:

. . . From thence I proceeded to Bustard Head where I found the buildings all completed except in one or two minor matters which are in dispute between the contractor and Mr Ferguson. We landed the oil and stores, and left the same night to bring the lightkeepers and their goods and chattels from Gladstone, and returned the following night to Bustard Head.

I found that the lenses all, more or less, showed traces of injury from being so long packed in tow and paper, and also there was some difficulty in getting the chain — by which the motion is given to the revolving apparatus — to work over the driving wheel, some of the links which were short, causing the chain to ride and jamb under the shafting above. This defect was lessened, but not removed, when I left, and since then some further improvement has been made, by reeving the spare chain.

Messrs. Chance, the manufacturers of the dioptric lenses, have promised that in future all the packing material shall be thoroughly heated and dried before being used when lenses are packed for long voyages, so as to prevent, if possible, the growth of the fungus which so seriously injures the surface of the glass.

One or two of the prisms have been slightly injured in putting together the Dioptric apparatus but nothing of any serious importance, and I believe that the contractor took every precaution in performing the work, though he had never seen anything of the kind before.

I found that the telescope, some lanterns and tools which are supplied with the Dioptric apparatus for the light service had been used by the contractor and which by the specification he appeared for the most part to have been entitled to do, but which on any future occasion he should be prevented from using. The tools sent from Chance Bros. should not be touched by the contractor, or the Spirits of Wine supplied for cleaning the lenses.

The contractor Mr Clark, appears to have carried out his work in the erection of the tower and buildings, very satisfactorily; but the dwelling-houses should have been lined, especially on the side exposed to the prevailing wet and south-easterly winds, and the floors should have been beech instead of hardwood, which always looks dirty, and is liable to cause splinters.

The road to the lighthouse is about 3 miles in length (Author's note: Heath is referring to the road from Pancake Creek, which is actually 3 kilometres long) *of loose sand and scanty vegetation and with two very sharp pinches up which few horses could take a dray load. I have purchased from the contractor his horse and dray for the use of the lightkeepers. The horse is a very excellent draught horse and is worth I believe the amount paid for the dray harness and all the timber left on the ground into the bargain.*

Frying Pan Creek gives a very convenient anchorage while communicating with the lighthouse. It has no bar at its entrance, but the water commences to shoal gradually at a distance of about three-quarters of a mile from its mouth. The entrance is narrow, giving us only just sufficient room to work in, in very fine weather, and is open to the north-west. I believe that no dangerous sea rolls in as far as the anchorage, even with that wind; while with all other winds it gives perfect shelter. For steamers especially, it offers capital shelter during heavy south-easterly winds, as it would not take them any distance out of their course, and they could steam head to wind into the anchorage; but sailing vessels would have some difficulty in getting in against a strong south-easterly wind blowing right out of the creek. I have had moorings laid down in the creek for the pilot vessel, so that she can lie inside with greater safety, and get under way without risk, and with less labor [sic] and loss of time.

As the formation of the headland itself is very incorrectly laid down upon the charts, I took the opportunity of making the necessary observations for laying down its general outline, and the relative position of the light from the outlying rocks, which information I have forwarded to the Hydrographer, for insertion upon the coast charts (Author's note: Heath calculated the position of the lighthouse as latitude 24° 01.2′ south, longitude 151° 42.0′ east. His latitude was correct within a fraction; but his longitude placed the lighthouse 3.8 nautical miles westward of its actual position. This was no slur on Heath, as precise longitude calculation depends on accurate time; Heath's chronometer was no more than 16 seconds out).

The lighthouse was first lit on the 26th June and has been burning every night since and it now seems to be in perfect working order. From the offing, the light given by the apparatus was most satisfactory; the flashes were intensely brilliant, being distinctly visible from the high land at Auckland Point at Gladstone, a distance of some 30 miles.[10]

Although the light was lit from 26 June 1868, the official Notice to Mariners advised that the light would be exhibited "on and after the 29th instant". Completed just over four months after expiry of the contract date, the establishment cost of the lighthouse was:

Cost of tower landed in Brisbane		£1,831.19. 9
Erection of iron tower on site		£1,970. 0. 0
	Total for tower	£3,801.19. 9
Lighting apparatus		£2,244. 1. 2
Fitting up		£30. 0. 0
		£2,274. 1. 2
Lightkeepers' houses		£800.16. 0
	TOTAL	£6,876.16.11[11]

The era of the lightkeeper was underway.

The heavy cast-iron wall panels were bolted together and set in red lead to waterproof the joints. The external staircase led to the main entrance door of the lighthouse. The ground floor was used for oil storage. During the day, curtains were hung on the inside of the lantern room to prevent the sun's rays becoming magnified by the prisms and causing damage to the lens.

Photograph provided by Mrs Birrell.

An early view of the lightstation. The lookout house and wind vane are to the left of the photograph. The Superintendent's cottage is to the immediate right of the lighthouse, while the two Lightkeepers' cottages stand close together in the foreground, a factor that later proved disastrous.

Photograph provided by Babs Atherton.

The start of a new era.

From the Queensland Government Gazette.

The Treasury,
Queensland, 30th June, 1868.

NOTICE TO MARINERS.

THE following Notice to Mariners respecting the Lighthouse recently erected at Bustard Head, and the Light to be exhibited therefrom, is published for general information.

R. R. MACKENZIE.

LIGHT AT BUSTARD HEAD.

ON and after the 29th instant, a dioptric light of the second order will be exhibited from the eastern headland of Bustard Head. It will shew as a fixed light every alternate minute, the intervening minutes being occupied by a bright flash, preceded and followed by a short eclipse.

The tower from which the light is exhibited is painted white and is thirty-three (33) feet high,—the light standing at an elevation of three hundred and twenty (320) feet above the level of the sea, and being visible from the deck of a small vessel about twenty-three miles.

The outer rock lying off Bustard Head bears from the Lighthouse N. five degrees E., distant about three (3) miles.

G. P. HEATH, Lieut. R.N.,
Portmaster.

Chapter 3

KEEPERS OF THE LIGHT

The man Portmaster Heath chose to be in charge of the new lighthouse at Bustard Head was thirty-seven year-old Thomas Rooksby. Like most men employed as lightkeepers at the time, Rooksby had spent much of his life as a mariner. Born in Gloucester, England in 1831, his early years were anything but privileged. Three months before Rooksby's birth, his father was killed in an accident, and nine years later his mother died. Cared for by relatives, he later took a position in a grocery business before becoming an apprentice on board a collier at the age of fifteen, eventually sailing to most of the world's major ports. While at sea he became absorbed in the study of navigation, a science that held his interest throughout his life. In 1861 he was appointed Master of the lightship *Rose*, situated at the Brisbane River Bar in Moreton Bay. Seven years later, with his wife Annie, Rooksby was transferred to Bustard Head as Supcrintendent on a salary of £190 per annum, a position he would hold for the next thirty-four years. Accompanying him were Light-keeper Daniel Gorman and Assistant Lightkeeper M. Morrison on yearly salaries of £108 and £96 respectively.[1]

It must have been a difficult first few months, settling in to a new environment and becoming familiar with what was then the latest in lighthouse technology. From fifteen minutes before sunset until sunrise, each man, with "unceasing watchfulness",[2] took his shift on the light, constantly ensuring that the wick burner — fuelled by China oil — was adjusted to the correct height and with just enough draught from the damper to produce the whitest light possible. And every two hours, winding the heavy weights to the underside of the lantern room floor, then letting them slowly fall again, to turn the clock-work mechanism that kept the giant crystal lens revolving once every eight minutes. The 2.4 metre high lens had eight panels; a fixed (constant) light of 2,700 candlepower occupied every alternate minute, while a bright flash of 20,000 candlepower, preceded and followed by a short eclipse, occupied the intermediate minute.

A most urgent problem for the lightkeepers was the wind erosion taking place around the lighthouse. During construction of the tower and cottages, the crown of the hill had been unavoidably stripped bare of vegetation, leaving nothing but fine drift sand which found its way into the lantern room with the potential for damaging the light and machinery. Rooksby applied for a temporary assistant to help cart up 150 loads of earth from Jenny Lind Creek for spreading over the site; but Portmaster Heath thought that the earth, when dry, would also blow away. Instead, Heath forwarded 12 lbs. of couch grass seed to the station, with the intention of re-establishing native grasses and shrubs to the area; as well, he suggested placing "rows of dead bushes stuck in the ground across the lines of prevailing winds".[3] Another of Rooksby's ideas was to lay stone paving over the site; and that is what finally happened. Over the next seven years, Rooksby, with the assistance of the lightkeepers, spent every spare moment quarrying, carting and laying hundreds of tonnes of stone.[4]

Although it must have been strange for the men settling into their new routine, it must have been more so for their wives, especially those with children. Annie Rooksby had no children, but Daniel Gorman's wife Hannah had three, all under the age of four. She went on to have a further eleven. Large families were normal in those days, but even so, remote from medical help, living in a one bedroom cottage with the south-east wind whistling between the weatherboards of the unlined rooms, illuminated at night by a flickering oil lamp, it must have tested the most robust of mothers. In an attempt to supply a little entertainment for the families, Heath forwarded a 'library' to the station, along with a book in which to enter the names of the persons who took the books to read. He also advised the Port Curtis Harbour Master that the crew of the pilot vessel could use the books "provided that they take proper care of them".

Isolation appeared to be having a detrimental effect on Lightkeeper Dennis McCarthy living on the single-family station at Gatcombe Head near the southern entrance to Port Curtis. For months he had been at loggerheads with the pilots over numerous minor matters. In an attempt to solve the problem, Heath arranged for Lightkeeper Gorman, who had been at Bustard Head for nine months now, to voluntarily swap places with McCarthy, hoping that he might become "more sociable" living on a three-family station.

Shipping was once again on the increase. The Australian Steamship Navigation Company ran a weekly service from Brisbane to Maryborough, Gladstone and Rockhampton. Vessels were regularly entering Eurimbula Creek, 9 miles from Bustard Head at the southern end of Bustard Bay, to load timber from a sawmill established there shortly before construction of the lighthouse began in 1867. Two beacons were placed at the mouth of Eurimbula Creek in 1869 to assist vessels crossing the bar.

The Port Curtis pilot schooner *Enid* often spent time in Pancake Creek while waiting for ships requiring pilotage. At 11.00 p.m. on Friday 6 May

1870 *Enid* was making her way from Gladstone to Bustard Head with Pilot Jansen. The night was very dark, and Jansen was hoping the moon would soon rise to help him enter Pancake Creek. Suddenly, the sky was illuminated for miles with a brilliant and dazzling light. It seems a large meteor travelling north to south, exploded over Bustard Head. Jansen later said that: "Every object on the shore was revealed as distinctly as by daylight, and about five seconds after the meteor burst, we were startled by a report which could only be likened to that following the discharge of a piece of the heaviest ordnance ... it was one of the grandest sights I've ever witnessed."[5] The noise was heard in Gladstone where it "shook every dwelling in the place".[5]

The rocks lying off Bustard Head still remained a problem for Heath. In his annual report to the Legislative Assembly in December 1871, he wrote:

> *At Bustard Head something still remains to be done. The light now shews [sic] the direction of the outlying rock, some three miles distant, but the intensity of the light tends, if anything, to mislead vessels as to their distance from the shore; so that, to avoid this danger, they often pass six or seven miles, or even more, outside the rock, which is steep to, and may be approached within a ship's length, and thus unnecessarily lengthen their passage. I had intended to place a bell upon it, to which motion was to have been given by the swell washing round the rock; but I found that the sea, at high-water springs, broke in bad weather too heavily over the rock to give such an apparatus any chance of permanence. The difficulty can probably be overcome by placing two small lights in such positions, that when in the same plane, and in line, they may cut the rock, and thus point out its distance from the shore; so that vessels passing, to insure being outside the rock, should merely keep the in-shore and upper light, above the lower and nearer light; while, to prevent these lights from being overpowered by the greater brilliancy of that shewn [sic] from the lighthouse above, I propose to reduce its intensity, by coloring [sic] red, a small arc of light in the direction of the rock. This arrangement could be carried out at a very small expense, and when at Bustard Head, the other day, I tested the possibility of effecting the proposed object as I have described.[6]*

Heath's proposal was put into action the following year on 4 December 1872. Two small white kerosene lights on poles were placed a short distance south-east of the lighthouse, while a red arc of 5° on the main light was centred on the outer rock. Another red sector was incorporated with the main light from W.N.W. westward until shut in with the high land of Rodd's Peninsula, thereby protecting vessels from the East Banks near the entrance to Port Curtis and the offshore dangers from Rodd's Peninsula.[7]

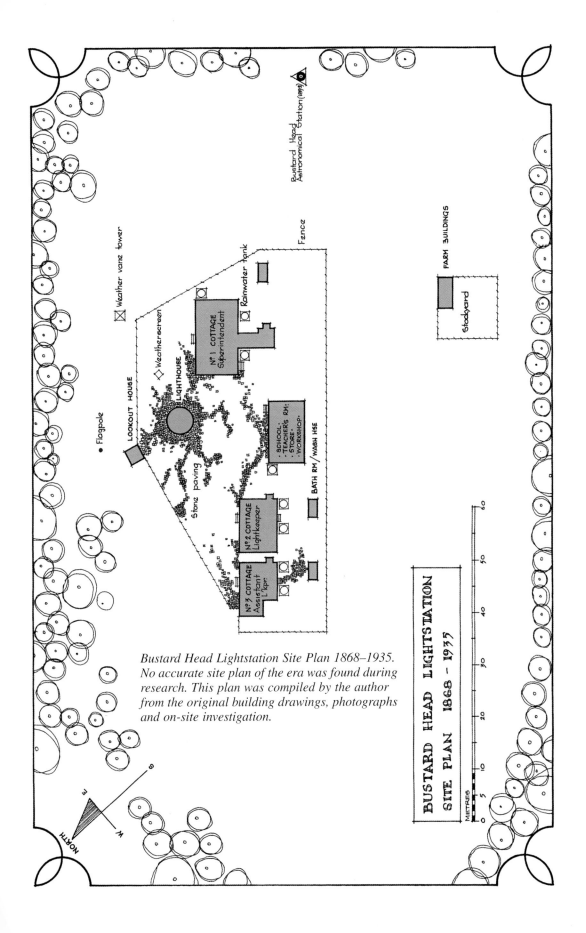

Bustard Head Lightstation Site Plan 1868–1935. No accurate site plan of the era was found during research. This plan was compiled by the author from the original building drawings, photographs and on-site investigation.

BUSTARD HEAD LIGHTSTATION
SITE PLAN 1868 – 1935

Bustard Head Astronomical Station (1872)

Weather vane tower

Weather screen

Rainwater tank

Fence

LOOKOUT HOUSE

LIGHTHOUSE

Flagpole

Stone paving

Nº 1 COTTAGE Superintendent

• SCHOOL.
• TEACHER'S RM.
• STORE.
• WORKSHOP.

BATH RM / WASH HSE

Nº 2 COTTAGE Lightkeeper

Nº 3 COTTAGE Assistant L'kpr.

FARM BUILDINGS

Stockyard

METRES

0 5 10 20 30 40 50 60

NORTH

Pancake Creek was becoming well known as a safe anchorage; the Sailing Directions of the time describe it as giving "capital shelter". One vessel to take refuge there in 1873 was the 66 ton schooner *Agnes*. Under the command of Captain Garcia, a man with years of experience on the Queensland coast, she left Mackay 8 June with twelve passengers bound for Brisbane. One of the prominent people on board was Mrs Philp, mother of Robert Philp who was later to become Premier of Queensland. A few days after leaving Mackay, *Agnes* met with heavy weather and took shelter in Pancake Creek for the purpose of taking on extra ballast. During her two day stay, Captain Garcia and a passenger, David Hume, went ashore where they met Superintendent Rooksby. The lightkeepers saw the schooner leave the creek on 16 June, heading into "very dirty weather". During the day the wind increased to gale force from the E.N.E. *Agnes* was never seen again.

When the schooner was overdue arriving in Brisbane, it was first assumed she was sheltering somewhere along the coast; however, as time went on, it was reported in newspapers that disaster had most likely befallen her. On 7 July an "influential deputation" requested the Premier to send the government steamer *Kate* in search of the schooner or its survivors. The Premier refused, saying it "would to all intents and purposes be a wild goose chase", but added that coastal shipping had been advised to keep a lookout. A lengthy and reproachful letter signed "Publicola" appeared in *The Brisbane Courier* on 5 August, part of which reads:

> . . . *Is not this conduct, both of the Government and the public, a disgrace — nay, a crime in a civilised community? . . . It is possible that twelve human beings, including several women, have been during the past month destitute, naked, shivering, hungry, starving and dying day by day by inches, on some rock or desert island. This is no fancy sketch, for have we not within the past few days the case of the* Alma, *whose crew of two men, after being four days subsisting on shell fish on a barren island in the north, was accidentally rescued by a passing vessel. On the other hand, the steamer (Kate) which might have rescued these poor destitute human beings (those aboard Agnes) is lying unemployed, or rather being cleaned, polished, fitted and victualled for a Vice-regal excursion . . . So much for the 'powers that be' in this matter. But what must be said of the citizens of Brisbane? I always thought we had a number of Christian clergymen in the city. If so, they have failed to appear or to interest themselves in one of their most important Christian duties — namely, to arouse the attention and feelings of their fellow-men in a case of life and death . . .*

"Publicola's" remonstrations, together with further deputation and appeals, failed to gain any assistance from the government or the clergy. Robert Philp spent much time and money organising lengthy search parties, but despite his efforts no survivors or trace of *Agnes* were ever found.[8]

Approaches were made during 1873 by Heath to the government to approve of a telegraph line extension from the existing Maryborough-Gladstone line to Bustard Head. Heath reasoned that the telegraph link "would apprise the pilots at Port Curtis and Keppel Bay of the approach of vessels from the southward".[9] The same year, the Superintendent of the Electric Telegraph Department made a similar proposal to the government.

At the Intercolonial Lighthouse Conference held in Sydney in September 1873, it was documented that Queensland was leading the way in regard to lighting the Australian coast. With a total of thirty-nine lights at an expenditure as low as any of the other colonies, Heath, now with the rank of Commander, was certainly proving his worth.[10]

During the three years since the two small kerosene lights were installed to provide a more precise location of the outer rock off Bustard Head, numerous complaints had been received from navigators regarding their positioning. It appeared the lie of the land had not afforded the lights to be placed far enough apart to be wholly efficient. Aware of the problem, Superintendent Rooksby, incorporating his navigational skills, submitted a unique design for a new light to Heath. Approval was given for Rooksby and the lightkeepers to construct it. The new 5.4 metre high square tower was built 457 metres S.E. by S. from the main light. Sheeted with iron and framed of bloodwood cut from the nearby bush, the tower was fitted with a fixed Fifth Order dioptric kerosene white light. A short distance in front of the tower, a 73 metre long curved screen, varying in height from 1 to just over 2 metres, was positioned to cut the light off before vessels approached dangerously near the rocks. The light, first exhibited on 3 April 1876, was a great success.[11]

Tenders were invited by the Electric Telegraph Department on 23 March 1877 for the construction of a telegraph line from Gladstone to Bustard Head. This was commenced on 3 July 1877 and completed on 24 October the same year for a cost of £1,263. 6. 6. The single wire was attached to existing poles for 48 kilometres on the Gladstone-Maryborough line, then a new line installed for the remaining 42 kilometres to Bustard Head. Along this new section, extensive mudflats — which flooded during spring-high tides and heavy rain — and two creek crossings had to be negotiated. The fact that Aborigines no longer frequented the area was a blessing for the workmen installing the line. About the same time, further north near Cooktown, the local tribe cut the line, stole insulators, pins, 64 metres of wire and speared one of the workers and two horses.[12] Bustard Head telegraph station was opened on 27 February 1878, and although all messages were in morse code and the service frequently unreliable, it proved a great benefit to mariners as well as reducing the isolation of the families on the station.

The first Superintendent of Bustard Head lightstation, Thomas Rooksby. He held the position for thirty-four years.

The East Auxiliary light, established in 1876, was designed by Thomas Rooksby and built by the lightkeepers.

The East Auxiliary light's cut-off screen is inspected by Superintendent Rooksby.

Those aboard the iron-built barque *Scottish Knight* during January 1880 were some of the first to benefit from the new telegraph. Heading south from Rockhampton, the vessel grazed Breaksea Spit at about 8.00 p.m. on the 9[th.] There appeared to be no damage, but next morning nearly 2 metres of water was found in the hold. Captain Lawson put the ship about to head for Port Curtis. Despite constant pumping, *Scottish Knight* took ever-increasing water; at 10.00 p.m. the level was less than two-thirds of a metre from the scuppers.

A horrendous night was spent as the ship, pushed along by a strong breeze, settled deeper and deeper in the water. Members of the well-known pioneering Archer family, who were passengers on board, vividly remembered the scurrying of panic-stricken rats as the encroaching water forced the family from their cabins to the higher level of the poop deck as the vessel rolled helplessly from side to side. At 7.00 a.m., now with a gale blowing, *Scottish Knight*, her deck awash, was close to and abeam of Bustard Head. Assisted by the Archer sons, Captain Lawson fired guns and displayed signals of distress. The lightkeepers replied, advising there was no pilot boat in Pancake Creek to give assistance, but they would telegraph Gladstone for help.

Doubtful that the vessel was capable of reaching Port Curtis, Captain Lawson put into Rodd's Bay, intending to go aground. Sheltered by the land the water calmed somewhat, but sounding the lead, only a rocky bottom was found. Lawson reluctantly decided to press on to Port Curtis, first disembarking the Archers and other passengers in a lifeboat. However, when the lifeboat cleared the protection of *Scottish Knight*, she was briskly whisked away from the intended landing shore some 3 kilometres distant. Now at the mercy of the sea, she was driven almost out of control towards a rock-strewn lee shore. A large wave smashed across the boat, bringing down the heavy mast on two of the Archer sons, knocking out a tooth from one of the boys in doing so. While struggling with the steering oar to keep the boat from broaching in the heavy seas, Tom Archer spotted a sandy beach. He made for this, safely landing everyone after five hours in the open boat.

In the meantime, alerted by the Bustard Head lightkeepers, the pilot schooner *Enid* had embarked Pilot Seeds on *Scottish Knight*. He eventually grounded her safely on the mud at the mouth of the Boyne River. Next day, *Enid* and the small steamer *Polly* rescued the passengers from Hummocky Island.[13]

Although Thomas and Annie Rooksby were still without children, the other two families at Bustard Head during 1880 weren't. Lightkeeper James Phillips and his wife Emma had six, while Assistant Lightkeeper Nils Gibson and his wife Kate had four. On 14 October the previous year, the Phillips' seven-week old son Henry died of "constitutional weakness". He was buried by his father next day 200 metres west of the lighthouse in a small clearing, the first recorded grave in what was to become the Bustard Head Cemetery.

Housing on the station, especially for the Phillips family with eight people living in a cottage containing one tiny bedroom, was totally inadequate. So much so, the previous year, Portmaster Heath had reported to Parliament that extra bedrooms were "urgently required, as the present accommodation is, for large families, hardly consistent with decency, and still less with comfort."[14] In 1880, additional bedrooms were built onto the cottages at a cost of £221.

The Fifth Order light, built in 1876 to warn of the rocks off the headland, although a great success, was slightly obscured by the land from one position. To compensate for this, in 1881, an additional small, fixed catoptric kerosene white light was placed on a mast 146 metres W.N.W. of the main light. A series of screens placed in front of it acted as staged warnings when approaching the rocks.[15] These two auxiliary lights were so functional they were to remain in use for the next sixty years.

With ten school-age children living at Bustard Head during 1882, it was decided to send a teacher to the station. In preparation for this, the store and workshop building was extended to accommodate a schoolroom and teacher's bedroom. At the same time, the shingles on the cottage roofs, which leaked badly, were replaced with galvanised iron. Total cost of the work was £88. 3. 3.

Bustard Head Provisional School No.391 opened on 1 September 1882. William Jackson was the first teacher on a yearly salary of £50, £10 of which was contributed by the pupils' parents. Free board and lodging to the amount of £25 was an extra benefit paid by the Marine Department. By the end of the year, thirteen children were attending the school. Two years later to the day, Jackson resigned due to ill health, a decision regretted by all at the station. In a letter to the Department of Public Instruction requesting another teacher, Superintendent Rooksby wrote that William Jackson's "kindness and attention to the school duties has secured for him the respect and good wishes of all, and all regret his departure". Regarding a successor, Rooksby wrote: "as girls preponderate, I beg leave to believe that a female protestant teacher would at this time more fully meet the requirements".[16]

The new teacher, Mrs Margaret Kenny, opened the school again five weeks later, but within a month sent in her resignation by electric telegraph. She believed the pupils' parents' contribution should have been £15 and not £10, as she had been receiving the higher amount at her last posting. Further, she found difficulty in controlling the children. The parents requested she withdraw her resignation; this she did, and remained teaching at Bustard Head for the next three years. It is not known if she was induced to stay by payment of the extra £5.

It is unrecorded whether the Bustard Head lightkeepers of the time received stores at regular intervals, but with the pilot schooner *Enid* frequently using Pancake Creek while waiting to deliver or pick up pilots from passing ships, they would never have gone wanting. Two white beacons were erected in

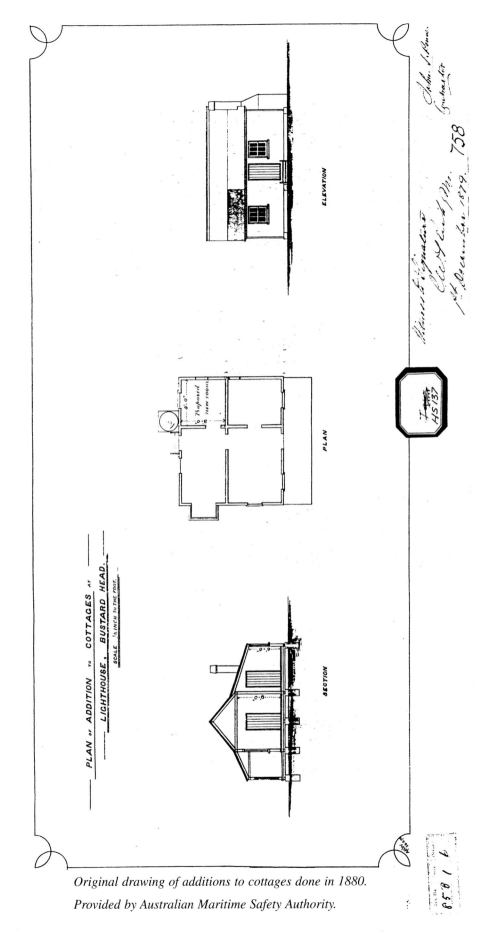

Original drawing of additions to cottages done in 1880.

Provided by Australian Maritime Safety Authority.

Thomas Rooksby beside the instrument he invented for accurately measuring time.

Station staff watch, as Superintendent Rooksby takes a reading from his time measuring invention.

A rare photograph of the West Auxiliary light established in 1881. Clews Point and Rodd's Peninsula in the background.

Photograph provided by Babs Atherton.

391.

School opened 1st Sept — &c, &c

T. Rooksby

Electric Telegraph, Queensland.

From Bustard Head

Dated 11·12 9 1882

Message for J. G. Anderson, BRISBANE. Board Instruction

School opened on first instant ten (10) scholars, regular attendance. Please advise if the new (10) pounds subscription residents to teachers paid to him or sent to you

T. Rooksby

13.9.82

Tel. parents. The contributions to the teachers' salary may be paid directly to the teacher

391
14.9.82

The telegram from Thomas Rooksby advising the Department of Public Instruction that the Bustard Head school opened on 1 September 1882 with ten scholars.

Pancake Creek in 1883 to assist vessels entering the channel. The Sailing Directions of that year state:

> The opposite or south-western side of the channel is formed by a sand bank, which dries at low water, and whose limits can easily be seen. In entering from seaward look out for two white beacons on Pancake Point, then follow round the north-west point of Bustard Head, keeping about 150 feet off from the shore until the two white beacons on Pancake Point come in line; then by steering for them on a South bearing a vessel will pass up in mid-channel, and bring up close to the mooring buoy, placed there for the use of the pilot schooner; be careful not to run too far past the buoy, as there are rocks lying abreast of the boat-shed. There is a good road from the boat-shed to the light-house about 2 miles distant, whence telegraphic messages can be sent.
>
> Fresh water can always be obtained at the back of the beach in the bay, abreast of the moorings.[17]

The Sailing Directions of 1884, in describing how to cross the bar into Eurimbula Creek to access the sawmill which was still operating, state for the first time there is "a heliograph by which telegraphic messages can be sent *via* Bustard Head." Passing messages by heliograph had been going on for some time. Bustard Head was often in contact with Gatcombe Head lightstation 23 nautical miles away, as well as "Turkey" cattle station, which lay 15 kilometres inland. Being adept at morse code was an essential requirement for lightkeepers.

To accommodate the ever-increasing family numbers, in May 1886, two rooms were added to the Superintendent's cottage, two to the Lightkeeper's cottage and one to the Assistant's at a cost of £250.

The China Oil, first used to fuel the main light, had been replaced by Imperial Oil. Experiments had shown the latter burnt with a much greater intensity, at the same time with less consumption. Testing was always being done on the wick burners. New, more powerful burners for use in bad weather were imported from England, some of which had up to six concentric wicks. The most up to date burner at the time was one designed by Sir James Douglass, the Engineer of Trinity House (Trinity House controlled the English light-houses). But Superintendent Rooksby modified an ordinary Trinity House burner to give as good a result as the Douglass burner.[18]

Rooksby was no novice at inventing things. His interest in celestial-navigation had led him to invent an instrument for accurately measuring time by the apparent movement of stars from east to west. This instrument, in conjunction with a simple form of sundial, also accurately measured time during the day.[19]

Following a visit to Bustard Head during 1886, Portmaster Heath reported to Parliament: "Everything is in excellent order at this lighthouse".[20]

Bustard Head could not have had a better man in charge.

Chapter 4

A CLOUD OF GLOOM

At first, nothing appeared unusual to Assistant Lightkeeper Nils Gibson on the morning of Thursday 5 May 1887. He had breakfast with his four daughters — Annie, Mary, Kate and Sarah-Jane — along with two young relatives, George and James Hay, who were living with the family. Nils' wife Kate was still in bed, but this was of little concern, as she often rested while suffering from one of her frequent headaches. After breakfast, eighteen year-old Mary took her mother a cup of tea. Shortly after nine o'clock, mother Kate came into the kitchen and began busying herself, the same as any other day.

That morning, Nils had been instructed by Superintendent Rooksby to collect a horse from "Turkey" cattle station, 15 kilometres inland from Bustard Head. Nils had planned to leave the lightstation about eleven o'clock, spend the night at "Turkey" and return the following day. About an hour before he was due to leave, nineteen year-old Annie saw her mother walk out of the cottage towards the calf pen and fowl house. When Nils returned to the cottage to say he was leaving, his wife Kate wasn't there, so he sent daughters Mary and Kate to look for her. They returned half an hour later without finding her. Although this appeared a little strange, Nils wasn't overly concerned, as his wife was often in the habit of going for a walk by herself.

Nils left for "Turkey" while Mary continued to look for her mother. About 3.00 p.m., Annie, now certain that something was wrong, joined the search. Superintendent Rooksby was informed at the same time; he immediately told the schoolteacher, Mrs Kenny, to dismiss the pupils and have them assist. The bush was searched until eight o'clock that night without success. An hour earlier, Rooksby had telegraphed the Port Curtis Harbour Master and sent a note to the Pilot on board *Enid*, which was moored in Pancake Creek, "earnestly soliciting his assistance for daybreak in the morning with as many men as he could spare".

The search continued next day, helped by the Pilot and every one of *Enid's* crew. At 2.00 p.m. Nils was sighted crossing the Jenny Lind Creek flats on his way home from "Turkey". Rooksby sent the boy George Hay to meet him and "break the news to him gently, that Auntie could not be found". Without returning to his cottage, Nils began combing the bush and kept doing so right throughout the night.

Next morning shortly after nine o'clock, near the telegraph line just over 700 metres from the lighthouse, Annie found her mother in the bush. Kate was lying on her right side, her right arm extended, with her other arm folded across her breast. She was dead.

"Here's Mother!" gasped Annie to George Hay who was with her. "You go home and tell the others."

George returned to the station and told the other lightkeeper's wife, Margaret Goodfellow. While she was informing those still on the station, George began cooeeing, summoning Nils and the other searchers. George led Nils down to where Kate was lying. As he bent down, lifting her into his arms, the movement exposed Kate's throat. It was slashed from ear to ear. Nils picked up the body and began carrying it back to the lightstation. He was met by Thomas Rooksby who immediately assisted him, but finding it difficult, he "sent for a hand barrow and by that means conveyed the body home". Kate was placed in her bed, and later put in an open coffin.

The previous day, Constable McKenzie from the Gladstone Police had been instructed by his Sergeant to go to Bustard Head and assist in the search. He arrived at 5.00 p.m. on Saturday, eight hours after the discovery of Kate's body.

In the meantime, Nils found one of his cut-throat razors missing. Accompanied by Annie Gibson and George Hay, Constable McKenzie went down to the thick scrub where Kate had been found. McKenzie saw a dried pool of blood and a trail of blood leading 8 metres to where the body had lain, but despite an extensive search, there was no sign of either a cut-throat razor or any other sharp instrument that could have been responsible for Kate's death.

Shortly after the discovery of Kate's body, Thomas Rooksby had telegraphed the Police Magistrate in Gladstone, who asked the Government Medical Officer of the Gladstone district, Dr Symes, to go to Bustard Head as soon as possible. The doctor left Gladstone at 12.30 p.m. and rode throughout the night, reaching the lightstation at five o'clock next morning. Dr Symes did a post-mortem examination on the body, stating:

> . . . There was an incised wound stretching obliquely across the throat from right to left six inches long. It severed the integument and the structures underneath severing the wind pipe and the external carroted artery and all neighbouring tissues. The cause of death hemorrage [sic] from the wound which must have been inflicted by some sharp instrument . . . the wound could have been self inflicted.

Another search at the death scene by Dr Symes, Constable McKenzie and others that morning proved unsuccessful. Later that day, Kate Gibson was buried in the Bustard Head Cemetery. At about 4.00 p.m., two hours after

Constable McKenzie left the station, Nils Gibson and George Hay resumed the search. Under the root of a little tree, almost at the spot where Kate's feet had been, George found Nils' bloodstained cut-throat razor.

At the inquest of 12 and 14 May the Coroner stated that no suspicious circumstances relating to Kate's death had been found. It was said she got on well with her husband and family as she did with the others at Bustard Head. Apart from some sleeplessness and frequent headaches, there was no obvious reason why Kate should have taken her life. But no-one will ever know what inner turmoil and anguish drove Kate to take her husband's cut-throat razor and, without a word to her four daughters, leave the cottage for that final desperate walk in the bush, to end her life in such a gruesome way.[1]

An epitaph written by Kate's daughters was placed in the *Gladstone Observer* newspaper:

> *We cooeed our best at dead of night*
> *The dead it could not hear us*
> *The children cry 'Oh Mother dear'*
> *What keeps you from us?*
>
> *With weary anxious eyes we search*
> *O'er sand, ridge, scrub, and bush*
> *But the warm heart was cold in death*
> *Of her who gave us birth.*[2]

Nils was fifty-four years old and had been stationed at Bustard Head for fifteen years when Kate died. A transfer to another station may have helped distance the dreadful memory, but it seems Nils preferred to stay where he was.

Dr Symes' 90 kilometre overnight horse ride from Gladstone to Bustard Head had been no mean feat. Although the rough track followed the telegraph line, the last half and most difficult part of the journey was done during darkness, where steep-banked tidal creeks and mudflats had to be crossed. The last creek to be forged before Bustard Head was Middle Creek (then known as Bustard Creek), which separated Middle Island and Bustard Head from the mainland. The telegraph line crossed Middle Creek at a point about 10 kilometres upstream from the lighthouse boatshed in Pancake Creek. When Electric Telegraph Department repairmen needed to fix faulty equipment at the Bustard Head end, they were usually met by the lightkeepers at the Middle Creek crossing and transported by boat to the lightstation.

Almost two years to the day after Kate Gibson's death, thirty year-old telegraph line repairer Alfred Power from Miriam Vale visited Bustard Head to repair some equipment. At the time, Superintendent Rooksby and his wife Annie were in Brisbane on leave. During his absence, Nils Gibson was in charge of the station. The new Assistant Lightkeeper John Wilkinson — a

Master Mariner — along with his thirty-nine year-old wife Elizabeth and their four children had only arrived on the station that year, 1889.

Power completed his repairs and was ready to leave on Wednesday morning 15 May. Early that morning Nils walked the 3 kilometres down to the boatshed at Pancake Creek to prepare the undecked sailboat for its trip to Middle Creek crossing. A little later, at about 7.30 a.m., Wilkinson and Power followed. They were accompanied by Elizabeth Wilkinson and Nils' twenty year-old daughter Mary, who were going with the men up to the crossing.

The party set off from the boatshed shortly after eight o'clock, with a fresh breeze blowing from the south-east. John Wilkinson was at the helm and the boat was moving briskly, close-hauled on a port tack (sailing as close as possible to the wind coming in on the port side). When they were about 450 metres from shore, Nils gave the order to go about, so they would get smoother water closer in. It took two attempts to get the boat's head around, and when it did, the sail filled on the other tack, tilting the boat over and shipping water to leeward. The passengers panicked and stood up. Alfred Power jumped up onto the mast thwart (seat) and took hold of the mast. Wilkinson immediately released the mainsheet and put the helm down. But it was too late — the top-heavy weight of the passengers caused the boat to capsize, throwing everyone into the water.

Wilkinson managed to scramble on top of the boat's keel, from where he saw the other four hanging onto the stern. He shouted at the two men, telling them to strip, and then took off his own shirt and singlet. Wilkinson's wife Elizabeth was closest to him; he removed his belt and fastened it around her wrist. With so much weight on the port side, the boat suddenly righted itself, then instantly turned over again. Elizabeth lost her grip and floated about 8 metres away from the boat. Wilkinson dived and found the painter (a rope attached to the boat's bow), then climbed back onto the keel. He coiled the painter and threw it to his wife. It landed right across her, but she took no notice of it. Wilkinson jumped into the water and swam towards her, took hold of his wife and, with great difficulty, towed her back to the boat. Once again he climbed back onto the keel and tried to keep Elizabeth's head clear of the water, as the boat drifted across the creek towards shore.

When the boat first capsized, Nils Gibson managed to take hold of his daughter Mary who he twice pulled to the surface, but, obviously fighting for her life, she clung to her father's jumper, often pulling him under before letting go at the last moment. Nils found it impossible to hang onto the boat; the wind and sea were against him. By this time, both Mary and Alfred Power had disappeared from sight. With the tide the only thing in his favour, Nils struck out for the western shore, eventually reaching it in an exhausted condition.

When Nils reached shore he saw Wilkinson on the boat's keel drifting towards him, but it took well over an hour before the mast of the upturned boat struck bottom. All that time, John Wilkinson had kept hold of Elizabeth by hanging onto the shoulder of her dress and her hair.

"Don't pull my hair!" she said.

And then shortly before the mast hit, she said:

"Give me your hand!"

As the mast took the ground, the boat began to right itself, making it more difficult than ever for Wilkinson to keep his wife's head above water. When the water was shallow enough, Wilkinson, assisted by Nils, dragged Elizabeth ashore. By this time she was unconscious, and all efforts to restore her failed.

John Wilkinson spotted something lying on a sandbank; it was found to be the body of Alfred Power.

Nils and Wilkinson continued to search for Mary Gibson, but did not find her.

The two bodies were placed in the boat, which was now high and dry from the outgoing tide. A further unsuccessful search was made for Mary until almost dark, when the tide was high enough to float the boat. The bodies were put in the boatshed for the night, then Nils and Wilkinson returned to the station to break the dreadful news to the families and telegraph the Port Curtis Harbour Master.

Early next morning the bodies were brought up to the station by dray. Nils and Wilkinson went back to the creek and spent all day looking for Mary, but still did not find her. When the men returned to the lightstation that evening they met the Government Medical Officer Dr Symes and Constable Moran, who had both travelled from Gladstone. Dr Symes examined the bodies, which were still in the dray covered by canvas, and gave the order for burial. A bruise was found on Power's forehead, perhaps the result of a blow from the mast.[3] Both bodies were buried in the Bustard Head Cemetery. In a fitting tribute to Alfred Power, who left a wife and two children, each of the four corner posts supporting the white paling fence around his grave was capped with a ceramic telegraph line insulator. The body of Mary Gibson was never found.

The Rooksbys' twenty-one year-old adopted daughter Grace, who had remained on the station during her parents' absence, wrote of the accident in her diary:

> *Wednesday May 15th 1889*
> *A very sad accident happened here today through the boat capsizing in Pancake Creek on the way up to Middle Creek to put Mr Power, Miriam Vale Telegraph Master, who had been here repairing telegraph instrument, across creek, causing the death of three persons, Mrs Wilkinson aged 39 years, Mr Power about 30 years and my dear friend Mary Gibson aged 20½ years. The men rescued both bodies but Mary never seen. The men returning home at 8 p.m. reporting the case, they were naked. The shock was almost unbearable for all here.*

Thursday May 16th
Men went down with dray to boathouse for dead bodies having been left there that night. After returning, partly made coffins and went in search of Mary, returning about 7 p.m. without success. About 5 p.m. Dr Symes and Constable Moran arrived overland to hold inquiry.

Friday May 17th
Day opens with dull, drizzly and miserable day. Finished coffins and prepared for burial. All went out (with Doctor's consent) to see the dead bodies who were then in coffins, and it will be remembered by all who were here as long as they live. No one could have recognised Mrs Wilkinson, but Mr Power was quite natural. It would touch the hardest heart to see those four little children take the last look at their mother. After coming in from seeing them I thought I should break my heart it was indeed dreadful. At 1 p.m. funeral took place all attending. Dr Symes reading funeral service. When we returned it seemed worse than ever. Today was my 21st birthday and will never be forgotten. Dr Symes was very kind to us all. They left here Sunday a.m. Mary's body never recovered. Bustard Head does not seem like itself now. It was very hard on us all single girls. No married woman here. I hope never to have the same again.[4]

Nils must have been devastated — first his wife, then his daughter. And to make matters worse for him, Portmaster Heath, in his 1889 report to Parliament stated:

A sad accident, causing the death of three persons by the upsetting of the boat, has cast a gloom over the establishment at Bustard Head Lighthouse. Unfortunately the Superintendent was absent at the time obtaining medical advice, or the accident probably would not have happened. The loss was not caused by any defect in the boat, but by want of ordinary care and presence of mind in those in her. Two of the bodies were recovered and buried at the lighthouse; one was not found.[5]

In his report, Heath most likely meant that if Superintendent Rooksby had been on the station he would not have permitted the two women to travel in the boat with the men. It was how things were in those days. Unfair criticism or not, it was something Nils Gibson had to live with for the rest of his life.

There was no doubt that a strong bond of respect had developed over the past twenty-eight years between Portmaster Heath and Superintendent Rooksby. On Heath's retirement, when he was leaving Queensland on 20 April 1890 on board the *Tara*, he wrote to Rooksby:

The tragic Gibson family. Nils Gibson with his three daughters (from left to right: Sarah-Jane, Annie and Kate).

Photograph provided by Catherine Mountford.

The lightstation stockyard and calf pen. Jenny Lind Creek is in the background.

Photograph provided by Norma Mills.

The Wilkinson family. Repeated attempts by Lightkeeper John Wilkinson to save his wife Elizabeth from drowning failed.

Photograph provided by Jill West.

Grace Rooksby, adopted daughter of Thomas and Annie Rooksby. Grace wrote in her diary of the shocking drowning accident in Pancake Creek.

Photograph provided by Rochelle Starr-Thomas.

I cannot, Rooksby, leave the waters of the colony without sending you a few lines to wish you good-bye, and to express my appreciation of your intelligent and faithful service in the department for so many years. There is nobody in the department for whom I have a greater respect, or in whom I have placed more confidence. I regret much that I will never have another opportunity of spending a pleasant hour at Bustard Head, which it was always very much a pleasure to me to visit, on account of the admirable manner in which the work there has been carried out. I can only now wish you many years — both you and your wife — of health and happiness.[6]

During Commander Heath's twenty-eight years' service as Portmaster, he was responsible for establishing fifty-eight manned lights in Queensland. Twenty-two of these were major coastal lights, including seven lightships. He left the colony with a fine record indeed.

Chapter 5

A TIME OF LEARNING

In an endeavour to more accurately plot the coastline of Australia on nautical charts, the Lords Commissioners of the Admiralty in 1891 requested the Surveyor-Generals of the various colonies to supply data regarding the position of prominent coastal features such as lighthouses. For this purpose, Queensland's Surveyor-General decided to establish astronomical observation stations at Cape Moreton, Sandy Cape and Bustard Head. The following year, an astronomical station — a simple, waist-high timber stump — was placed 202 feet South, 108 feet East of the Bustard Head lighthouse, and a number of observations taken. The results, compared to today's charts, show the latitude as identical, while the longitude was only a fraction out.[1] Superintendent Rooksby would have been in his element during that time.

Meteorological records show that the Bustard Head lightkeepers first began recording rainfall in 1885. However, it wasn't until the charismatic Clement Lindley Wragge, F.R.G.S., F.R. Met. Soc., Honorary Corresponding Member of the Scottish Geographical Society, Gold Medallist of the Scottish Meteorological Society, was appointed Government Meteorologist of Queensland in January 1887, that weather reporting in Queensland came into its own. Within a year of taking office, Wragge reported to Parliament:

> . . . *That, despite the meteorological systems of other colonies, which are excellent enough in their way, Queensland proves to the scientific world that she will be second to none; that she has, in fact, spirit enough to establish a meteorological organisation of her own, even better than any of them . . . so that whereas, on December 31ˢᵗ 1886, no meteorological organisation existed in Queensland, by December 31ˢᵗ 1887, Brisbane had become, as a matter of fact, the Chief Weather Bureau for all Australasia, by reason of Queensland having taken the entire initiative in issuing Australasian and inter-colonial forecasts.*[2]

His enthusiasm for establishing Climatological stations was inexhaustible. He hoped:

> *... eventually to place one in every township throughout the Colony, and in the forest lands, on open plains, in valleys and on the ranges, with a rain gauge at every Post and Telegraph Office, so that each variety of climate may be practically investigated with reference to agricultural, hygienic, pastoral and other interests ... When these have been established, no country in the world will possess a meteorological service more complete than that of Queensland.[3]*

Despite the flamboyant rhetoric, in between compiling an unrelenting flood of maps, tables, diagrams, charts and synopses, the ever-optimistic Wragge *did* manage to establish hundreds of weather stations providing daily reports and forecasts throughout Australia. In 1888, Bustard Head was classified as a 3rd Order B station, supplied with only a rain gauge which was read every day at 9.00 a.m. In 1892 it was upgraded to a 2nd Order station, supplied with a standard barometer, Stevenson's double-louvred thermometer screen, hygrometer, maximum and minimum self-registering thermometers, solar and terrestrial radiation thermometers, earth thermometers, wind-compass and rain gauge. Readings were taken each day at 9.00 a.m. and 9.00 p.m., also when it was mean noon at Greenwich.[4]

In addition to becoming an important weather station, Bustard Head became a storm signal station on 12 January 1893, displaying a cone and/or a ball from the quarters of the yard-arm (flagpole) to warn mariners when bad weather was anticipated.[5]

The new Portmaster, Thomas Almond, was as impressed with Bustard Head as Heath had been. In his 1893-4 report to Parliament he stated:

> *At Bustard Head the lighthouse and station generally are maintained in a state of great efficiency, reflecting great credit on the Superintendent and his staff.[6]*

The tragic death of Kate Gibson and her daughter Mary, understandably had a deleterious effect on Nils Gibson. Six years after Mary's death, Nils, who was still at Bustard Head, became ill. He died on the lightstation a few months later on 25 February 1896 from cirrhosis of the liver, and was buried in the Bustard Head Cemetery the following day. A headstone in memory of the three Gibsons was placed on Nils' grave.

Two months after Nils' death, Paulina, wife of Assistant Lightkeeper Ernest Waye, gave birth on the station to a daughter they named Milly. At the age of twenty months, Milly was accidentally scalded with boiling water on 6 January 1898. Far from medical help, the poor child suffered excruciating pain for nine hours before finding relief in death. Superintendent Rooksby was the Lay Reader for her burial in the Bustard Head Cemetery two days later.

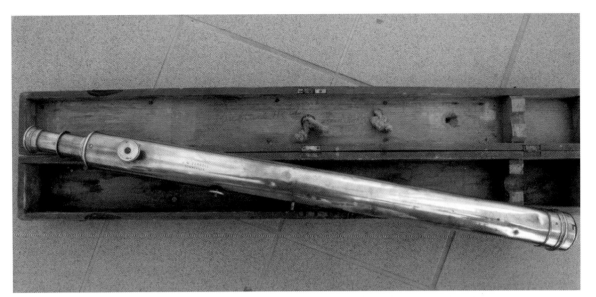

This brass telescope was put under the charge of Superintendent Thomas Rooksby on 1 June 1889 by the charismatic Clement Lindley Wragge, Queensland's Government Meteorologist. Some time after Rooksby's retirement in 1902, the telescope disappeared from the station. No more was heard of it until 1968, when Joan Oliver, the "antique mad" publican of the Horse and Jockey Hotel at Warwick, Queensland, was given the telescope by "one of the lads who drank at the pub". It cost Joan only a few drinks. Twenty-six years later, Joan passed the telescope on to her son Ian who, in 1999, donated it to the Miriam Vale Shire Historical Society for display in their museum at Agnes Water.

The inscription inside the telescope box reads: "Given in my charge at Brisbane by Mr Wragge June 1st 1889, also Stevensons thermometer screen and all other instruments. Thomas Rooksby, Bustard Head".

Photograph provided by Ian Oliver.

The telescope is used by a lightkeeper to identify a passing ship. Circa 1895.

Photograph provided by John Christensen.

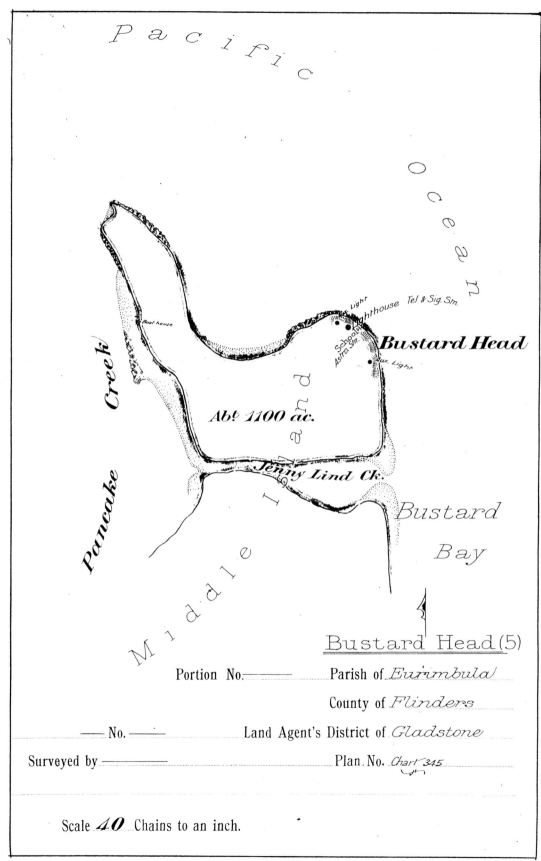

An early survey plan of Bustard Head.

Provided by Australian Maritime Safety Authority.

The wind vane and Superintendent's cottage.

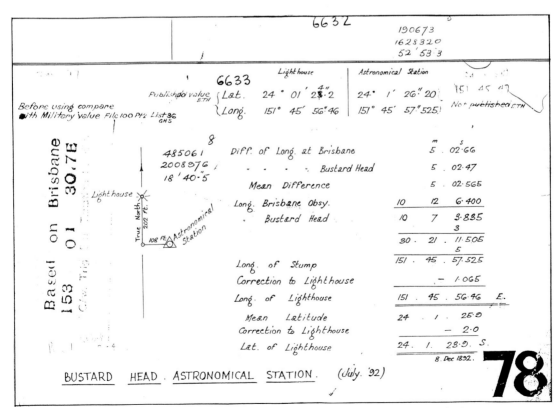

Site plan of Bustard Head Astronomical Station showing latitude and longitude calculations.

Provided by Department of Natural Resources.

All flags flying. Circa 1900. Superintendent Rooksby is on the first floor landing of the lighthouse.
Photograph provided by John Christensen.

As the twentieth century approached, lighthouse technology was improving in leaps and bounds. Early in 1900, Engineer of the Marine Department, Edward Cullen, departed on an overseas voyage to investigate some of the world's harbours and navigational aids. In Paris at the premises of Messrs Sautter, Harle and Company, the Engineer-in-Chief, M Jean Rey, showed Cullen a newly developed light — an incandescent mantle powered by high pressure vaporised petroleum — to replace the oil fuelled wick burner. Experiments had shown that the new light was four times brighter than a six-wick burner and used only one-sixth the amount of fuel consumed by the latter. In his report to Parliament later that year, Cullen advised that it was "one of the most important developments in lighthouse illumination that has occurred for a long time".[7] He was to be proven right.

Age had caught up with the Port Curtis pilot schooner *Enid*. She was replaced in 1901 by a new cutter *Jessie*, which continued to provide the monthly stores service to Bustard Head. The faithful old *Enid* suffered the indignity of being transformed into a barge for carrying gas holders for the Rockhampton gas buoys.

The end of an era arrived in June 1902 with the retirement of seventy-one year-old Superintendent Thomas Rooksby. In his annual report regarding a visit to Bustard Head that year, the recently appointed Portmaster John Mackay stated:

The buildings here with lighting arrangements were found to be in excellent condition, the surroundings giving evidence alike of official activity, and domestic happiness and comfort. This station is now in charge of Captain Bowton, late Harbour Master, Townsville, who I think, will prove a worthy successor to Mr Rooksby, retired after a service of forty-three years, during which long period he did honour to the lighthouse service, supplementing an intelligent discharge of his duties by an able grasp of the technical problems concerned in successfully providing for the perfect combustion of illuminants when used under conditions of temperature, &c., differing from those for which the appliances in which they were used were originally designed. In this, and meeting the new requirements demanded by the use of more refined illuminants as time proceeded, Mr Rooksby was signally successful. These questions, on which the value of a light so largely depends, are of the very first importance amongst those connected with the subject.

Mr Rooksby also interested himself with success in the subject of practical astronomy, and is the author of an ingenious instrument for use in connection therewith.[8]

After thirty-four years at Bustard Head, Superintendent Thomas Rooksby had the privilege of not only being the first Superintendent, but would retain the record for being the longest serving lightkeeper in the station's history.

The new Superintendent of Bustard Head, sixty-nine year-old Master Mariner Frederick James Bowton, arrived at the station with his wife Katherine and their three children, Frederick, Bertha and Elsie, aged fourteen, nine and seven respectively. Katherine, twenty-three years younger than her husband, was the Captain's second wife. The Lightkeeper, Charles Rasmus, who had been at Bustard Head for nine years, bitterly resented the fact that the Captain, with no prior experience of working on lightstations, was made Superintendent. The two men did not have a good relationship.

It was decided by the Marine Department in 1902 to stop the practice of sending relief lightkeepers to most stations, including Bustard Head, when the permanent keepers were on leave, resulting in an annual saving of £500.

The new pilot cutter *Jessie* was soon found to be unsuitable for the handling of buoys in Port Curtis and was sold in 1903. Subsequently, Bustard Head was serviced by the steamer *Fitzroy* from Rockhampton. Bustard Head, together with other lights in the vicinity, although controlled by the Portmaster in Brisbane, was now under the supervision of the Rockhampton Harbour Master, who visited the station each month on the stores boat.

White ants had eaten into the frame of Superintendent Bowton's cottage. In 1904 the Harbour Master wrote to the Marine Department requesting urgent repairs, as the building was "in danger of collapse". An inspector from the Works Department was sent to investigate and repairs were effected the following year. As well, an additional horse was supplied to convey oil and stores from the boatshed to the station.

A little over three years after his arrival on the station, Superintendent Bowton died suddenly from a heart attack on 17 October 1905. He was buried the same day in the Bustard Head Cemetery (Author's note: Superintendent Bowton's Death Certificate shows his date of death and burial as 17 October 1905. However, his headstone inscription mistakenly states he died on 5 October 1905). The Marine Department advised his wife Katherine that she could stay on the station until the family had found another home. This infuriated Lightkeeper Rasmus, who was now in charge, and after a while he began badgering the Bowtons to move out of their cottage so he could move into the designated Superintendent's quarters. Despite Rasmus's insensitivity, to a certain extent his urgency could be understood — with a wife and eight children, the much larger Superintendent's cottage must have appeared extremely appealing.

In 1975 the author was told by Captain Bowton's daughter Bertha, then eighty-two years of age, that, after her father's death, Rasmus had made life so miserable for the family, they moved down to Pancake Creek and camped near the boatshed for some months before moving to adjoining Middle Island to run

The new Superintendent of Bustard Head, Captain Frederick James Bowton. His family went on to have a long association with the lightstation.

Photograph provided by Kathy Mian and Boyd Rich.

The Captain's wife Katherine, twenty-three years younger than her husband.

Photograph provided by Kathy Mian and Boyd Rich.

The Bowton children. Frederick, Bertha and Elsie (sitting on the chair).

Photograph provided by Kathy Mian and Boyd Rich.

cattle. However, records show that Bertha's brother Fred was employed as Assistant Lightkeeper at Bustard Head a fortnight after his father's death, and Mrs Bowton was acting as his housekeeper. Bertha had obviously forgotten the chain of events, but by March 1907 the Bowtons had moved to Middle Island and were establishing their cattle property. They set up camp on the banks of Middle Creek, 3 kilometres upstream from the Middle Creek telegraph line crossing, and over the next seventy years remained an integral part of life on Bustard Head.

Charles Rasmus was officially appointed as Superintendent on 1 November 1905 "a promotion fully merited by his long and faithful service combined with a thorough knowledge of the duties devolving upon him".[9]

A brief description of life on Bustard Head in those days was given by journalist John Munro during a visit in June 1907. Munro was accompanying Portmaster John Mackay on a coastal voyage aboard the government steamship *Albatross*. Part of Munro's article which appeared as a series in *The Brisbane Courier* states:

> *On Wednesday, 5th we arrived at Bustard Head at 7 a.m., and anchored at Pancake Creek. On landing we were met by the superintendent (Rasmus) with a spring-cart, and conveyed along a heavy bush road to the lighthouse, which, with cottages, outhouses and stockyard, cattle and horses quietly browsing on the succulent grass and herbs, carried one back to pioneering times, when on a cattle station on the frontier of civilisation. The gloom of the morning ushered in with rain was dispersed by the innocent jubilance of a troop of children, who with expectant glances gathered round the Portmaster for the usual distribution of lollies — a time-honoured custom in the department. The school is in charge of Miss Crawford, from Brisbane, and I believe her successful efforts in the cause entrusted to her is deserving of all praise.[10]*

The schoolteacher mentioned in Munro's article, Margaret Crawford, was one of the few to last four years on the station. Since the school's inception twenty-four years previously, Margaret was the thirteenth teacher. All but the first teacher, William Jackson, had been female. For most of these young, single teachers, life at Bustard Head, after a while, must have become terribly monotonous. In an internal Department of Public Instruction memo regarding a resignation from Bustard Head it was stated:

> *It is very difficult to get persons to take such places, difficult to get persons suitable, and difficult to get suitable persons to stay for any length of time, without complaints and petty quarrellings and squabblings, seeing the life is of much the same nature as life on board ship, with only a few on board.[11]*

The memo went on to suggest that a past teacher at the station, Marianne Hensley, be asked to return. Miss Hensley pulled no punches in her reply:

> *. . . It may be remembered that I was appointed to the position of teacher at that school in the early part of May 1888. It was my first school, and my recollections of the place are such as do not, by any means, create a desire to return.*[12]

While at Bustard Head in 1889, Miss Hensley had written to the Department of Public Instruction suggesting the school be closed, as there were only four school-age children on the station. She also requested a transfer to a school "more accessible". Neither request was met, but the number of school-age children was increased to eight, by a change in personnel.

It was difficult obtaining a transfer, but resigning was easy, and some of the reasons given were delightful. After only eight months at Bustard Head, eighteen year-old Amy Joyner stated in her letter of resignation:

> *. . . My reasons for taking the above steps are, that I do not enjoy the best of health, as the sea air is too strong for me.*[13]

Shortly before the end of five weeks Christmas vacation in January 1905, schoolteacher Lavinia Anna Summers, who had taught at Bustard Head during the latter half of the previous year, wrote to her Department requesting six weeks leave of absence because she was "very ill, and my doctor says that I am quite unfit to return to my duties at present, and will be for some weeks to come". The accompanying doctor's certificate, written in an extremely shaky and spidery hand, stated that Lavinia was suffering from Nefritis and Parametritis.

The Department of Public Instruction granted her only three weeks, as they considered six weeks on top of the vacation was too much. At the end of the three weeks, Lavinia applied for, and received another three weeks. At the end of the six weeks, she applied for "one week or ten days leave". The accompanying doctor's certificate, written in an even more shaky hand than before, stated that Lavinia was now suffering from Dengue Fever. Lavinia was granted a further one weeks leave, ending on 10 March.

However, on 21 March, when the stores boat arrived at Bustard Head, Lavinia wasn't on board. Lightkeeper Rasmus, who was Secretary of the School Committee, wrote to the Department of Public Instruction advising them of this, and said he had "strong reasons to believe she is not returning here". He requested another teacher be sent, as the ten children on the station had now been without schooling for four months. The Department wrote to Lavinia (her address being c/o Rockhampton G.P.O.):

Superintendent Charles Rasmus and his family. His urgency to move into the much larger Superintendent's cottage could be understood.

Photograph provided by John Christensen.

The Superintendent's cottage, showing the detached kitchen at the rear.

Photograph provided by John Christensen.

POST & TELEGRAPH DEPT.
01701 A 16 FEB. 1902
QUEENSLAND.

COMMONWEALTH OF AUSTRALIA.

Bustard Head Lighthouse

POST AND TELEGRAPH DECLARATION.

EDWARDI SEPTIMI REGIS.

No. 12, SECTION 9, SECOND SCHEDULE.

I, Charles Rasmus.

do solemnly and sincerely declare that I will not willingly or knowingly open detain return or delay or cause or suffer to be opened detained returned or delayed any postal article which shall come into my hands power or custody by reason of my employment relating to the Department except by the consent of the person or persons to whom such postal article shall be directed, or by an express warrant in writing for that purpose under the hand of the Postmaster-General or unless otherwise in pursuance and under the authority of any of the provisions in that behalf contained in any Act law or duly authorised regulation of the Department passed and made for or in relation to the postage and conveyance of postal articles. And I further declare that I will be true and faithful in the execution of the telegraph duties intrusted to me and that I will hold strictly secret all telegraphic or other communications that may pass through my hands in the performance of my duties. I also further declare that I will not give any information directly or indirectly respecting any telegrams or despatches transmitted or intended to be transmitted by telegraph except to the persons to whom such telegrams or despatches may be addressed or to their recognised agents.

Charles Rasmus

DECLARED before me, one of His Majesty's Justices

of the Peace for the State of Queensland

this   day of

The School Committee at Bustard Head writing to this Office under date the 21ˢᵗ instant report that you have not yet re-opened the school.

You are requested to report forthwith whether you intend to resume duty, and if so, on what date.

If you do not intend to resume duty, you should notify the Department immediately and tender your resignation, otherwise it will be necessary to take action which will not be to your advantage.[14]

No answer was received, so the Department "wrote her off" as "Deserted", and began making arrangements for another teacher to replace her.

A week later, on 6 April, out of the blue, Lavinia arrived at Bustard Head. The same day, she wrote to the Department:

I have the honour to report that school was resumed to-day.

Leave of absence was granted to me till the 10ᵗʰ ultimo, but owing to an attack of dengue fever following on my recent indisposition, I was unable to travel by the steamer which arrived here on the 21ˢᵗ ultimo.

As the vessel would not be leaving again for here before early in May next, I have had to take the overland route, and have lost as little time as possible in re-assembling the school.[15]

The Department of Public Instruction replied:

. . . As a communication had not been received from you . . . Thereupon by direction of the Minister you were written off in the Registers of the Department as having deserted duty and steps were taken to appoint another teacher to the school.

The Minister views with strong disapproval your action in absenting yourself from duty without leave and in not notifying the Department immediately of your extended absence and he directs me to reprove you for your remissness and for the trouble and inconvenience you have caused the Department.

Mr Barlow is reluctant to terminate your services and he therefore permits you to continue duty but he directs that salary be withheld for the period of your absence without leave . . . [16]

Lavinia responded:

. . . In reply I have to say that I regret extremely your having had occasion to so severely reprimand me for neglect of duty. In extenuation of my conduct I can only say that I was too ill to write and report my incapacity to you.

So that I might re-open school with as little delay as possible, I undertook a long and tedious ride and drive of nearly 50 miles overland before I was hardly recovered enough to travel.

I can only repeat how sincerely I regret the trouble and inconvenience caused to the Department.

Kindly convey to the Minister my sincere thanks for allowing me to continue duty.[17]

The Department had the last word:

. . . I am directed by the Minister to intimate that your neglect to report your further absence from duty and to advise the Department of your address and of your movements is inexcusable.

If you were not able to write, you should have asked some person to notify the Department in your behalf.[18]

Lavinia taught for a further six months at Bustard Head before resigning to accompany her parents to Western Australia. Before leaving, she requested a reference from the Department of Public Instruction. This was forwarded, simply stating she was "a fairly capable teacher".

Lavinia was followed by Margaret Annie Matilda Crawford who, on 14 August 1908, applied to the Department of Public Instruction for a transfer:

I have the honour to state that I am desirous of a transfer from the Bustard Head Provisional School, and I hereby apply for the same.

For the past 2 years and 8 months I have endured the hardships and disadvantages of lighthouse isolation, on a salary of £40 per annum.

Bustard Head is distant from Gladstone 57 miles by land and 32 miles by water. The settlement consists of three families, who are employed in the lighthouse service. The next nearest residence to Bustard Head is a cattle station, which is 15 miles distant.

Although the Marine Department is supposed to supply the teacher here with free board, this does not include washing and scrubbing expenses. The teacher is compelled either to do her own washing and scrubbing or to incur further expense by having it done. This is only one of the many inconveniences which belong to this place.

The only occurrence which breaks the gloom and monotony of Bustard Head is the arrival once a month of the storeboat with provisions for the lighthouse keepers.

It will be learnt from the departmental records that, when three weeks have elapsed, I shall have put in the longest term as teacher of this school for the last twenty years.

After remaining here under the foregoing circumstances for the period mentioned, and having laboured unceasingly for the betterment of everyone, parents and children combined, I feel that I am fully justified in applying for a transfer to a better school, and I trust that the Department may see good cause for my application and that they may therefore favourably consider my request.[19]

Margaret's application was rejected. An internal Department note attached to her letter stated: "I would think she'd be glad to wash her own clothes and keep her room clean to help her to fill in the time".

Nine months later, on 1 May 1909, Margaret once again applied for a transfer in a letter exuding the quiet desperation she must have been suffering:

I have the honour to again apply to you for a transfer from the above school.

For nearly 3½ years I have endured the hardships and inconveniences of teaching at this lighthouse school at Bustard Head, and have put in the longest term as teacher here since the opening of the school in 1882.

The circumstances under which one finds it necessary to live and work are known only to those, whose lot it is, to be isolated in such a place for a number of years.

I do not feel prepared to resign, although I feel that I cannot live under my present surroundings for a much longer period, and I therefore again request the Department to grant me a transfer to a school in the Darling Downs or Moreton District, and I trust that this time my request may meet with the Department's favourable consideration.[20]

It was. Four months later, Margaret received her transfer and was replaced by Eva Mary Rowe. Bustard Head was Miss Rowe's first school. On 12 April 1910, after Miss Rowe had been on the station for nine months, Superintendent Rasmus, who was still Secretary of the School Committee, reluctantly wrote to the Department of Public Instruction saying that since the new teacher's arrival there has been "neither discipline nor progress" at the school. The following month, District Inspector Clement Fox was sent out to investigate; he submitted his report a fortnight later:

. . . There appears to be ground for Mr Rasmus' complaints for Miss Rowe's disciplinary control is weak and the progress of her pupils slow; moreover, in some branches of instruction there is a decided falling off in the class work. However I consider Miss Rowe, with due exercise of care, capable of improving most of the deficiencies in her teaching and of eventually producing results at least fairly satisfactory.

Her ill success in the control of her pupils has been intensified by her want of tact and discretion in her dealings with the parents. She is addicted to violent displays of temper, and at such times lets her tongue run loose. From the first, she appears to have resented any favourable allusion to her predecessor's work, and to have spoken disparagingly of the many successes Miss Crawford achieved. She did not keep up the needlework: Miss Crawford was highly successful in this subject. Miss Crawford looked well after children's Home Exercises: Miss Rowe rather neglected them until the parents remonstrated, and since then she has given them satisfactory attention. Miss Crawford advised "writing pads" for the children, instead of slates. The pads arrived sometime after Miss Crawford's departure: Miss Rowe "did not believe in pads" and made the children continue the use of slates. Miss Crawford placed suitable pictures on the walls: Miss Rowe had them removed. In these matters I fear she has been prompted by jealousy of Miss Crawford's reputation.

When the parents have mildly remonstrated or simply asked for an explanation regarding anything that wanted clearing up she has burst into a violent temper and drowned further talk from others by administering a 'tongue thrashing' all round; and now the people are almost afraid to mention school matters to her.

I think this feature in her character has told against her almost as greatly as any. The parents here seem amenable to reason and are not a difficult lot to get along with.

I was myself witness to one of Miss Rowe's silly displays when investigating the following matter brought before me.

Mr Anderson complained of the treatment he had received from Miss Rowe, so I asked him to the school to state his case in her presence.

He said: His boy had been punished and he went to ask Miss Rowe further about it. She was in her private room which opened to the yard. The door was open. She saw him coming and before he could speak she banged the door in his face. From the inside of her room she called him a "low ignorant man" and used other offensive expressions; and refused to hear what he had to say. When she got quieter he said "Well, it was not the action of a lady to bang the door in my face". This was all he got a chance to say to her, and he finally went home. He simply wanted to know from her why the lad had been punished.

Next morning she came to him in the workshop and abused him. When he attempted to reply she refused to listen and rushed back to her room.

His son was 'kept in' that day, so he went to the school door and called him out. Miss Rowe was in school but not the other pupils. He did not ask Miss Rowe to let the boy go. He believed she kept him in from spite, hence his action.

I pointed out to Mr Anderson the impropriety of his conduct and how it would injure the authority of the teacher. He said in palliation that he could get no satisfaction from Miss Rowe. She would not listen to him. He honestly believed she kept the boy in through spite, or he would not have done it. He did not object to punishment when necessary. He thought the children had been treated too indulgently even by Miss Crawford, and had told Miss Rowe so.

When Mr Anderson was making his statement and replying to my questions Miss Rowe jumped up and interrupted by shouting at him: "How dare you interfere with the school? You low ignorant man. You are no gentleman. What right had you to speak to me? There was nothing to complain about. How dare a man like you address me? I won't stay here to listen to you. etc.etc."

I had some difficulty in calming her, but eventually she cooled down, and in reply to my questions, said: She had shut the door quickly because it was her bedroom. She did not tell Mr Anderson to go to the school and wait for her there. She did not listen to Mr Anderson. She thought he had no right to interfere.

Mr Anderson said: He meant no offence in going to that room. Where else should he go? The door was wide open until she shut it.

In this case the lad probably deserved the punishment he got; and I think the matter would have ended had Miss Rowe simply and quietly given her version of the trouble. No one here accuses Miss Rowe of giving excessive corporal punishment.

Other cases were brought before me where Miss Rowe had undoubtedly acted unwisely.

I have given her suitable admonition and advice. I believe she sees she should have been more discreet. Things have gone too far for her ever to be of much service here, for she has lost the respect and confidence of both parents and scholars. She will, I think, try to do better in future, and may succeed if she be given a chance in another place.

I suggest she be transferred to Keppel Bay in place of Miss Hansen. She will have younger children to deal with there.[21]

When advised by the Department of Public Instruction of the transfer and the reasons for it, Miss Rowe replied:

Regarding your letter of 17th concerning complaints from committee about me, there has been better reason of complaint from me about

Bustard Head Provisional School of 1911. The teacher is Irene Sedgman. The Department of Public Instruction found it very difficult to get teachers to stay on the station for any length of time.

Photograph provided by Australian Maritime Safety Authority.

The Anderson family. Lightkeeper Frederick Anderson received a "tongue thrashing" from schoolteacher Eva Rowe. Much worse was yet to happen to the Andersons. Daughter Edith 'Edie' Anderson is second from the left. Her sister Ethel is to her right.

Photograph provided by Nell Thwaite.

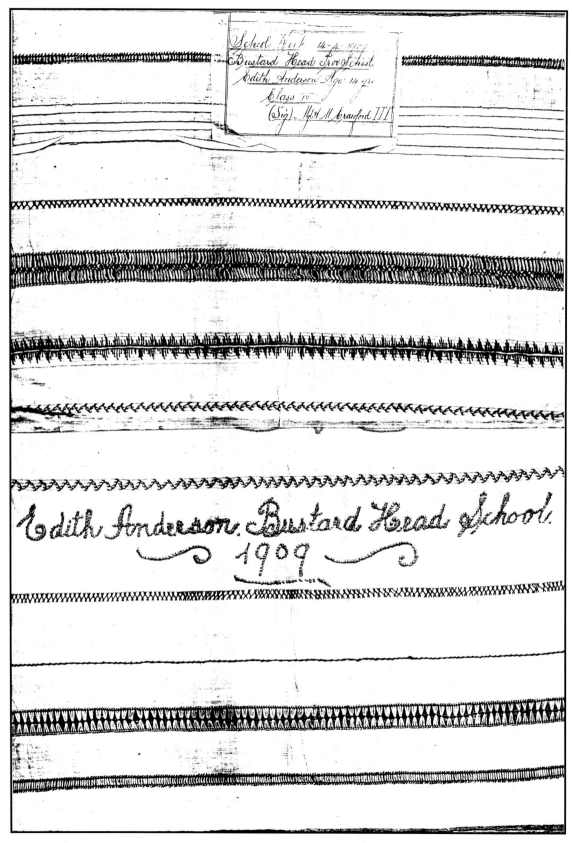

Edie Anderson's needlework, a school subject encouraged by teacher Margaret Crawford.
Provided by Nell Thwaite.

them. There has been interference with me in the discharge of my duties by one and another, and I shall be extremely sorry for any teacher who takes my place. The conduct of two girls called Rasmus aged 12 and 14 has been utterly disgraceful and for many months I have been on the point of writing to you for a transfer on that account. I spoke several times to the parents about it, and they told me not to show them any of my temper, and that their children had not been to blame. I shall be extremely thankful for a transfer from you, and would not care to live on a lighthouse station again.[22]

Mr Anderson, who Inspector Fox referred to in his report regarding the complaints against Miss Rowe, had been stationed at Bustard Head as Light-keeper for five years. Before his posting there, Swedish born Frederick Anderson had spent most of his life at sea. Prior to his arrival in Australia in 1881, he was shipwrecked in the South Seas during the days of the Kanaka trade, and was rescued by the government vessel *Sandfly*. In 1882 he served on board the pilot vessel *Clara*, before spending a year on the Proudfoot Shoal lightship moored in Torres Strait. He married Mary in 1884, and remained in Brisbane for a number of years engaged on the Brisbane Corporation steam launches. After obtaining his pilot's certificate from the Marine Board of Queensland he worked for three years as a pilot out of Bowen. He then returned to the lighthouse service, where he was stationed at Dent Island, Cape Moreton and Double Island Point, before arriving at Bustard Head in 1906.

Life hadn't been kind to Frederick and Mary Anderson. Since their marriage, six of their children had died, the last occurring on 3 February 1908 at Bustard Head. Five month-old Mary had died of chronic enteritis. She was buried the same day in the Bustard Head Cemetery.

Much, much worse was yet to happen to the Anderson family.

Chapter 6

THE "TURKEY" STATION TRAGEDY

Complaints about the isolation and hardships at Bustard Head made by some of the schoolteachers in the early 1900s were no doubt justified, as most of those young women, used to a more social life, had only accepted the position as a stepping stone in their careers. Nevertheless, isolated as it was, there was usually some sort of activity happening in the area. Apart from the monthly stores boat from Rockhampton, sailing boat charters with fishing parties from Bundaberg were frequent visitors, as were the owners and their friends of "Turkey" cattle station, who often visited the lightstation for picnics. By 1909, oyster leases at Bustard Head were being worked by the Moreton Bay Oyster Company; and a Chinese group, based on Curtis Island, were using the ketch *Economist* to harvest bêche-de-mer in Pancake Creek. The small creek known as Chinaman's Creek on the southern side of the 445 hectare lighthouse reserve, was most likely named for that reason.

There were some permanent residents living nearby too. Thomas and Margaret Kettlewell with their three young children lived at Pancake Point on Rodd's Peninsula, almost opposite the boatshed in Pancake Creek. In 1899, Thomas and his family had travelled from Tinana near Maryborough to Pancake Point, where they built a slab hut. Thomas was employed as a fencing contractor on "Turkey" cattle station, and in his spare time shot kangaroos for their skins. Every so often, Margaret and her six year-old son Albert would travel to Gladstone by horse and cart to sell the tanned skins, the round trip taking about a week.

One night, some tanning liquid, which had been left in the hut on a shelf above the food, leaked into the oats. Next morning, after a breakfast of porridge, the whole family became violently ill. Margaret managed to attract the attention of the lightkeepers by flashing a mirror into the sun. Relief Light-keeper Tripcony and his wife rowed 2 kilometres across Pancake Creek to find out what was wrong. The lightkeeper had to return to duty, but left his wife with the Kettlewells to nurse them back to good health.

Picnickers on board Wave, *homeward bound from Pancake Creek. The boat was owned by the Worthingtons from "Turkey" cattle station.*

Photograph provided by John Christensen.

Accidentally poisoned, Thomas and Margaret Kettlewell were nursed back to good health by the lightkeepers.

Photograph provided by Roger Eason.

Jerry Wirth, a stockman from "Turkey" cattle station, visits Bustard Head.

Photograph provided by Norma Mills.

Thomas and Margaret produced a further three children while living in the hut at Pancake Point. Although the family returned to Maryborough in 1906, their name is still remembered — a reef 5 kilometres along the ocean beach from Pancake Point is known as The Kettlewells.[1]

The isolation at Bustard Head was somewhat reduced in 1902, when the electric telegraph was converted to telephone. Up to the date of conversion, the Superintendent was paid a yearly allowance of £40 for being the official electric telegraph operator. After that date, the less skilled position of telephone operator and postmaster — or in some cases postmistress — paid a yearly allowance of only £5. Salaries for the lightkeepers had increased little since the establishment of the station in 1868. In 1902, the Superintendent's yearly salary was £231 (which included an allowance for quarters of £26, and a telephone operator's payment of £5); the Lightkeeper's salary was £134 (which included an allowance for quarters of £16); and the Assistant Lightkeeper's salary was £112 (which also included an allowance for quarters of £16).

Living conditions on the lightstation were still quite primitive. Without bathrooms in the cottages, bathing a family of twelve in a tub on the kitchen floor was something that just had to be accepted; as was cooking for the same number on the aptly named "No.8 Albion Beacon Light" wood stove.

New 1000 gallon galvanised rainwater tanks were requested by the lightkeepers in 1903; but Captain Sykes the Rockhampton Harbour Master, on his monthly inspection of the station, recommended the use of 400 gallon iron ships' tanks, as these were easier to transport and would last three or four times longer than the galvanised ones. Six ships' tanks were bought for a total cost of £20.

A new pilot launch, the 12 metre *Annie* with "good motor power", was supplied to Gladstone in 1910. Together with her sister ship *Edith*, which went to Maryborough, these were the first motor launches owned by the Marine Department. They were powered by three-cylinder Wilson kerosene engines, one of which is on display at the Queensland Maritime Museum. *Annie* replaced the *Fitzroy* on the stores run to Bustard Head and, together with her pilot duties, was a regular visitor to Pancake Creek. So much so, the first edition of the *Australia Pilot Volume IV* published in 1917, in regard to Bustard Head, states:

> *If bound for Port Curtis and requiring a pilot, the signal should be made off this head, as sometimes the pilot is there.*[2]

Well before the Commonwealth of Australia was proclaimed on 1 January 1901, many discussions had taken place by the colonies regarding the funding of lighthouses. Sharing the cost of lighthouses nationally would be beneficial to a colony like Queensland, which had a high need for lighthouses but a low population to pay for them. Discussion had also taken place on what lights should be controlled by the Commonwealth — coastal lights, harbour lights, or both. With Federation, came Australia's Constitution, part of which stated:

> *The Parliament shall, subject to this Constitution, have power to make laws for the peace, order, and good government of the Commonwealth with respect to . . . (vii) Lighthouses, lightships, beacons and buoys . . .*

But for the first few years after Federation, little was done in regards to deciding *what* should be done. The Commonwealth was short of funds and had more important national matters to attend to. Eventually, by 1911, the Commonwealth Government submitted a list of 120 coastal lights —twenty-eight of those in Queensland, including Bustard Head — to the States for their agreement to transfer them to the Commonwealth. Light dues to shipping would be charged on a tonnage basis for the whole coastline, making the service self-sufficient.

However, before anything was finalised, a retired naval surveyor, Commander C.R.W. Brewis, R.N., was commissioned by the Commonwealth Government to report on the condition of existing coastal lights, make recommendations for alterations, and proposals for new lights. In this regard, on 8 August 1910, Queensland Portmaster John Mackay, accompanied by Commander Brewis, left Brisbane on board the *Excelsior* for an inspection of the coast from Cape Moreton to Torres Strait.

Meanwhile, the white ants had been busily eating away at the Bustard Head cottages and outbuildings. In 1908, Portmaster John Mackay reported to Parliament that:

> *The buildings at this station are in need of extensive repairs, which, consistent with the comfort of the staff, must receive early attention, for not withstanding their attempts at sundry repairs the limited time at their disposal can scarcely arrest the dilapidation from white ant and other natural causes.[3]*

During the next two years, minor repairs were done to the cottages and extensive repairs to the boatshed; a new earth closet was built at the back of each cottage, but the old lookout house was beyond fixing. Superintendent Rasmus ordered the materials for a new lookout house, which was built by the lightkeepers in early 1912 for a cost of £16.10. 0. A replacement horse was sent to the station "as the long drag from the beach to the station through heavy sand is too much for one". And finally the cottages were painted, as recommended by the Government Architect, with the lethal addition of "equal proportions of white lead and white zinc, tempered with raw linseed oil". In those days, red or white lead and white zinc were sent to the station by the hundredweight. The authorities were unaware of the dangers of using lead in paint.

The new lookout shed built by the lightkeepers in 1912.

Photograph provided by Mavis Ord.

Another death occurred on the station on 5 January 1911. Frederick Hovell, son of Assistant Lightkeeper Henry Hovell and his wife Elizabeth, died seven hours after a premature birth. He was buried the same day in the Bustard Head Cemetery.

On 18 June 1911, sixteen year-old Edith Anderson, daughter of Lightkeeper Frederick Anderson, left her home at Bustard Head to take up a position as a domestic servant at "Turkey" cattle station. The same year, twenty-one year-old Henry Rasmus, son of Superintendent Charles Rasmus, was employed at "Turkey" as a rouseabout. By 1912, "Turkey", with an area of 21,343 hectares carrying about 4,000 head of cattle, was one of the most prosperous holdings in the district. "Turkey" was managed by William Worthington, who lived in the station homestead with his newlywed wife Susan. Worthington owned a half share in the property; the other half was owned by John Kessell the Mayor of Gladstone and proprietor of the town's newspaper the *Gladstone Observer*. The same year, Kessell won the seat of Port Curtis in the Queensland Parliament.

Although the number of employees on "Turkey" varied with the seasons, at the beginning of February 1912, apart from Edith Anderson — who was known as Edie — and Henry Rasmus, there were two other regular wage earners. Willie Yow Yeh was sixteen years of age and employed as a rouse-about. His father was a full blood Kanaka and his mother a full blood Aborigine. Willie had been at "Turkey" for just over six months. The other was twenty-one year-old George Daniels, who had worked at the cattle station for over a year as a stockman and horsebreaker. George's father was a full blood Kanaka, and his mother a half-caste Chinese.

George Daniels had worked on various stations in the district for the past six years, and had gained a reputation as an expert horseman and rifle marksman. He also had achieved a certain proficiency in reading and writing, which was unusual in those times for someone with his background. He took pride in writing letters for the mainly illiterate half-caste Aborigines and Kanakas with whom he associated. He was self-assured with a swaggering manner, and was regarded by whites as being "a bit flash".

William and Susan Worthington were well liked by their employees, at the same time retaining the balance of social distinction of that period between employer and worker. Edie Anderson had settled in well to her duties and appeared to be relishing her new independent lifestyle away from Bustard Head. Hardly a day passed at "Turkey" without a visitor, many of them men from nearby cattle stations. Edie, not an unattractive girl, enjoyed their visits and reciprocated their banter and good-natured flirting.

A frequent visitor to "Turkey" was thirty-two year-old Arthur Cogzell, the youngest son of William Cogzell who owned "Eurimbula" station which adjoined "Turkey". Arthur had often worked for the Worthingtons and was highly regarded in the district. He and Edie got on well together. Perhaps due to Edie's cloistered upbringing on lightstations she treated Willie Yow Yeh and George Daniels similarly to any white person. This was unacceptable behaviour in those days. White society condemned the mixing of the races. It was bad enough for a white man to mix with a half-caste or black woman, but for a white woman to associate freely with a black man meant ostracism from white society.

With unease, the Worthingtons had been watching the relationship between Edie and George Daniels develop over the few months prior to February 1912. It was obvious Daniels was infatuated by Edie, made even worse by Edie not rebuffing his advances. Once, at six o'clock in the morning, William Worthington saw Edie opening the door of the iron-sheeted lean-to at the rear of the homestead where Daniels slept, but when she saw Worthington she quickly closed the door and ran round the back. Another time he saw Edie in the kitchen with her arms around Daniels' neck. Worthington later spoke to Daniels about this, saying:

"I won't have this sort of thing going on here. One of you will have to leave."

Daniels denied that anything was going on between him and Edie. Worthington wasn't convinced of Edie's innocence; he described her as a "fast sort of girl with boys . . . and cunning in regard to her behaviour with Daniels".

So typical of human nature, Willie Yow Yeh and Henry Rasmus were quick to tell the boss whenever they saw anything untoward. Rasmus told Mr Worthington he had seen Edie sitting on Daniels' knee on the old stretcher under the kitchen window. And Willie Yow Yeh told Mrs Worthington he had seen the two lying together fully clothed on Daniels' bed. Daniels found out that Willie had reported him, and gave him "a chop with his stockwhip". At the time, Daniels had a horse for sale that Willie wanted, but couldn't afford the £5 price. The two agreed that if Willie would tell Mrs Worthington he had been mistaken about seeing Daniels and Edie on the bed together, Daniels would sell Willie the horse for half-price. The deal went through, but it's doubtful if it changed Mrs Worthington's mind.

Daniels began to resent Arthur Cogzell's visits to "Turkey" and his interest in Edie. He was convinced Cogzell was trying to take Edie away from him, and as well take his job.

Three brothers, Tom, Harry and Albert Tapper, had been engaged by William Worthington to build some cattle yards and fencing on "Turkey". They were camped at Captain's Creek some kilometres away from the homestead, and each Sunday afternoon, Daniels, on his day off, would ride over and visit the men. Daniels became friendly with Tom Tapper, and eventually poured out to him his infatuation for Edie and his consuming hatred for Arthur Cogzell. Tom Tapper advised Daniels to leave "Turkey" and get a job somewhere else. Tapper told him that Edie was underage and said:

"Her father is in a government billet here. You're a black man and you know that they wouldn't have you in the family."

"Edie likes me and I like her," Daniels replied. "She is mine and I'll have her and somebody will go under yet."

Next time Tom Tapper saw Arthur Cogzell, he warned him of the hatred George Daniels felt for him:

"By God Arthur you had better look out. George has got you dead set."

"That's all right. I'll settle him," Cogzell laughed.

Increasingly concerned, Mrs Worthington wrote to Edie's mother Mary Anderson ("Turkey" did not have a telephone) telling her that Edie was being overly familiar with Daniels. Frederick Anderson visited "Turkey" on 26 December 1911 and reprimanded his daughter for her behaviour. It was decided that William Worthington would sack Daniels and Edie could stay. However, in January, Worthington decided to keep Daniels on, and left it to Mary Anderson to decide if Edie should go home. Mary replied that Edie could stay until Mrs Worthington got another girl.

On Friday 2 February 1912, Arthur Cogzell left his home at "Eurimbula" to ride to Bustard Head. Cogzell was extremely friendly with the Anderson family and visited them frequently. Cogzell said to Anderson:

"You ought to take Edie away from "Turkey". It's like a blackfellows' camp. She has nothing but blacks around her."

That convinced Frederick Anderson to bring Edie home on his next day off, but Cogzell offered to escort her back to the lightstation in a weeks time when he returned to "Turkey" after a trip to Gladstone. Anderson readily accepted.

From Bustard Head, Cogzell rode to "Turkey" and informed Worthington of his plans. While Cogzell was in the kitchen at "Turkey", Daniels returned from a day's mustering. Edie met him and told him to bring the 'night horse' into the yard.

"I've done my day's work," replied Daniels. "Let them get the horse in that want to use it."

Edie explained that Arthur Cogzell wanted to use it.

"Then let him bloody well get it in!" exploded Daniels.

Cogzell came storming out of the kitchen.

"If I hear you talk to a girl like that again, I'll screw your bloody neck, you black bugger!" shouted Cogzell.

Next day, when Daniels rode out to the Tapper brothers' camp with some meat, he told Tom Tapper about the previous night's incident with Arthur Cogzell.

"If Cogzell had hit me I would have bashed his brains out," Daniels said. "I've got him dead set. He gets everything out of Edie and then runs to Mr Worthington with it. Worthington hasn't spoken to me for a week. If Edie goes I'll make somebody sit up for it."

Arthur Cogzell left "Turkey" for Gladstone on Wednesday 7 February, advising William Worthington he would be back on the following Saturday or Sunday to take Edie to Bustard Head. On Friday, William Worthington's partner in "Turkey", John Kessell, arrived at the property, as did George Watt, the owner of nearby "Rodd's Bay" station. Both men had been invited by the Worthingtons to spend the weekend at "Turkey".

Next morning, Willie Yow Yeh had a disagreement with Worthington and immediately quit his job. He packed his belongings and then went to say goodbye to George Daniels.

"Where will I meet you again next?" Willie asked.

"In hell," replied Daniels.

Later that Saturday afternoon, Daniels asked Henry Rasmus to accompany him to 'the target' for some shooting practice. 'The target' was on a mudflat about 800 metres from the homestead. Henry declined, so Daniels went alone, carrying his .32 calibre repeating Winchester rifle. The rifle's magazine held six rounds, but as the ejector mechanism was defective, the spent shells had to be extracted using a penknife. Daniels fired about a dozen shots and returned to the homestead, where he asked Henry Rasmus to go kangaroo shooting with him next morning. It was Daniels' practice on Sunday mornings to take his two kangaroo dogs and go shooting. Again Henry declined.

A leaden sky greeted the dawn on Sunday 11 February 1912. Those at "Turkey" knew it would develop into a hot, oppressive day. George Daniels rose early, saddled the 'night horse', then rode down to the horse paddock and ran up the station's working horses, including his own piebald filly. When he returned to the homestead he was told to run a bath for John Kessell. While doing so, Henry Rasmus came to the bathroom door. Daniels looked up at him and said with a sardonic laugh:

"This is the last bath I will fill up for Mr Kessell."

Arthur Cogzell arrived at the station about 7.00 a.m. and was invited in to breakfast by William Worthington. Edie was all packed up and ready for her trip back to Bustard Head. Most of her belongings were in a wooden box, which would be sent to Gladstone and returned to the lightstation by the pilot launch. She had made up a roll of clothes to carry with her on horseback. Wrapped in this was an envelope containing Edie's wages, a cheque for £7. 7. 0. Edie appeared quite excited about going home to be with her family again.

After breakfast, Arthur Cogzell went down to the yard and saddled a mare for Edie. At the time, George Daniels was in the horse paddock breaking in two young station horses, alternately riding one and leading the other, all the time glancing up towards the house. Worthington, who could see Daniels from the homestead, found this strange, as Daniels didn't usually work on Sundays. Shortly before 9.00 a.m., Daniels came up from the horse paddock and saddled his piebald filly.

"Where are you going today?" asked Worthington.

"I'm going to Tappers' camp after dinner," replied Daniels.

He then mounted his horse and cantered away along the road towards Iveragh, but after about 400 metres he wheeled round and returned to the homestead. He went into the saddle room and took his Winchester rifle and some cartridges, remounted and set off again. Worthington thought it strange that Daniels hadn't taken his kangaroo dogs with him.

Ten minutes later, Edie and Arthur Cogzell mounted their horses ready for the ride to Bustard Head.

"You can come back to us later when Daniels has left," said Mrs Worthington.

"I will not come back to "Turkey" while George Daniels is here," replied Edie as they rode off.

It's highly likely that Edie had come to realise the advantages of a friendship with the sociably acceptable Cogzell and wanted to break her association with Daniels.

The timing of the 24 kilometre trip to Bustard Head was dictated by tides. Two tidal creeks — Worthington (known locally as the Danube) and Middle — had to be crossed at low tide. It was 6 kilometres from "Turkey" to the Danube, and then a further 5 kilometres to Middle Creek. From the Danube, the track followed the telephone line to the lighthouse.

At about eight o'clock that same morning, Fred Bowton (son of the late Captain Fred Bowton, who had been Superintendent of Bustard Head) had left his Middle Island property to ride to "Turkey" in regards to some contract work that William Worthington was offering. Working the tides, he crossed Middle Creek and then the Danube. At Scrubby Creek, about 4 kilometres from "Turkey", he met Arthur Cogzell and Edie riding towards him. They spoke for a while before continuing on their way.

Fred Bowton spent only a short time at "Turkey" before heading back to Middle Island. As he approached the Danube around 11.30 a.m., he was surprised to see Edie Anderson's mare standing on the left hand side of the track about 40 metres from the crossing, the reins hanging on the horse's neck. Then Fred saw Arthur Cogzell sitting on the lower bank of the creek on the right hand side of the track. The front of his shirt was saturated with blood and he was moaning. Arthur's horse was standing on the creek bank about 15 metres upstream. Fred leapt from his horse and rushed over to Cogzell.

"Good God Arthur old man, what's the matter!" exclaimed Fred.

"I'm shot," replied Cogzell.

"Where?"

Cogzell pointed to his stomach.

"Who shot you?" continued Fred.

"That black bugger."

"Who?"

"George."

"Where's the girl?"

85

"That black bugger has taken her."

Fred Bowton tried to make Arthur more comfortable by shifting him slightly, placing his back against a tree, then told him he would ride to "Turkey" for assistance.

"I'll be dead before you get back," gasped Arthur.

Fred galloped back to "Turkey" and told Worthington. Worthington immediately ordered Henry Rasmus to run up the station's sulky horse. But visitor George Watt intervened, saying he would get his two buggy horses. When he brought them up to the yard, in the haste, one of them broke away, crashing into a fence and staking its chest. This caused a considerable delay while Henry Rasmus rigged up the sulky. At last, John Kessell and George Watt set off in the sulky accompanied by Fred Bowton riding his mare. Worthington stayed behind to heliograph Bustard Head. A young lad, Wilf Crow, who was visiting the lightstation with his father, saw the heliograph flashes and alerted Superintendent Rasmus. Worthington signalled the tragic news to Rasmus, requesting he telephone the Gladstone Police. The nearest police station to "Turkey" was about 45 kilometres away at Miriam Vale, but the officer usually stationed there was on police business in Rockhampton. Within thirty minutes, two armed constables had left Gladstone and were on their way to "Turkey". Frederick Anderson, when informed of his daughter's disappearance, immediately saddled a horse and set off for the cattle property.

Arriving back at the Danube, Fred Bowton found Arthur Cogzell still sitting against the tree. Arthur was dead. Edie and Arthur's horses were standing where Fred had last seen them. Edie's roll of clothing was still strapped to the saddle, and on investigation the cheque for £7. 7. 0. was found inside. George Watt and John Kessell searched up and down the creek a short distance, but couldn't find any sign of either Edie or Daniels. They lifted Arthur's body onto the sulky, and while Watt and Kessell returned with it to "Turkey", Fred rode off to "Eurimbula" cattle station to advise William Cogzell of his son's death.

The two Gladstone police constables, Kreutzmann and Murray, arrived at "Rodd's Bay" cattle station shortly before dark that evening. Unfamiliar with the country, they were doubtful if they would reach "Turkey" on the same day. Luck was with them; Willie Yow Yeh, after quitting his job at "Turkey", had gone to "Rodd's Bay". Accompanied by Willie, the three reached "Turkey" just before midnight to find William Cogzell, Fred Bowton and Frederick Anderson waiting for them.

During the night, Frederick Anderson made a rough wooden coffin. Early next morning, Cogzell's body was placed in it, loaded on a buckboard and taken to Iveragh for transportation by rail to Gladstone. About 3.00 p.m. the Government Medical Officer Dr Taylor conducted a post mortem examination on the body. He found two entry wounds in the back and two corresponding exit wounds in the front of the torso. Dr Taylor found that Arthur Cogzell had died from haemorrhage and shock occasioned by gunshot wounds, and that the delay in receiving medical attention at the scene of the incident had not contributed to his death. Arthur Cogzell was buried in the Gladstone Cemetery that Monday evening.

On Sunday evening, the day of Cogzell's death, Inspector Quilter of Rockhampton wired the Commissioner of Police in Brisbane, informing him of the tragedy. The Commissioner instructed Inspector Quilter to remain in Rockhampton and direct search operations from there. He was told to employ such resources from his own district as necessary, and to wire the Commissioner if further were required. By next morning, four constables and two Aboriginal trackers had begun the search. Quilter had chosen the best men under his command. They were all good horsemen and bushmen, were well armed and provided with good horses. Quilter believed it would only be a matter of a day or two before the murderer Daniels was apprehended, but his main concern was the welfare of Edie. Daniels now must have known that, if caught, he would hang. He had nothing to lose.

Unfortunately it rained heavily throughout Sunday night, and continued intermittently during Monday. Any tracks that had been there, were now lost. On Monday afternoon, Daniels' piebald filly was found tethered to a tree up a blind gully about 200 metres downstream from the Danube crossing. The filly had pawed the ground all round the tree and eaten much of the bark from its trunk; it had obviously been there since the shooting.

Despite torrential rain throughout Tuesday, the search continued. On Wednesday, about 30 metres from where Cogzell had been shot, Constable O'Grady found a felt hat, a handkerchief, an opened penknife, a rifle pull-through and four empty .32 calibre cartridges at the base of a large gum tree. It was apparent this had been the spot where Daniels lay in wait for Arthur Cogzell, before cowardly and cold-bloodedly shooting him twice in the back.

The search continued relentlessly. By the end of February there were ten police officers and four trackers engaged in the search, assisted by numerous civilian volunteers including William Cogzell, William Worthington, Willie Yow Yeh and Edie's father Frederick Anderson. A police camp was established at "Turkey" and other strategic places throughout the district. Food, forage for the horses and supplies were brought in from Miriam Vale and Bororen. Horses and equipment were loaned to the police by owners of local cattle properties. Mudflats, creeks, forests, rocky mountain ranges, abandoned gold mines and nearby islands were thoroughly investigated. Aboriginal camps were visited and the persons there interviewed. The heavy rain continued, hampering the searchers and adding to the misery they were already suffering from hordes of sandflies and mosquitoes.

It was discovered that, the week before the murder, Daniels had written several letters to some of his acquaintances. The letters gave no indication that he planned to kill Cogzell or abduct Edie, but all ended with the words: "Goodbye now and forever". In Daniels' room at "Turkey", William

Worthington found a copy of *The Queenslander* newspaper dated 9 December 1911. At the top of the front page Daniels had written "I am a fool to do this on Sunday so goodbye now and forever", and under it signed his name.

Rumour and speculation grew as the search continued. Some believed that after shooting Cogzell, Daniels had shot Edie, thrown her body into the Danube, then followed her in and shot himself, knowing that the fast flowing ebb tide would carry their bodies into Rodd's Bay. Others thought that Daniels had taken Edie into the bush, shot her, then made his escape. The Danube was searched using a boat and grapple. Nothing was found.

Photographs of Daniels and Edie and their descriptions were published in the *Queensland Police Gazette* on 24 February 1912. Police throughout the State were instructed to watch all roads, ports and railway stations.

Hopes of a breakthrough arose at the end of February. Police received a report that a woman, Mrs Kate Leslie, who lived alone in a slab humpy in the Milton goldfields, had sighted Daniels and Edie. When interviewed by Constable Schnitzerling, Mrs Leslie claimed that Daniels had called at her place early on the morning of 19 February and asked for bread and some lead to make bullets. He said he was going to Colloseum Creek. Daniels then walked away towards a nearby creek where a white girl was waiting. Although Mrs Leslie gave a fairly accurate description of the clothes they had been wearing, Constable Schnitzerling seriously doubted her story. Mrs Leslie had given her age as thirty-nine, though she was obviously more than seventy, and admitted that some gold miners working in the area had told her of the murder and described the clothing the two were wearing. Constable Schnitzerling reported that Mrs Leslie was "not in full possession of her senses", and had fabricated the story to gain some notoriety. Later, at the Inquest of Arthur Cogzell, a police witness described Mrs Leslie as "an imbecile".

The search went on for three months, much of it done in uninhabited wilderness. Inspector Quilter reported to the Commissioner that if the search was to be continued, fresh men and horses would be required. The Commissioner authorised the withdrawal of the search parties on 8 May.

Then, for some unknown reason, on 12 June the Commissioner directed Quilter to renew the search. The old search area was re-examined and expanded, and a more extensive search done of nearby islands. Nothing was found. By the end of July the men and horses were again at the point of exhaustion. The search was cancelled on 5 August.

During the second search, Inspector Quilter died from a sudden illness. He was replaced by Inspector Masterson who examined the witnesses at the Magisterial Inquiry beginning on 28 August 1912. It was no surprise that the Coroner's finding was that Arthur Cogzell died from haemorrhage and shock caused by gunshot wounds inflicted by George Daniels.

Inspector Masterson, with fresh enthusiasm, requested the Commissioner to authorise a new search in the Cania and Monal districts where it was believed "half-castes and undesirables" lived, and a more extensive search of the coast-line and offshore islands. Permission was reluctantly given. Seventeen men from Brisbane were sent up to join those from the local District. Even the pilot launch *Elsie* arrived from Brisbane to assist with the search of the islands. On 3 December the third and final search was abandoned. Again, nothing was found.

The ten-month search for George Daniels and Edie Anderson had proven to be the most expensive search undertaken by the Queensland Police Force to that date. On 30 November 1912, the Queensland Government offered a reward of £500 for information leading to the conviction of George Daniels. The reward posters brought numerous reports of sightings from all over the State, interstate and even overseas — as far away as northern Canada. All were investigated. All proved fruitless.[4]

It must have been devastating for Frederick and Mary Anderson not to know what happened to their daughter Edie. At the inquest, Frederick Anderson said: "I am of the opinion that Daniels shot Edie the same day as he shot Cogzell and then did away with himself". But the Andersons could never be really sure.

And as if the abduction of Edie wasn't enough for the Andersons to bear, just a few weeks after Edie's disappearance, Frederick and Mary's twenty-one year-old daughter Ethel suffered an epileptic fit and died. She was buried near her baby sister Mary in the Bustard Head Cemetery on 1 April 1912.

Almost a small village. Seventeen children lived at Bustard Head in 1908. Superintendent Charles Rasmus and his wife Alice at centre of back row. Lightkeeper Frederick Anderson wearing cap in centre of second front row, with his wife Mary to his left. Edie Anderson standing behind her father, while her sister Ethel sits at the left-hand end of second front row.

Photograph provided by John Christensen.

In the early 1900s, the shingle roofed "Turkey" cattle station was the centre of social activity in the area. Even the sulphur-crested cockatoo on the verandah railing appears to be joining in.

Photograph provided by John Christensen.

The lightkeepers join a picnic party on the banks of Pancake Creek.

Photograph provided by John Christensen.

Frederick Bowton, who found Arthur Cogzell shot at the Danube.

Photograph provided by Kathy Mian and Boyd Rich.

Edie Anderson. Her father decided she must return to Bustard Head.

Photograph provided by John Christensen.

George Daniels. His passion for Edie led to cowardly murder.

Photograph provided by John Christensen.

"Seconds before Tragedy". A sketch by Tim Welch.

"I am a fool to do this on Sunday so goodbye now and forever". Daniels' words written on a newspaper found in his room after the shooting.

£500 REWARD.

Home Secretary's Department,
Brisbane, 28th November, 1912.

HIS Excellency the Governor, with the advice of the Executive Council, has been pleased to direct that a Reward of £500 be paid for such information as will lead to the apprehension and conviction of a half-caste named GEORGE DANIELS, who is alleged to have shot, on Sunday, the 11th February, 1912, one Arthur Cogzell, while the said Arthur Cogzell was accompanying a girl named Edith Anderson from Turkey Station, where she was employed, to her home at Bustard Head, and who, after shooting the said Arthur Cogzell, took the girl away with him, neither of whom has since been seen nor found; and that a Pardon be granted to any person who may be concerned in the crime, not being the principal offender, who may give such information.

J. GEO. APPEL.

DESCRIPTION AND PORTRAIT OF GEORGE DANIELS.

GEORGE DANIELS, otherwise George Douglas, is wanted for the murder of Arthur Cogzell, near Turkey Station, Gladstone District.

Offender at the time was 18 years of age, 5 feet 7 inches high, slight build, 9 stone 7 lb. weight, smart appearance, dark hair inclined to be straight, very small dark moustache, dark eyes; a stockman or horse-breaker; a native of Murray's Creek, between Miriam Vale and Bundaberg; was dressed, when last seen on the 11th February, 1912, in a grey crimean shirt, brown beaver trousers, elastic-side boots (size 6), no hat; can read and write. His mother is a half-caste Chinese and his father is a Kanaka. Any person having information regarding the above should communicate with the nearest Police.

The reward poster for George Daniels was displayed at police stations, courthouses, railway stations, post offices and all public buildings throughout Queensland.

Chapter 7

PARTING OF THE WAYS

Five months after Edie's disappearance, Frederick Anderson was transferred to Gatcombe Head at the southern entrance to Port Curtis and put in charge of the No.2 lead light. In June the same year, Commander Brewis's report to the Commonwealth Government on the lighting of the Queensland coast was published. In regard to Bustard Head, he stated that the period of the light was too slow for modern requirements and recommended that:

> (a) *The present optical apparatus (eight panels) be used, but the speed of the light be increased by inserting new mechanism (pedestal and clock), altering the period of the light from fixed and flashing every two minutes to fixed and flashing every twenty seconds, duration of the flash about one second.*

> (b) *The power of the flash be increased from 20,000 c.p. to 120,000 c.p., by installing an 85 millimetre incandescent mantle. Illuminant, vaporized kerosene. Visible — white, 24 nautical miles; red, 10 miles.*[1]

He remarked that the lighthouse and apparatus were in good order, but the cottages were very old and would need replacing in the course of a few years. Commander Brewis's suggestions weren't immediately acted upon. However, on 5 March 1914, tenders were invited for "improvements and repairs" to the lightstation buildings. The successful contractor was V.C. Wye with a tender of £225. A new room was added to Superintendent Rasmus's cottage, the verandah floor was replaced and the ceiling lined, and a new 1000 gallon rainwater tank installed. The main bedroom lining which had been badly eaten by white ants was relined with 6″ × 1″ grooved, tongued and beaded pine, and a portable shower and footbath was provided for an existing shed recently built by Rasmus. A new rainwater tank was installed at the Assistant Lightkeeper's cottage and the verandah ceiling lined. And the two lightkeepers' cottages were each provided with a wash shed and bathroom, complete with portable shower and footbath. To protect the schoolroom from the hot afternoon sun, a new verandah was built along one side of the building.[2]

On 1 July 1915 the Queensland State Government officially handed over control of the coastal lightstations to the Commonwealth, and so Bustard Head became a part of the newly formed Commonwealth Lighthouse Service. To mark the end of that era, the recently appointed Portmaster, Vassal Forrester, said in his 1914-15 report to Parliament:

> *The coast lights from Cape Moreton to Booby Island, 28 in number, have now passed from State to Federal control, but until the end of the present calendar year the State, at the request of the Commonwealth Government, will attend thereto and transport all maintenance stores.*
>
> *At this 'parting of the ways' I should like to place on record my appreciation of the good work performed by the keepers of the coast lighthouses, amongst whom are faithful officers who for many years have, during their solitary vigils, kept devoted watch and ward and given their best attention to the lights for the benefit of 'ships that pass in the night'. I would add that the Department is loth to part with such men, but is happy in the knowledge that they pass away from State control with good records and are taken over by the parent Government, which there is every reason to believe will be equally solicitous for the future welfare of these guardians of the deep as has been the State.[3]*

For compensation purposes payable by the Commonwealth to the State, a valuation of Bustard Head lightstation was done in 1916:

Valuation of site
1100 acre lighthouse reserve	£550

Valuation of tower and auxiliaries   £2,344

Valuation of optical apparatus
2nd Order Chance Brothers	£500
5th Order auxiliary	£40
Hinck's duplex burner, auxiliary	£5

Valuation of quarters and schoolroom   £650

Valuation of other structures
Boat Shed, Lookout Shed, Screen Mantlet	£85

Valuation of Plant, Tools, Etc.   £93

TOTAL   £4,267

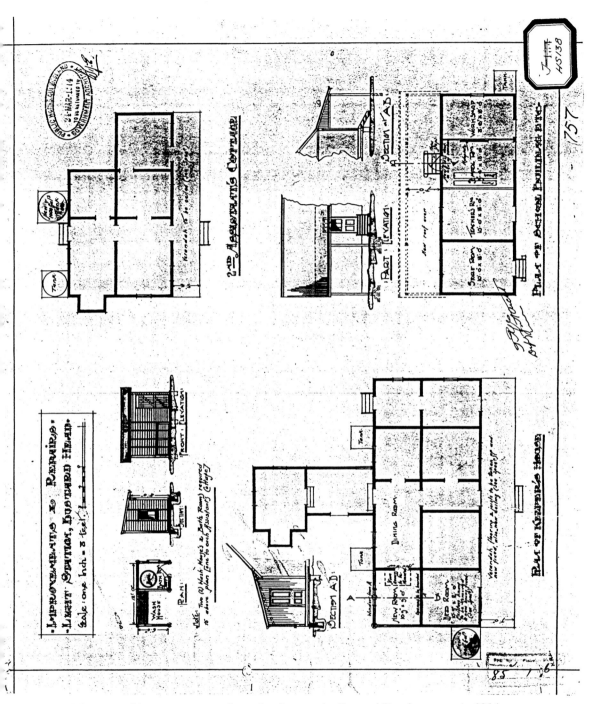

Original drawing of improvements and repairs done to the Bustard Head cottages in 1914.

Provided by Australian Maritime Safety Authority.

At the time of transfer, the Queensland lightkeepers had a choice of working on either the State or Commonwealth lights. Most remained where they were, their choice of employer being influenced by the station they were on. Commander Brewis's recommendations for establishing the Commonwealth Lighthouse Service bureaucracy was basically adhered to. A central office was formed in Melbourne under the control of its first Director, British engineer Joshua Ramsbotham. The Australian coastline was divided into four districts. No.2 district covered the Queensland coast from Torres Strait to Cape Moreton, and was controlled by a District Officer and a District Engineer based at Townsville, with another officer in Brisbane.

The First World War had a temporary effect on the staffing at Bustard Head. A day after the outbreak of war between Britain — therefore Australia — and Germany on 5 August 1914 Superintendent Charles Rasmus was suspended from duty because of his European background. Although it only took until the end of September that same year for Australian and New Zealand troops to occupy the German island possessions in the Pacific, it wasn't until the following year that Rasmus was reinstated. Even so, Rasmus's troubles weren't yet over. On 15 December 1915, a Mr Nagle from Capella wrote to the Minister of Public Instruction the Hon. H.F. Hardacre, M.L.A., regarding a schoolteacher at the lightstation:

> *I have a favour to ask of you. Mrs Moran of this place has a daughter Miss Margaret Willmott, who is at present in charge of the small school at Bustard Head. The man in charge of the lighthouse is a German, and from some patriotic remarks made by Miss Willmott, who is only a girl of 18 or 19 years, he has taken a great dislike to her and has made her life most unpleasant.*
>
> *Miss Willmott, who is a one time pupil of mine, wishes a transfer from there, as she says she cannot endure any longer the life she was compelled to put up with during the last six months. Her mother would naturally prefer a transfer to some place in Central Queensland, and would have her home, but she has three daughters of a second marriage.*
>
> *Hoping you will be able, without undue inconvenience, to effect this.[4]*

Mr Nagle was advised that Margaret Willmott would receive a transfer "without unreasonable delay". She was replaced by Edith Cronin, who was to be Bustard Head's last schoolteacher. At the beginning of the 1917 school year, only three children were on the roll. Bustard Head Provisional School No.391 closed on 6 November 1917. Over its thirty-five year history, nineteen teachers taught at the school, only one of them a male.[5]

In accordance with Commander Brewis's report, the power of the main light at Bustard Head was increased "on or about" 15 May 1917.[6] The wick burner was replaced by an 85 millimetre incandescent burner fuelled by vaporised kerosene, which increased the power of the flash from 20,000 to 120,000 candlepower. But Brewis's suggestion of shortening the time between flashes from two minutes to twenty seconds was not acted upon, no doubt because of the substantial amount of money required to replace the clockwork mechanism during a time of economic hardship.

Nevertheless, by May 1918, enough money was available for the Commonwealth to pay £8,392 for 2 acres 2 roods 14 perches of prime Brisbane River frontage land at New Farm, acquired under the *Lands Acquisition Act 1906* for the establishment of a lighthouse depot and workshop.[7] By 1920 the District Officer and District Engineer had moved from Townsville to Brisbane and established Queensland's Commonwealth Lighthouse Service headquarters.

In 1917, the 46 kilometre section of branch telephone line from Iveragh to Bustard Head was rented by the Lighthouse Service from the Postmaster-General's Department for an annual fee of £112. Shortly afterwards, it was decided that the telephone line be made "available for public business". The new Head Lightkeeper of Bustard Head, John Kent, who had replaced Charles Rasmus the previous year, complained of persistent troubles with the line (Following the Commonwealth takeover of lighthouses in 1915, the name Superintendent was changed to Head Lightkeeper). On 18 March 1918, Kent wrote to the District Officer:

> *It is urgently necessary that some action should be taken without delay, to have the Telephone Line and Instruments at this Station seen to, as at present it is almost impossible to get a message through to Gladstone; in fact several times the Postal Officials have given up trying; thereby at times putting me to great inconvenience.*
>
> *This morning the trouble was actually worse, and a message to the Postmaster at Gladstone had to be given up in despair; the whole thing in fact is beyond the Limit.*
>
> *I may state in all fairness that before 9.0 am and after 7.0 pm it is possible to get a message through. These times for business are of course out of the question.*
>
> *Hoping some action will be taken.*[8]

Action *was* taken and the line repaired by the Postmaster-General's Department, but over the next few years they must have found it a costly and difficult item to maintain for such a small annual rent, because early in 1923 the Postmaster-General's Department offered to waive the rent in return for the Lighthouse Service bearing the maintenance costs of the line, which included an immediate payment of £802. Baulking at this proposal, the Lighthouse Service offered to pay a share of the maintenance costs. The Postmaster-General rejected the offer, stating that "the line is being practically handed over to the Lighthouse Service without payment of any capital expenditure" and if the

The new incandescent burner fuelled by vaporised kerosene. Installed in 1917, this more powerful light replaced the original oil wick burner.

Photograph provided by Neville Murphy.

Relief Lightkeeper Arthur Riley from Gladstone at the back of his cottage. Note the extensive stone paving and washtub.

Photograph provided by Norma Mills.

Little Nesta Simpson meets the new Head Lightkeeper John Kent. He replaced Charles Rasmus who was transferred after twenty-three years at Bustard Head.

Photograph provided by Norma Mills.

The lighthouse supply ship Cape Leeuwin *arrives at Bustard Head.*

Photograph provided by Kevin Urban.

proposal wasn't met, there would be no alternative but to dismantle the line. Reluctantly, the Lighthouse Service agreed to pay. Of course, the Postmaster-General's annual fee of £68 for removal of faults and line inspections still applied.

Since the closure of the Bustard Head school in 1917, the children were being taught by correspondence lessons. With only a monthly stores service, it was up to eight weeks before their lessons were returned to the station for correction. At that time, the least frequent postal services in Queensland, other than to lightstations, were fortnightly, and even those were few. The Department, which regarded the education of lighthouse children as an "absolute necessity", was aware of this problem, and at the end of 1918 approved the granting of a £30 per annum education allowance for each lightkeeper's child between the ages of seven and fifteen. This only applied where educational facilities were not available at the station and necessitated living away from home. At first, the Bustard Head lightkeepers were reluctant to send their children away, and in 1920 requested the Department to provide a live-in governess. This was refused. Two years later, the Department, still aware of the schooling problems, asked a senior Head Lightkeeper's wife, Nellie McDonald, to submit a letter stating her opinion of correspondence schooling. She replied:

> *In the morning the children has [sic] two hours home lessons, the afternoon three hours, and in the evening two hours. They will not sit for any length of time alone to do their lessons. Some-one has to be constantly with them and consequently it interferes greatly with household duties. We have to do all our own cooking (bread bakeing [sic] included).*
>
> *Washing day for instance, very little or no work is done by the children, and a day is lost.*
>
> *The least thing their attention is drawn off their work, any noise outside, or any person coming into the room will disturb them, besides they will not learn for their parents as they would for a teacher, also there is no competition, as there would be if attending a school.*
>
> *The school work completed the first week after the storeboat, it is seven, and sometimes eight weeks before they look at it again, consequently they have apparently forgotton [sic] it, also any mistakes has [sic] to be corrected by them, and also the comeing [sic] week's work.*
>
> *The corrospondance [sic] papers in my opinion, are good in themselves with some one to supervise them and be with the children when doing the work, and with weekly mail.*

I believe the children are doing fairly well at their lessons, but it will only be for a time as sewing must be done, and other work. Being with the children it falls behind at times. I am teaching two children now and after this comeing [sic] March I shall have two more children of an age to be taught.

I will not be able to teach all four of them and do my household duties satisfactorily and to make a success of the corrospondance [sic] school the children must have at least five hours a day school lessons.[9]

The Department issued an official memo the same year which stated that, because of the monthly stores service, correspondence schooling was less beneficial to lightkeepers' children than to any others. Boarding school was recommended and where a child showed special promise the education allowance could be continued beyond fifteen years of age so secondary school or college could be attended. As well, an amount exceeding the annual allowance was paid in "special circumstances".

Under State control, only the minimum of furniture had been supplied to lighthouse cottages; it was mainly left to the lightkeepers to provide their own. Under the new Commonwealth regime, a schedule of substantial furnishings was approved for all cottages in 1922. Due to a shortage of funds, it took many years to implement the plan, but it was a move in the right direction in regard to the comfort of the lightkeepers.

Since the Commonwealth takeover in 1915, the lightkeepers' stores continued to be delivered to Bustard Head by State vessels chartered by the Commonwealth. In Commander Brewis's report of 1912, he had suggested that a steam vessel of about 600 tons and 200 feet long be obtained for use in Queensland waters. The duties of the ship would "include supplying the lighthouses with stores, periodical visitation of unattended lights, &c., prevention of smuggling, &c., removal of wrecks that may be a menace to navigation, searching for missing vessels, and rendering assistance to vessels in distress". In 1914, tenders were called for three such ships to cover Australia's coastline, but with the outbreak of the First World War these plans were deferred until 1924 when three much larger ships were ordered. *Cape Leeuwin* and *Cape York* were delivered in 1926, and the smaller *Cape Otway* delivered in 1931.

The 1500 ton *Cape Leeuwin* was based in Brisbane at the Commonwealth's New Farm Depot. About once a month she arrived at Bustard Head, anchoring well outside the mouth of Pancake Creek. Fuel, stores and mail were loaded into one of the ship's workboats, then delivered to the boatshed in Pancake Creek. If *Cape Leeuwin* was unavailable, *Cape Otway* often stood in for her. On the rare occasion that neither vessel was available, a private launch was chartered.

In July 1923 the flash of the main light was increased in power from 120,000 to 191,000 candlepower. This was achieved by replacing the vapour burner's incandescent Collodion type mantle with a recently introduced Auto-form mantle. Although the new mantle was much smaller than the Collodion, its intrinsic brightness was very much greater.[10]

By 1929, Bustard Head lightstation was in dire need of major repairs. The Head Lightkeeper's cottage (called No.1 Cottage) and No.2 Cottage were in "fair condition", but No.3 Cottage, where the white ants had once again become active, was in a "disgraceful" state. Parts of walls, eaten by these voracious insects, had been patched with hessian and wallpaper. The station's rainwater tanks were in poor condition, and the auxiliary light to the south-east of the main light, built by Superintendent Rooksby and the lightkeepers in 1876, was in disrepair. Even the lighthouse was suffering the effects of time and weather: the external landing and staircase from the ground to first floor was badly corroded, and rainwater had seeped through the door opening and behind the internal steel sheet lining, also causing corrosion.

Plans to build new cottages and replace the south-east auxiliary light with a concrete structure had been under discussion for some time. But as Australia entered the worst economic depression in her history, these proposals were put on hold.

Chapter 8

FIRE!

The crew of the 8.2 metre fishing boat *Laurel*, accompanied by *Anemone*, were trolling for mackerel in the vicinity of Outer Rock off Bustard Head on Wednesday afternoon 21 May 1930. A strong current was running and the seas were heavy. Both vessels were owned and operated by professional fishermen from Gladstone. Around 4.00 p.m. *Anemone* headed inshore towards Inner Rock, where her crew fished for a while before returning to Pancake Creek to anchor for the night. As *Anemone* left Inner Rock, her skipper Alfred Haack noticed *Laurel* fishing between Inner and Middle Rocks.

There were three men on board *Laurel* — brothers Allan and Thomas Williams, and Sidney Bickle. At about 5.00 p.m., when the launch was close to Inner Rock, her motor failed. The strong current, aided by the wind and waves, quickly swept her towards the rock. An exceptionally large wave lifted her up and threw the helpless vessel on top of the oyster-covered platform. Waves continued to dash the boat, but *Laurel* remained stuck fast on a falling tide. To lighten the boat in the hope it would float off the rock at high tide later in the evening, the three men dumped their catch of fish and jettisoned the engine.

Their efforts were rewarded at about 2.00 a.m. the following morning when *Laurel* slid off the rock into deep water. But the pounding she had taken had weakened the hull, and before long the vessel began to break in two. The men lashed the two sections of wreckage together and, using pieces of timber, started paddling towards the beach. A large wave crashed over them, releasing the anchor which fell quickly to the bottom and dug into the sand. With *Laurel's* progress now checked, she was pounded even more by the waves. Eventually the lashings gave way and the two pieces of wreckage parted. Brothers Allan and Thomas Williams were on the part of wreckage still anchored, but Sidney Bickle, who was clinging to the other half, began drifting out to sea.

During the night, Allan Williams became delirious, interspersed with bouts of unconsciousness during which times his brother Thomas revived him by blowing down his nostrils. Thomas, although exhausted by the ordeal, continued to hold onto his brother throughout the night and into the morning. But shortly before 9.00 a.m. his strength gave out. Allan slipped from his grip and disappeared into the water.

Earlier that same morning, Alfred Haack up-anchored *Anemone* from Pancake Creek and headed for Outer Rock to do more trolling. Unaware of the disaster that was taking place nearby, and with no sign of *Laurel* either in Pancake Creek or at the rocks, Haack assumed she had returned to Gladstone during the night. Haack fished for a while before heading in to Gladstone.

Another vessel fishing off Bustard Head that morning was *Roamer* from Bundaberg. She had also spent the night in Pancake Creek. There were seven crew on board *Roamer*, including her part owner James Brunke. Only ten minutes after Allan Williams had slipped from his brother's arms and drowned, one of *Roamer's* crew spotted something east of Middle Rocks that he thought was a small rock. Almost at the same moment, the crew noticed the frantic signalling of a morse lamp coming from the lightstation. Lightkeeper Eric Rapkins, who had sighted the shipwrecked fishermen, had been trying to attract *Roamer's* attention for some time.

Now aware that something was amiss, *Roamer* motored across to the 'small rock', which the crew discovered was Thomas Williams.

"Thank God you are here!" Williams gasped. "Another ten minutes and I would've been gone. My poor brother has just gone."

Williams was lifted aboard in an exhausted condition and given some brandy, as he explained that Sidney Bickle had drifted out to sea on the other half of the wreckage. As *Roamer* motored over towards Middle Rocks in search of Bickle, one of the crew spotted something in the distance. It turned out to be Bickle clinging to the remains of *Laurel*. He waved feebly. The waves were much too large for *Roamer* to pull alongside Bickle with safety, so a line was thrown to him with instructions to fasten it to the wreckage. He had difficulty catching the line, and when he did eventually take hold of it, it quickly slipped out of his grasp. In a desperate move, Bickle abandoned the wreck and started swimming towards *Roamer*; but after only three strokes he crossed his hands above his head and sank out of sight. *Roamer* searched for Bickle for a considerable time without success. The crew were convinced he had been taken by one of the many huge sharks that frequented the area.

On their return to Pancake Creek, two of the crew, August Brunke and Neville Downing, walked up to the lightstation to phone the Gladstone police, only to discover the telephone out of order. There was little they could do but return to *Roamer* and motor in to Gladstone. In the meantime, the Bustard Head telephone fault was rectified and the news passed on to Gladstone. An anxious crowd waited on the Auckland Creek Jetty for the arrival of *Roamer* that evening. Only then were the full details of the tragedy revealed.

Next day, a party of police arrived at Bustard Head. Assisted by the light-keepers, they searched in vain for the bodies.

Thirty-three year-old Sidney Bickle was a single man, but thirty year-old Allan Williams left a wife and two young children who, according to Gladstone's newspaper *The Gladstone Observer*, were "in somewhat straitened circumstances". The Mayor of Gladstone, Walter Ferris, opened a relief fund to assist the widow; within a fortnight, a total of £23. 8. 0. had been donated.[1]

As Australia's depression worsened, only the most essential of repairs to the lightstation were effected. In 1929 Head Lightkeeper Archie Henderson installed new bearings to the main light's revolving apparatus and fitted a new chain and chain wheels to the clockwork mechanism. During February 1930, Foreman Mechanic Potter from the New Farm Depot came ashore from the lighthouse ship *Cape York* to replace the main light's two red glass sector panels which were "cracked and badly broken". He temporarily fitted the new sectors until their correct positions were confirmed by the officers aboard *Cape York*. Only then were the sectors secured to their metal frames. He also adjusted the height of the light's kerosene vapour burner, which he discovered was slightly lower than the focal plane.

While Mechanic Potter was on the station, Head Lightkeeper Henderson discussed with him the poor condition of the external steps and landing to the first floor of the lighthouse, and pointed out the corrosion taking place behind the internal steel sheet lining, caused by rainwater seeping through the door. Potter, in his inspection report of the station, suggested to the Deputy Director (previously called the District Officer, the man in charge of navigation and lighthouses in Queensland) that the first floor external door opening be sealed with a metal plate, and the external steps and landing discarded. Potter proposed to build a new set of steps inside the tower from the ground to first floor, into which a trapdoor could be formed. The main and only entry would then be through the existing, more weather protected, ground floor door. The Foreman Mechanic's suggestions were approved in theory, but with little money to put them into action, nothing was done for the moment.

Continual faults with the telephone line necessitated the replacement of 4 kilometres of wire during February 1931. The lighthouse ship *Cape York* stood by for four days while five of the crew came ashore to do the work. They were assisted by the lightkeepers who provided the station's horse and cart to help move the heavy coils of wire.

During those harsh economic times, rather than employ new personnel as relief lightkeepers, the Department utilised the services of crewmen from the lighthouse ship *Cape Leeuwin*. This was the case at Bustard Head at the beginning of May 1932, when Ship's Steward Harold Deasey and Fireman Lionel Elkington were working there as reliefs. The Acting Head Lightkeeper Tom Shanahan, his wife Mary and their four children, were living in No.2 cottage. Mary, who was the only woman on the station, was three months pregnant. But rather than the author describe what happened, I'll let Philip Shanahan do that. At the time, Philip was the baby who Mary was carrying:

The great depression of the 1920s and 30s had a profound effect on the lives of many Australians. My father Tom Shanahan was no exception.

Dad was a merchant seaman, but when he married in 1922, he quit the sea and secured a shore job to be with his wife.

Like many others in 1928, Dad was out of work, and with a wife and three children to support he had no choice but to go back to sea. In 1929 he signed on as Able Seaman on the Commonwealth Lighthouse Service supply ship S.S Cape Leeuwin.

A year later, Dad was offered a position as Lighthouse Keeper at Bustard Head. The salary of £248 per annum was £40 less than that of an Able Seaman, but he would be living with his family and there was the added bonus of free accommodation and free fuel for the stove and lighting.

So, on 15 September 1930, my father, mother and their children — Winnie, Tommy and Alan — along with their furniture, food and luggage arrived at Bustard Head on board Cape Leeuwin. The ship anchored a mile off Clews Point, where the family was offloaded into a lifeboat and taken to the boatshed in Pancake Creek. The lightkeepers were waiting with the horse and dray to transport them up to the station. They moved into No.2 cottage, which had just been vacated by Eric Rapkins.

My family shared their isolated life at Bustard Head with Head Lightkeeper Archie Henderson, his wife Ada and daughter Nellie, and Lightkeeper Francis Barton and his wife.

After living in the city, my mother found housekeeping on the lightstation quite difficult for a while. Without refrigeration, our staple diet was corned beef and cured bacon. A lot of our supplies came in bulk: butter in large tins, cases of assorted canned meat, 140 pound sacks of flour, 70 pound bags of sugar, 4 gallon tins of honey, and 7 pound tins of syrup. Of course, fresh fish, crabs and oysters were always plentiful, and in winter, turtle or pigeon soup was popular. My mother baked bread in a removable oven, which sat on two burners of the Blue Flame kerosene stove.

The health and schooling of the children were a worry for my mother, but with regular doses of castor oil for their health, and Nellie Henderson's help to supervise correspondence lessons, Mum managed quite well.

But her greatest fear was the prospect of childbirth on an isolated lightstation. Always on her mind was the fate suffered by her grandmother, Mary Ann Griffin, who died in childbirth, far from medical help, at the lonely Cape Moreton lighthouse in 1876.

Commonwealth Lighthouse Service policy decreed that pregnant women must leave a lightstation at least one month before the baby was due. So, when Mum was six months pregnant in 1931 she and the children sailed on Cape Leeuwin *for Brisbane to await the birth and to enrol Winnie at Lourdes Hill boarding school to begin her formal education.*

By May 1932, Head Lightkeeper Archie Henderson had retired after thirty-five years in the service, and Lightkeeper Francis Barton was away on his annual holidays, leaving my father as Acting Head Lightkeeper and Postmaster. Harold Deasey and Lionel Elkington were his assistants.

My family were enjoying a pleasant Saturday afternoon on 7 May. The boys were riding their pedal toys on the lawn near the lighthouse, while Winnie, home from boarding school for the end of term break, was playing with baby Keith on the verandah. Because there were only kerosene lamps and candles for lighting, my mother always liked to finish the evening meal before darkness set in. That afternoon the family sat down to supper at 5.20 p.m. Harold was in his cottage, and Lionel, who was on light-up duty, was in the lighthouse. Lionel was well known for having just two speeds — dead slow and stop. So, when Dad saw Lionel running towards the cottages, he remarked:

"Look at creeping Jesus move, there must be a fire."

Then Dad heard Lionel shouting:

"Tom! Tom! No.3 cottage is on fire!"

That's when all hell broke loose.

Dad leapt from his chair and ran outside. As No.3 cottage was built very close to our cottage, Mum rushed to get the children out of the house. She told nine year-old Winnie, who was carrying the baby in her arms, to take the boys and stand beside the lighthouse where they would be safe.

Within minutes the tinder-dry timber cottage had become a roaring inferno. The men tried desperately to control the blaze, but the station's fire extinguishers were useless against the flames. In an attempt to stop the fire spreading to our cottage, Dad grabbed an axe and holed the rainwater tanks; the water poured onto the flames with little effect, and the second cottage began to burn. Dad managed to rescue Mum's Singer pedal sewing machine from the front verandah before he was driven back by the intense heat. There was nothing more they could do but stand and watch in disbelief. In fifteen minutes both cottages were burnt to the ground.

Apart from the clothes they were wearing and Mum's sewing machine, the family had lost everything. All Mum's cherished

109

photographs and Dad's war medals were gone and could never be replaced. Winnie was upset at the loss of her doll's pram, especially brought out for her from Scotland by a doting aunt.

No-one knew for certain what caused the fire, but it was thought it could have been started by rats chewing on waxed matches.

The family moved into the remaining No.1 cottage with the two lightkeepers. Winnie and the boys had to sleep on the floor; and for two nights, Mum had little sleep as she kept watch in case rats tried to bite the children.

Two days later, a launch was sent from Gladstone to evacuate my mother and the children. The kindly Gladstone Harbour Master Mr Whelan took them into his home and supplied clothes from his own family's wardrobe. After shopping for clothing and other necessities, Mum and the children left by train for Brisbane, while Dad stayed at Bustard Head as Head Lightkeeper until September.

At least there was one happy event for Mum and Dad that year. On 8 October I was born. Well, I hope it was.[2]

Lightkeeper Francis Barton, who had lost all his possessions in No.3 cottage, didn't bother to return to Bustard Head. Instead, at the end of his leave he transferred to Gabo Island lightstation in Victoria. Tom Shanahan remained in the service for the next twelve years, during which time he was in charge of Caloundra Head and Dent Island lightstations. Both men wrote to the Department claiming compensation for the items destroyed in the fire, but their requests were refused. A short time later a memo was issued to all stations advising that it was the responsibility of the lightkeepers to insure their belongings.

Supplies are carried ashore from the Cape Leeuwin's *workboats to the boatshed in Pancake Creek.*

Photograph provided by Cheryl Nugent.

In dry times, water was transported in a steel tank from springs to the station. Here, Lightkeepers Shanahan and Barton prepare horses Duke and Nugget for another trip.

Photograph provided by Philip Shanahan.

Visitors to the station provided a welcome change for the lightkeepers. And they arrived by various means: by horse . . . (Bertha and Elsie Bowton with their niece Daphne).

Photograph provided by Philip Shanahan.

by boat and foot . . .

Photograph provided by Cheryl Nugent.

and by . . . ah . . . canoe?

Photograph provided by Philip Shanahan.

In 1930 the Shanahan family shared their lonely existence at Bustard Head with the Henderson and Barton families. Back row from left to right: Head Lightkeeper Archie Henderson, Mrs Barton, Lightkeeper Francis Barton, and Lightkeeper Tom Shanahan. Front row from left to right: a visitor, Mary Shanahan with her son Alan looking through the lifering, Tommy Shanahan and Winnie Shanahan.

Photograph provided by Philip Shanahan.

Even on isolated lightstations little girls loved their dolls and prams. Nesta Simpson was no exception.

Photograph provided by Norma Mills.

Fire!
Cutting provided by
Philip Shanahan.

DAILY MAIL, BRISBANE, TUESDAY, MAY 10, 1932.

FIERCE FIRE AT LONELY OUTPOST

The lighthouse and cottages at Bustard Head, near Gladstone. The two cottages on the right were destroyed by fire at the week-end.

After the fire. The Head Lightkeeper's cottage to the immediate right of the lighthouse and the old schoolroom and workshop to the right of the photograph escaped undamaged.

Photograph provided by Neville Murphy.

Chapter 9

A SOUTHERN VISITOR

The fire couldn't have happened at a worse time for the Department. The two cottages weren't insured, and the Commonwealth didn't have enough money at the time to replace them. For the next three years Bustard Head remained a 'bachelor station', the three men living in the remaining cottage.

Two years after the fire, towards the end of 1934, twenty-six year-old Neville Murphy was in Sydney preparing his motor cycle to set off on a life-long dream to visit Bustard Head lightstation. Neville's grandfather and grand-mother, George and Margaret Goodfellow, had been lightkeepers on the station between 1886 and 1889. Neville's mother Grace was seven when she arrived with her parents at Bustard Head (The Goodfellows were on the station at the time of Kate Gibson's death). Grace's childhood stories of her life on the light-station had inspired Neville to plan what was then a very adventurous trip covering thousands of kilometres over atrocious roads. By 1934, after com-pleting ten years study of electrical engineering at Sydney Technical College, it was time for Neville to put his plan into action. Leaving Sydney he rode out to Bourke in western New South Wales, across the border to Charleville in Queensland, then east to Brisbane before heading north to Miriam Vale. The story of Neville's visit to Bustard Head is best told in his diary and a letter he wrote to his mother during October 1934:

> *The weather cleared up so I was able to ride on from Miriam Vale to the turn-off leading east to "Turkey" station. For the first few miles the road was pretty fair. After that there were stony ridges and some bad creek crossings but it was no worse than many of the main roads I had traversed. I was in good spirits because I was on the last lap of my journey to the lighthouse. I passed through a wide gate above which a sign read:*

> *TURKEY STATION   PLEASE SHUT THE GATE*

I must have ridden for about another hour and then as I was rounding a grassy hill, there, suddenly ahead of me was "Turkey" station homestead. I parked the bike and walked up towards the homestead. I saw one man on the verandah and another at the gate. There was also someone at a window, watching me through binoculars. I realised they must have heard the sound of my bike when it was a fair way away and wondered what it was. Probably the first time such a noise had been heard at "Turkey" station. I approached the man at the gate and asked if he could show me the way to Bustard Head lighthouse.

"You can't ride there on your bike. There's only a bush track," he replied.

"How far is it?" I asked.

"Fourteen miles and there are a couple of tidal creeks, so you've got to pick the right time. Why do you want to go to the lighthouse?"

"My mother lived there when she was a child. Her father was one of the lighthouse keepers. I've always wanted to come and visit Bustard Head lighthouse."

"What was his name? He'd be your grandfather, wouldn't he?"

"Yes, his name was George Henry Goodfellow and my name is Neville Murphy. I've come from Sydney."

"Well my name is Worthington. But come in and have a cup of tea and we'll think out what's the best way to go."

On the way into the house he introduced me to the man on the verandah, as Harry Bloomfield. He was in his late twenties, I think. They were amazed I'd come so far on my frail looking motor bike.

While we were having a cup of tea, Mr Worthington said I'd be welcome to stay the night and that Harry Bloomfield would guide me to the track in the morning.

"Turkey" station homestead is very large with many bedrooms and is well furnished. I accompanied Mr Worthington and Harry Bloomfield while they killed a calf for meat. Then, after a shower and a change of clothes we had tea. There were eight of us at the table, most related to Mr Worthington, plus Harry Bloomfield who I think is a station hand, but seemed to be treated as one of the family. Then there was Bill Emerson, a PMG linesman who had just returned from the lighthouse and was staying the night. From the verandah the light could be seen flashing. It was 10 miles away as the crow flies, I was told.

In the morning, breakfast finished, Mr Worthington said:

"If you come outside, Bert's waiting for you. He's going to show you the way."

I picked up my rucksack and followed Mr Worthington. I saw Bert with a couple of horses, both saddled.

"You'll be riding a horse. That all right with you?" said Mr Worthington with a grin.

"That's a marvellous idea, Mr Worthington. You're very kind."

He smiled an acknowledgment and handed me a parcel.

"Can you put that in your rucksack? It's some meat. They'll appreciate some fresh meat out there. No need for you to go empty-handed. I'm sure they'll ask you to stay with them."

"Thanks Mr Worthington," was all I could say, but it seemed so inadequate. I had arrived at "Turkey" station only yesterday as a complete stranger, and Mr Worthington had provided me with first-class accommodation, a man to show me the way to the lighthouse, meat to take with me, and in addition to all that, a horse for as far along the track as a horse could go.

I didn't tell them I hadn't ridden a horse before, but I thought it couldn't be harder than riding a motor bike. I mounted the horse. I was aware that, whereas I always mounted the bike on the right-hand side, a horse had to be mounted on the left-hand side. Bert led the way, my horse followed and we went at a walking pace for about 5 miles, following the telephone wires. The track was a bit rough but the horse seemed to cope without any effort on my part. We came to a creek.

"They call this the Danube," said Bert.

It was getting on to low tide and the water was only knee-deep. Two miles further on we came to some mangrove flats and another creek.

"Well, Neville," said Bert, "this is as far as I can take you. It's called Middle Creek. It's a bit muddy, but when the telephone line was built they cut a lot of saplings and laid them down to form a corduroy crossing."

I removed my shoes and socks and made my way across. The corduroy track wasn't much help because many of the logs had sunk down into the mud. I found a spot where I could wash the mud off, put my socks and shoes back on and started to walk the remaining 7 miles that lay between me and the lighthouse. The walking was through scrub, a lot of which had recently been cut down, so I had to continually change direction to find the easiest way.

I kept on walking and walking until eventually I came up over a rise and out of the scrub and could see the lighthouse about a mile away. I kept on walking. I was on the last lap and was eager to complete it. I passed a small cemetery and a small structure containing a kerosene lamp. The lighthouse tower looked solid and authoritative in its isolation. The tower is white with a red top. The walls at the top gave place to glass, carried in metal frames, and inside the glass, canvas hangings could be seen. A balcony encircled the tower, near the top. A cottage and some outbuildings occupied land near the tower and a fence enclosed the lot. I approached the weatherboard cottage; it was old but well maintained. All seemed deserted. After some repeated knockings a smallish man in khaki shirt and shorts emerged, looking as if he had just been wakened. He appeared to be about fifty-seven.

"My name is Neville Murphy," I said. "My mother lived at the lighthouse and went to school here many years ago. Her father was a lightkeeper. His name was George Henry Goodfellow. I've always wanted to visit the lighthouse."

"Come in, come in," he replied affably. "My name is Walter Powell. I'm the Head Lightkeeper. But hang on a minute, I'll call the other two lightkeepers, they'll be interested. We don't often get visitors here."

He returned with his assistants and introduced me to them. One was Lionel Elkington, a man of about fifty-five, and the other was Allan Nugent who would have been about twenty-two. It was obvious they had just been wakened, but before long we were like old friends, sitting around having cups of tea and comparing experiences.

Afterwards Mr Powell took me over to the lighthouse and explained the salient features. The lighthouse is circular in shape and 58 feet high. Standing as it does on a hill close to the water, the light is exhibited at a height of 320 feet above sea-level. On the ground floor is stored the kerosene. This comes to the lighthouse in oil drums. The first floor is entered from a staircase running up the outside. On this floor there is only a bookcase and the original wick oil lamp. From the first floor, a steel stairway which follows the curve of the wall, leads up to the second floor.

On this floor there are two cylindrical steel tanks about 3 feet high and 1 foot in diameter, each of about eight gallons capacity. These tanks contain kerosene, and by means of a hand-pump alongside them, the air pressure in the tanks above the kerosene is raised to about 80 pounds per square inch. From the bottom of each tank comes a small copper tube. By means of a two-way cock, the tube from either tank can be connected to a long thin copper tube which goes up to the lamp. There is also a table and chair on this floor, where the man on watch usually sits.

On the next floor up is located the driving mechanism or clock. The purpose of this clock is to rotate a system of lenses and prisms around the light proper. The driving force of the clock is provided by weights which travel slowly down a tube in the centre of the tower between the clock floor and the ground floor.

One duty of the man on watch is to raise these weights each hour, by giving a crank handle on the clock twenty turns. If allowed to fully unwind, it would take forty-six turns of the crank handle to raise the weights from the ground floor. The clockwork machinery is housed in a glass-doored cabinet about 3 feet square and 4 feet high. On top of this structure, rotates the lens and prism arrangement, the body of which is in the next floor up, i.e. the top floor.

The top floor is arrived at by ascending a set of steep steel steps. The walls of this are of plate glass, carried in brass frames. The floor is just a steel grating that extends in from the walls for a distance of 2 feet. The circular hole thus formed, which is about 6 feet in diameter, is occupied by the light system. In the centre, supported by a stationary structure at a height of about 4 feet is a kerosene vapour burner and silk mantle. The mantle is about 3 inches in diameter and spherical. The kerosene that comes up the copper tube from the storage tanks passes through a regulating valve and enters a heated vaporising tube. The vaporised kerosene is ejected through a nipple and directed into the vapour burner and mantle. The vaporising tube is kept heated by a bunsen tube fuelled by a small amount of vapour diverted from the main flow to the mantle. Each night, when starting up, the vaporising tube is first heated by a methylated spirit lamp for about twenty minutes. The principle is similar to that of a blowlamp. The mantle lasts for about fourteen nights and consumes 2.25 pints of kerosene per hour.

Around this light rotates a great cage about 5 feet in diameter and 9 feet high. This cage has eight sections, divided by vertical brass bars, which carry the lens and prism structure. In four of these sections the prisms and lenses are arranged to throw a powerful beam like a searchlight, the light being concentrated at the centre of the section. While the remaining four sections, placed alternately between the former four panels, are such that the beam is uniform and less intense. This system is turned by the clockwork mechanism at one revolution per eight minutes.

When the light is observed from a distance, as the concentrating section comes around, the light is very dim for 25½ seconds. Then it flashes very bright (191,000 candlepower) for 9 seconds, then becomes dim again for 25½ seconds. When the next section comes into line the light remains bright (31,000 candlepower) and steady for a minute. This cycle of changing light is repeated over and over again. Standing at the bottom of the lighthouse on the ground outside, the four great beams can be seen moving slowly around.

119

The combined efforts of station horses Duke and Nugget were needed to haul the stores up the steep road from Pancake Creek. Head Lightkeeper Walter Powell sits in the cart, while Lightkeeper Allan Nugent stands beside Duke.

Photograph provided by Cheryl Nugent.

Part of the sandy track that led from Pancake Creek to the lightstation.

Photograph provided by Cheryl Nugent.

After an arduous trip from Sydney by motorbike, Neville Murphy achieved a lifelong dream when he arrived at Bustard Head. From left to right: Lightkeeper Allan Nugent, Lightkeeper Lionel Elkington, Head Lightkeeper Walter Powell, and Neville Murphy.
The 1932 fire began in Lionel Elkington's cottage.

Photograph provided by Neville Murphy.

The lighthouse at the time of Neville Murphy's visit, showing the entrance to the ground floor of the tower.

Photograph provided by Cheryl Nugent.

An extremely high tide in Jenny Lind Creek. The photograph, taken from the lighthouse balcony in 1934, shows how little bush there was on the headland.

Photograph provided by Cheryl Nugent.

Fixed to the boatshed at Pancake Creek, this sign greeted visitors for decades.

From Lighthouse Historical Society of Queensland collection.

Inside the plate glass panels of the lantern room there are two red glass sections which are arranged in such a way that they can be seen by a ship when in the vicinity of the dangerous outlying rocks.

Situated a few hundred yards each way from the main light are two kerosene wick lights. They are known as the East and West auxiliary lights. Each has a cut-off screen at some distance in front of it, positioned so that when the light, as observed from a ship, can no longer be seen, the vessel is too close to the rocks.

There is only one cottage now. The other two were destroyed by fire in 1932. The three lightkeepers live in the remaining cottage. In front of the cottage is the flagpole and over near the tower is the watchroom. This has sliding windows and contains a telescope. One of the duties of the lightkeepers is to convey commercial and other messages to and from passing ships. This is done by flags during the day and by lamp at night. Another of their duties is to take readings of wind, rainfall, barometer, maximum and minimum temperatures, wet and dry bulb temperatures and to report cloud and visibility. The results are passed on to the Department of Navigation and to the Weather Bureau.

Apart from keeping a watch on the light at night, each lightkeeper is also supposed to do four hours work during the day each weekday. A continuous watch is supposed to be maintained throughout each day as well as at night. Mr Powell 'lights up' a quarter of an hour before sunset. One of the others takes over at 8.00 p.m. until midnight, and the third from midnight till 4.00 a.m. when Powell comes on again.

The night after I arrived, I got up at midnight with young Allan Nugent and accompanied him on his watch until 4.00 a.m. His duties were to wind the clockwork mechanism, keep up the air pressure in the fuel tanks, watch and log the passing of any ships, and read various weather indicators.

The supply ship calls at the lighthouse every six weeks. The beach where it delivers stores is 2 miles away. The lightkeepers keep a couple of horses and a cart to bring them up. The track comes up to the station past the little cemetery. All the foodstuffs come by sea with the exception of a few eggs and some honey. Mr Powell bakes some very good bread. All the cooking is done on kerosene Blue Flame stoves.

Neville stayed at Bustard Head for five days, during which time he explored much of the area, often accompanied by the lightkeepers. At sunset, on the night before his departure, Neville went up to the lantern room alone to capture the unique soul of the lighthouse and its surroundings:

It is now about 6.00 p.m. on Sunday 21 October. I am in the light room of the lighthouse. It is sunset. The sun is going down in a flame of red. The sky is clear except for a few scattered clouds low down.

Looking inland, beyond the inlets and mangrove flats rise range after range of mountains, wreathed in a soft blue. Everything is clear cut and fresh. The deep blue of the sea is pierced only where the jagged rocks of the reef lift out of it and the sea shows an angry foam.

The trees below are bowed before a wind from the east. The wind hums around the tower with a peculiar undulating hum. From here a view can be obtained in every direction by walking around the lamp. Though the wind outside is cool and crisp, none is to be felt up here. The tower is warm after the day's sun and this warmth is maintained by the light, which is now burning.

From within the lighthouse there comes the hiss of the light, like the steady hiss of escaping steam. Then there is the metallic clap, clap, at second intervals of the great clock mechanism which rotates the lens and prism system.

My light is provided by the light itself, and this is continually changing as the mechanism rotates. As darkness closes in, the moon lights up and carpets the velvet sea with silver. This silver path is occasionally broken by a shape as the clouds move across the moon.

Next morning, Neville prepared to set off for "Turkey" station. His diary continues:

Because of the tides in the creeks, it was no good going too early. I offered to pay the lightkeepers for their hospitality, but they wouldn't hear of it. I was sorry to be going. I think that my friends felt the same, for Mr Powell said:

"Neville, as you'll have to get away about midday, you'll need something to eat, so I think we'll all have lunch at eleven-thirty as a farewell gesture."

I don't even remember what was on the menu, but what I do remember was the way the conversation went on and on until I had to force myself to go. I thanked them for their hospitality and said:

"I looked forward to making a trip to the lighthouse for many years. I can say now that it exceeded my expectations and all because you three have been so helpful. Thanks again."

I departed from Bustard Head about 12.30 p.m. and walking at a good pace I arrived at "Turkey" station at 5.15 p.m.

Mr Worthington and all the others welcomed me back and seemed to be as pleased as I was that my trip had been so successful and enjoyable. I had a shower and then it was teatime. Soon after tea, tiredness caught up with me so I decided to go to bed; but before I did so, I went out onto the verandah and, for about five minutes, watched the Bustard Head light flashing and flashing.

I wondered if I would ever see it again.[1]

Chapter 10

WAR AND PEACE

The most significant change to Bustard Head lightstation since its establishment occurred during 1935. By that time, Australia was on its way to economic
recovery after years of depression, enabling plans for long awaited public
works to be put into action. At the end of January 1935, Supervising Foreman
Albert Swingle from the New Farm Lighthouse Depot arrived at Bustard Head
to set out the site for a new cottage and its associated concrete rainwater tanks.
While there, he repaired a "motor truck" that had been landed by the lighthouse
steamer in December the previous year to ease the difficulty of transporting
building materials up the steep road from Pancake Creek. Swingle examined
two wells in the vicinity of the lighthouse, which he believed would supply
sufficient water for the concrete, eliminating the need to bring water ashore
from the ship. During the next few months, the building materials were landed
at the boatshed and taken to the station by the lightkeepers.

On 12 May, Swingle returned to the station with a team of men employed
by the Department to begin construction. Built on massive concrete stumps
about a metre high, the new, two-bedroom, timber framed cottage was sheeted
with asbestos cement wall sheeting, and roofed with corrugated sheets of the
same material. The two bedrooms, a lounge room and office opened onto an
enclosed verandah which ran round two sides of the house, and a pantry and
laundry were positioned close to the kitchen. Although a bathroom was built at
the end of one verandah, the toilet remained as an outdoor earth closet. Two
2,600 gallon concrete rainwater tanks were constructed close to the cottage.
Another tank, built on a high concrete stand, provided gravity water pressure
to the cottage, the water being pumped to the header tank by means of a semi-
rotary hand-pump.

Simultaneously to the cottage being constructed, major alterations were
underway at the lighthouse. The external stairs leading to the first floor were
removed and the door opening blocked by a steel plate. Apart from the
external landing, which was cracked and badly corroded, the stairs themselves
were found to be in reasonable condition. So much so, they were reused inside

A "motor truck" is carefully unloaded from the lighthouse supply ship onto two workboats lashed together. The truck was used to cart building materials from the beach to the lightstation.

Photograph provided by Queensland Maritime Museum.

The start of major alterations in 1935. An engine room, built close to the lighthouse, receives its finishing touches.

Photograph provided by Cheryl Nugent.

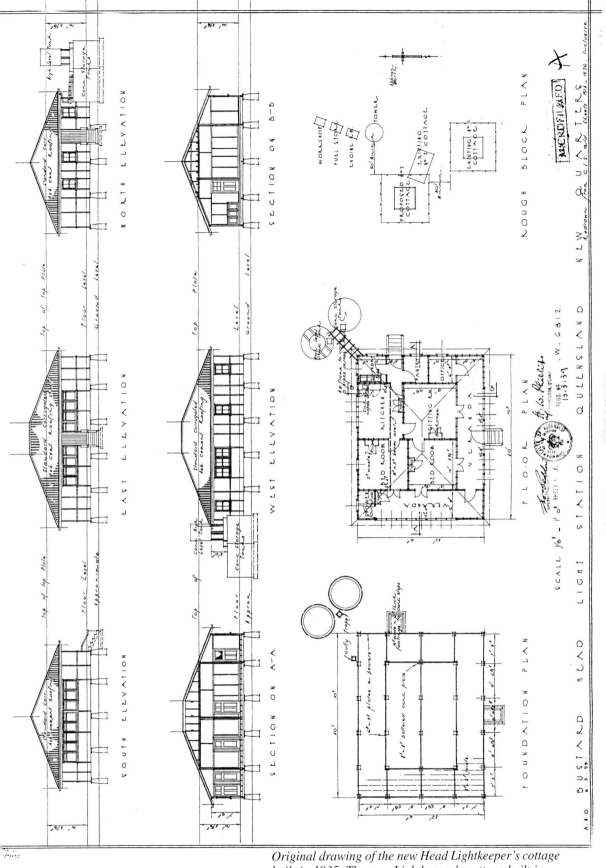

Original drawing of the new Head Lightkeeper's cottage built in 1935. The new Lightkeeper's cottage built in 1939 was of similar design.

Provided by Australian Maritime Safety Authority.

View from the lighthouse balcony showing the workmen's tents, and piles of gravel for use in the new cottage.

Photograph provided by Cheryl Nugent.

Inside the lantern room, showing the bullseye panel of the huge Second Order lens shortly before its removal.

Photograph provided by Cheryl Nugent.

The new Head Lightkeeper's cottage built in 1935. The roof of the old Head Lightkeeper's cottage is at the bottom right-hand side of the photograph.

Photograph provided by James 'Lofty' Hayes.

The new automatic light built at Clews Point in 1935 to replace the East and West Auxiliary lights.

between the ground and first floor, into which a large access hole was cut in the steel chequer-plate flooring. Some of the internal steel sheet lining was removed to check the extent of corrosion that had occurred due to rainwater seepage. Little serious damage was found, but nevertheless it was decided to remove all the internal lining from inside the tower in case of future problems. The panes to the lantern room, which also leaked, were reglazed with non-setting putty; and at the same time, three of the glass panels that faced inland were replaced with solid panels of asbestos cement.

Undoubtedly, the most crucial change to take place was the conversion of the main light from kerosene to electricity. A temporary light was erected and exhibited on 30 May while the alteration was being done. The main light's vapour burner, huge Second Order lens and clockwork mechanism were removed, and replaced by a much smaller Fourth Order Swedish AGA lens. This eight-sided lens was designed to revolve once every forty seconds, giving two successive flashes every ten seconds. Although the lens was much smaller than the original, the power of the flash increased from 191,000 candlepower to 560,000 candlepower. With so much space remaining in the lantern room, a suspended metal platform was built above the AGA lens to carry a central light source that illuminated two red sector lens panels. The new light was first exhibited on 26 June 1935.[1]

The light was powered by a single cylinder 5 horsepower Ronaldson and Tippett water-cooled petrol motor, coupled to a generator that produced 110 volt DC power. Two of these motors and generating sets were housed in a new, timber framed, asbestos cement sheeted engine room built beside the lighthouse. The petrol generators were run on alternate days from light-up until close-down. But on the off-chance of both sets failing, a huge bank of Britannia batteries was installed for emergency power. In case of a total electrical breakdown, two emergency pressurised kerosene Tilley lamps were supplied to replace the bulbs from the main light and red sector, and the lens had to be revolved by hand. No matter what the circumstance, it was impera-tive that the light continued to be exhibited.

In a similar design to the engine room, a new boatshed was built at Pancake Creek, while a workshop, fuel shed and stable were built in the lightstation precinct. To make way for the new works, the old watchroom was demolished. The stable was originally designed to accommodate the two station horses, spring cart and feed room. But due to the recently improved road from Pancake Creek to the station, only one horse was now needed to pull the cart; which was just as well, as the older horse Duke was almost too feeble to be of any use. Also, it was thought that in the not too distant future a motor vehicle would replace the horse and cart. So, it was decided to build a stable with sections for one horse, a cart, feed room and motor truck.

The two auxiliary kerosene fixed lights near the lighthouse were dis-continued and replaced by a single, automatic, acetylene powered flashing light positioned on Clews Point, 3 kilometres north-west of Bustard Head lighthouse. The Clews Point light, called "the auxiliary", was established on 28 June 1935.[2]

Although the main light was powered by electricity, kerosene lamps were still used for lighting in the new cottage, as was the Blue Flame kerosene stove for cooking and the Coolgardie cool safe for refrigeration. However, the new laundry was supplied with a kerosene fuelled "Steemkleen" boiler.

For the first time since the lighthouse was established, a nightly watch by the lightkeepers was no longer necessary. Instead, a battery alarm system was installed, designed to activate an alarm in each of the cottages if the light should fail, stop revolving or change its speed of revolution. If the red sector light failed, the main light would automatically cut out as well. This was done as a safety precaution for any vessel approaching the rocks; otherwise, if the red sector light failed and the main light remained lit, those on board the vessel could wrongly assume they were out of the danger area, possibly with disastrous results.

With no night watches on the light, Bustard Head was reduced to a two-man station. Supervising Foreman Swingle and the last of his work party left Bustard Head on 19 July 1935. After his departure the lightkeepers were kept busy cleaning the new cottage, packing the Foreman's equipment and transporting it to Pancake Creek ready to be collected by the lighthouse ship. The original lens apparatus was packed in crates and sent to New Farm Depot. Total cost of the new works and alterations, excluding the new lens, was £2,846.

On 9 August 1935, Head Lightkeeper Charles Woodhead, accompanied by his wife Frances, arrived at Bustard Head to take charge. After three years as a 'bachelor station', Bustard Head was once again graced by a woman's presence. No night watches meant that more time was available during the day for maintenance. The last remains of the two cottages that had burnt down were now removed, the stumps dug out and the site cleaned up. On 4 October, after many years of faithful service, the old station horse Duke was destroyed.

Throughout the year, faults had been occurring regularly to the telephone line, due to badly corroded wire on the Bustard Head to Middle Creek section, which was "easily broken by birds and high winds". Supervising Foreman Swingle and a party of workmen arrived later in the year to replace almost 7 kilometres of wire and a few bloodwood poles.

Since the installation of the motors, it had become obvious that on-site repairs and maintenance by lighthouse mechanics would be required more often than when the light was kerosene. Urgent repairs could be needed when neither the lighthouse ship nor stores boat was available to assist with the transport of mechanics. This problem was solved by the presence of the Bowton family who had been living on Middle Island for the past twenty-eight years. In 1917, Mrs Katherine Bowton had officially taken up the grazing lease on the 3,432 hectare Middle Island (called the Red Hill run). Her daughters Bertha and Elsie, now forty-three and forty-one years old respectively, still lived with their mother, while Katherine's son Fred, now forty-eight and married, lived on the nearby 6,736 hectare Rodd's Peninsula (called the Bray Hills run), the lease of which he had taken up in 1925.

Katherine and her daughters offered to assist with the transport and accommodation of mechanics. It was arranged that mechanics would travel from Brisbane to Iveragh by train, then by truck to "Turkey" station. There, they would be met by Bertha Bowton and taken by horseback to the Middle Island homestead to spend the night. Next day, Bertha would lead them on horseback up to the lighthouse.

The system worked well, and was used frequently by the Department to transport engine parts as well as mechanics. The Bowtons thought the system could be further improved by connecting their homestead to the Bustard Head telephone line, a distance of only 2 miles. The Deputy Director of Navigation and Lighthouses in Queensland, who was now answerable to the Commonwealth Department of Commerce, supported the Bowtons' proposal and wrote to the Posts and Telegraphs Department requesting their approval and a quotation for the work involved. Approval was given, together with a quote of £89. 5. 0. Bertha Bowton confirmed her proposal in a letter dated 22 March 1938 to the Deputy Director:

> . . . *I would like to draw your attention to the advantages to be derived should you decide to connect our homestead with the Bustard Head 'phone line:*
>
> 1. *There is at present a decided risk that I may not receive notice to meet the lighthouse mechanic as hitherto, as I understand the future mail service is to be run by horse buggy or packhorse and not by the much quicker car and truck and with phone connection I could always arrange for a car to bring the mechanic from Iveragh to a point where I could connect with horses and so expedite his arrival at Bustard Head and it would not be necessary to wait until mail day (Saturday) to get word through.*
> 2. *Should the line break down between here and Bustard Head, as it frequently does, I could at once investigate and mend the break, this I would undertake to do without expecting payment.*
> 3. *There would be no timber to clear between here and the line to Bustard as the whole of the distance, approximately 2 miles, could be along salt pans, or if that is not desired, the wire could be run through the timber from tree to tree.*
>
> *With the earnest desire that you will give this appeal your early consideration . . .* [3]

However, it was not to be. The Acting Secretary of the Department of Commerce, who was in a more senior position than the Deputy Director, wrote to the latter:

> . . . It has been ascertained, however, that the cost of providing this communication would be a great deal higher than it was first anticipated, and it has been decided to abandon the proposal.
>
> As it is realised that the above telephone line, in addition to providing emergency communication for this Service, would also have made available to Miss Bowton a convenience which we should have been only too happy to provide, it is with great reluctance that the decision not to provide the above communication has been arrived at. The services rendered by Miss Bowton to this Department in the past are greatly appreciated, and it is very much regretted that we have perhaps caused her hope for the provision of a communication which would have been of some convenience to her but which we are unable to provide.
>
> Will you please forward a copy of this memorandum to Miss Bowton.[4]

Although communication between the Department and the Bowtons regarding the telephone had come to a standstill, communication between some of the more isolated lightstations had improved. In 1937, when pedal radios were installed at six stations — Dent Island, Pine Islet, North Reef, Cape Capricorn, Lady Elliot and Sandy Cape — the lighthouse radio network was formed. Cape Capricorn, the only station of the six connected to the mainland by telephone, was selected as the base station for transmitting and receiving messages to and from the other five stations. The pedal radios could transmit and receive voice, but when reception was bad, morse code was used. The network proved a vital link for the lightkeepers in times of emergency. As well, general messages could be sent, and weather observations forwarded to Brisbane.

The rocks off Bustard Head were still making their presence felt. At 2.29 p.m. on 20 March 1939, the lighthouse steamer *Cape Leeuwin* hit an underwater obstruction while passing midway between Outer and Middle Rocks, a course the vessel had taken many times before. The chart showed a clear passage and no breakers had ever been observed there. At the time, *Cape Leeuwin* was drawing 4.5 metres and the moderate following sea had a lift of about 1.5 metres. Although it was dead low tide, there should have been a depth of at least 22 metres beneath the keel. Second Mate Sydney Griffith immediately took three cross bearings to fix the ship's position. During the next four hours, as *Cape Leeuwin* made for Gladstone, the shipwright took regular soundings inside the vessel; the results showed she was not taking water.

A rare visit to town for Bertha Bowton from Middle Island.

Photograph provided by Kathy Mian and Boyd Rich.

Carting firewood at the Bowtons' Middle Island property.

Photograph provided by Cheryl Nugent.

Day and Date.	Hour.	Wind.		Weather.	Bar.	Ther.	Remarks.
		Direction.	Force.				
Wed 16th	9 a.m.	SE	3	C	2994	73	Employed in engine room
	3 Noon	"	3	C	" 90	81	Painting at No 1 cottage
	6 p.m.	"	4	C	" 91	75	& various other jobs
	Mdgt.						
Thu 17	9 a.m.	SSE	3	OC	2988	72	Employed in engine room
	3 Noon	E	4	BC	" 85	80	Cape Leeuwin arrived at 1500
	6 p.m.	E	3	C	" 87	75	& landed stores mail &
	Mdgt.						Keith Foster, the vessel departed
							for Lady Elliot Isl at 2130
Fri 18	9 a.m.	S	3	OP	2983	72	Employed in engine room,
	3 Noon	ESE	5	CQ	" 82	79	carting stores & carting
	6 p.m.	"	4	C	" 83	76	Abbetts effects to boatshed
	Mdgt.						
Sat 19	9 a.m.	SSE	3	C	2982	74	Employed in engine room
	3 Noon	ESE	3	BC	" 78	82	attention to generators, batteries
	6 p.m.	"	3	"	" 80	77	etc & testing engines
	Mdgt.						
Sun 20th	9 a.m.	S	4	B	2979	76	Engine room duties &
	3 Noon	ESE	5	BCQ	" 77	82	watches
	6 p.m.	SE	6	"	" 79	77	
	Mdgt.						

Lightstation daily logbook 1942. Entry on 17 December notes that Keith Foster, son of Head Lightkeeper Sam Foster, arrived at Bustard Head on board Cape Leeuwin *to spend the school holidays.*

Provided by Australian Maritime Safety Authority.

A good supply of fresh milk wasn't a problem for the lightkeepers in 1938. Here, Pat Casey milks the station cow.

Photograph provided by Keith Foster.

Lightkeepers' wives Jean Foster (left) and Dot Abbott take it easy as station horse Darkie earns his keep. Jean and Dot chose to remain with their husbands on the station during the critical years of the war.

Photograph provided by Keith Foster.

However, next day, while steaming out of Gladstone, it was discovered that the domestic water from the forepeak tank tasted brackish. When the tank was pumped dry, Captain George Clinch and Chief Engineer Nye found water seeping in between the concrete lining and the shellplate. After consultation with the Deputy Director, it was decided to continue on the ship's itinerary and take no further action until *Cape Leeuwin* returned to Brisbane. Each day, over half a tonne of water leaked into the vessel.

On her return trip south, *Cape Leeuwin* anchored off Bustard Head on 2 April to offload some building materials. While there, Captain Clinch and Second Mate Griffith took the ship's launch to sound the area where *Cape Leeuwin* had struck, but no obstruction could be found.

At a Preliminary Inquiry conducted by the Deputy Director of Navigation and Lighthouses on 26 April, Captain Clinch gave evidence that he still considered the passage between the rocks was clear, and that *Cape Leeuwin* had struck a submerged log or a whale.

When the vessel was slipped on 3 May, Engineer and Ship Surveyor Miller discovered an isolated crushing of the after portion of the stem shoeing. He reported that:

> *. . . The marking of the steelwork in way of this damage appears to be the result of striking a hard object, and considering that the damage is above the keel line and also that the vessel would trim by the stern, it would not appear possible for this vessel to have struck an immovable object and to have passed over that object without further damage to the hull unless it was in the nature of a pinnacle which fractured on impact, or a portion of the steelwork of a sunken vessel, such as a mast or superstructure which collapsed on impact . . .* [5]

The Australasian United Steam Navigation Company was employed to repair the damage for the cost of £16.10. 0. Queensland's Deputy Director I.J. Burch issued the directive that:

> *. . . Although the soundings taken by the Master and Second Mate on the vessel's return from the north indicate that the depths are approximately as charted, the fact that the vessel struck something leaves an element of doubt in one's mind regarding this and therefore it is considered that until a survey of the vicinity is made, a notice to mariners should be issued warning masters of vessels of the danger in using the passage . . .* [6]

On 29 March 1939, a week after *Cape Leeuwin's* accident, a works party from the Department of the Interior landed at Bustard Head to begin construction of a second cottage, almost identical to the one built in 1935. At the same time, a truck was brought ashore to assist with the transportation of materials. The new cottage was completed within three months for a cost of £2,226. 1. 4. The works party departed the station on 23 June, leaving the lightkeepers to dismantle the original Head Lightkeeper's cottage and dig out the stumps. Most of the old timber was taken by truck down to the boatshed at Pancake Creek, where it was stacked ready to be returned to Brisbane on board the lighthouse steamer. The remainder was bought by Bertha Bowton from Middle Island for £3, together with one spring cart for £1.10. 0 and two corrugated iron tanks for £3 each.

The death of Katherine Bowton on 5 March 1940 left her two daughters Bertha and Elsie to run the Middle Island property by themselves. Katherine was buried beside her husband Captain Frederick Bowton in the Bustard Head Cemetery.

Bertha, more than Elsie, was a frequent visitor to the lightstation. At that period, the lighthouse steamer delivered fuel and supplies to Bustard Head about every three months. In between times, a boat from Gladstone would be chartered for the monthly stores run. Bertha and Elsie had permission from the Department to transport some of their bulk provisions from Brisbane to Bustard Head on board the lighthouse steamer. The sisters would collect these provisions from the lightstation by horse, or sometimes by rowing boat — a round trip of 24 kilometres.

Well before 3 September 1939, the day Great Britain and Australia declared war on Germany, discussions had taken place between the Commonwealth Lighthouse Service and the armed forces regarding the protection of coastal lighthouses in a national emergency. In a secret memorandum dated 31 August 1939 from the Department of Commerce (Lighthouse Service) to the Attorney-General's Department, following a meeting between representatives of the Army, Navy and Lighthouse Service, it was decided that:

> . . . *Although the importance of providing protection for lighthouses was agreed upon and the heavy loss of life and property that could be entailed by interference with navigational lights was realised, the Conference was of the opinion that it would be impracticable to provide full protection for a number of the more isolated lights.*
>
> *It was accordingly decided that Lt. Commander Burrell (Navy) and Mr Laycock (Principal Lighthouse Engineer) should again meet to consider which of the automatic lights and manned lights staffed only with one man or two men could and should be fully protected, but in regard to stations staffed with three or four lightkeepers, immediate action should be taken to have all members of the staff sworn in by your Department as Special Commonwealth Peace Officers and supplied with firearms.*
>
> *Possibilities that can be visualised are that lightstation staff may be overpowered by enemy agents in order that:*

(a)   *Lights which should be exhibited may be extinguished to cause shipping losses or that lights which by direction have been temporarily extinguished may be exhibited to aid an enemy.*

(b)   *That lights may be altered in character so that they may be confused with other lights or so that white light is shown over dangerous waters which normally would be covered by a red light.*

(c)   *That a light which with another light forms a line of leads to shipping may be extinguished and replaced by one in a nearby locality so that shipping might be directed into dangerous waters.*

(d)   *That signalling equipment at lightstations may be used to communicate with enemy ships.*

Whilst these possibilities are perhaps remote, and the protection afforded by the supply of (say) one rifle and one revolver with fifty rounds of ammunition for each, to all lights would not be great, it would provide at least some measure of protection at little cost.

In regard to one-man and two-man stations, the question of whether additional staff should be provided in a national emergency is now being considered and in this connection you will be further advised, but in the meantime it is considered that the existing staff at these stations also should be sworn in as Special Commonwealth Peace Officers and supplied with firearms . . . [7]

In December 1939, the Department decided that, for the present, no extra personnel would be sent to assist the two lightkeepers at Bustard Head. For the past year, little signalling had been done between the lightstation and shipping, so Bustard Head was categorised as a "defence watching" station only. It was decided that the main light and automatic acetylene Clews Point light should be exhibited as normal, unless otherwise directed by the District Naval Officer. Head Lightkeeper Sam Foster was instructed to keep the telephone handy at night, and was shown by a lighthouse mechanic how to extinguish and relight the Clews Point light.

Circumstances changed drastically on 7 December 1941 when the Japanese launched their surprise air attack on the United States' base at Pearl Harbour. The following day, Australia formally declared war on Japan. As the Japanese moved relentlessly southward across the Pacific, Australia realised she faced the threat of invasion, the like of which she had never experienced before.

The wives and children of lightkeepers on Booby and Goods Islands in Torres Strait were compulsorily evacuated and both lights extinguished on 16 December 1941, while at all other stations evacuation was voluntary and the lights lit as normal unless otherwise ordered. The wives and children of the Bustard Head lightkeepers chose to remain on the station. The older children

The pilot of an RAAF plane sent this photograph to Head Lightkeeper Sam Foster during the Second World War. Jenny Lind Creek is to the left; Pancake Creek is at the top right.

Photograph provided by Keith Foster.

The second of the new cottages (right-hand side) was built in 1939. The two timber horizontal rails around the walls of the fuel shed, workshop and engine room were fitted to prevent the station horses rubbing and damaging the asbestos cement wall sheeting.

Photograph provided by James 'Lofty' Hayes.

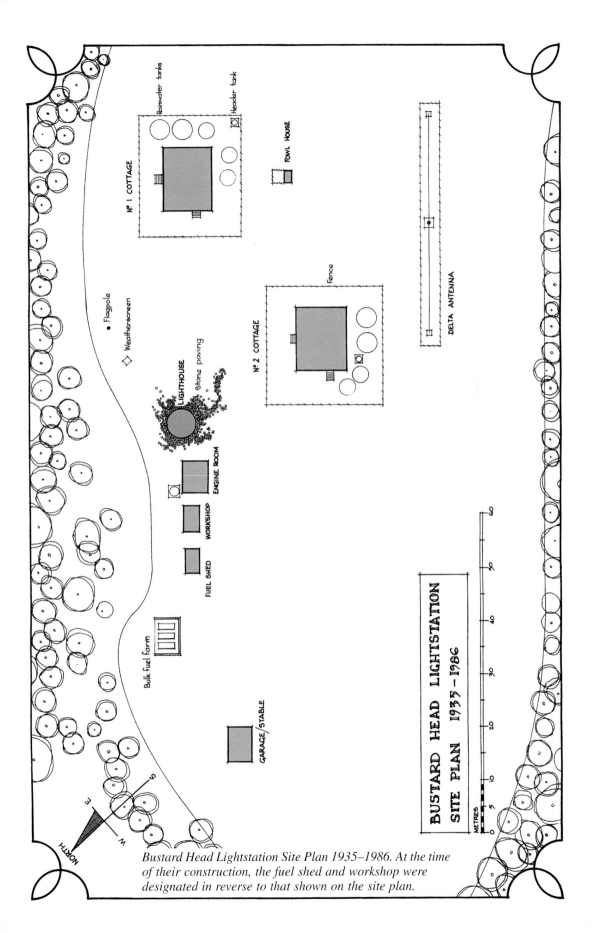

Bustard Head Lightstation Site Plan 1935–1986. At the time of their construction, the fuel shed and workshop were designated in reverse to that shown on the site plan.

BUSTARD HEAD LIGHTSTATION
SITE PLAN 1935 – 1986

Rainwater tanks
Header tank
Nº 1 COTTAGE
FOWL HOUSE
DELTA ANTENNA
Fence
Nº 2 COTTAGE
Flagpole
Weatherscreen
LIGHTHOUSE
Stone paving
ENGINE ROOM
WORKSHOP
FUEL SHED
Bulk fuel farm
GARAGE/STABLE
NORTH
METRES
0 5 10 20 30 40 50 60

continued to attend boarding school, sometimes returning to the station for school holidays on board a naval vessel. An extra lightkeeper was sent to the station and a continuous watch kept for aircraft, shipping, submarines and mines, all of which had to be reported immediately. If the naval authorities (Fighter Sector Headquarters in Brisbane) required the light to be extinguished, the Head Lightkeeper was advised of the order by telephone accompanied by the code word for the month (the code word for January 1943 was "Jericho") followed by the words "Fighter Flash Lighthouse". As well, all weather reports were sent by code. A sergeant and five men from the Volunteer Defence Force were sent to the lightstation to assist with the watches. The two Blue Flame kerosene stoves were put into one cottage, which was used as the 'mess'.

But despite the Japanese threat, the decision to provide lightkeepers with revolvers and rifles was rescinded. The Department reasoned that:

> . . . it would appear that the nature of any attack likely to be made on a lightstation would be of a very different nature from that of the attacks first contemplated and that arms of the above type (revolvers and rifles) would not only be inadequate for the protection of property but, through their inadequacy, be a source of danger to the lightkeepers themselves.[8]

In the event of an enemy raid by a landing party, a plan was devised that, if time permitted, the lightkeepers should make the main light inoperable by smashing the bulbs and emergency lamps and removing vital parts from the motors and generators. In the case of Clews Point, it was planned to release the acetylene gas from the cylinders. Fortunately no such action was necessary, as the allied victory at the Battle of the Coral Sea in May 1942 relieved the threat of a Japanese invasion of the Queensland coast. But in May 1943 security and surveillance were tightened after a Japanese submarine torpedoed and sank the hospital ship *Centaur* off Cape Moreton lighthouse. The same year, the lighthouse steamer *Cape Leeuwin* joined the United States Seventh Fleet, engaged in hydrographic surveys in enemy waters. During her absence, *Cape Otway* took over the duties of delivering fuel and supplies to Bustard Head.

As the war neared its end in 1945, Bustard Head's Volunteer Defence Force and third lightkeeper were removed, the 'mess' discontinued and one stove returned to its rightful cottage. In February of that year, Lightkeeper William Chapman was taken in to Gladstone for medical treatment after badly cutting his shin with a hoe. Shortly afterwards, Head Lightkeeper William Smith became ill and was also told to go in to Gladstone. It was arranged that a Relief Lightkeeper would arrive at Bustard Head on the same boat that was taking Smith off. However, as the Relief Lightkeeper knew nothing about running the station, the Department employed Mrs Smith as Acting Head

Lightkeeper, the first and only time in the station's history that a woman was officially in charge of Bustard Head.

Victory in Europe was declared on 9 May 1945, but the war in the Pacific dragged on. Japan still refused to surrender, until August 1945 when America dropped atom bombs on Hiroshima and Nagasaki. The end of the Second World War was celebrated by the lightkeepers on 14 August 1945. After six years of fear and uncertainty, the small community of Bustard Head, having escaped the horrors of war, could now look forward to a peaceful future.

Chapter 11

ROCKS OF WRATH

A number of technological innovations developed for use during the Second World War proved to be very useful for the Commonwealth Lighthouse Service in peacetime. One of these was the ex-Army amphibious vehicle called a DUKW.[1] Until the end of the war, fuel and supplies delivered to Bustard Head were offloaded from the lighthouse steamer into workboats and taken to Pancake Creek, where they were offloaded onto the beach then transported by horse and cart up the steep, 3 kilometre road to the station. The four-wheeled DUKW, equally at home on land or water, could go straight from the ship to the lightstation. The DUKW also proved invaluable at Clews Point automatic acetylene light, where once a year at least a dozen gas cylinders, each weighing 100 kilograms, had to be replaced. Before the introduction of the DUKW, these cylinders were landed on the closest beach to the light and manhandled 400 metres up a steep slope; then the empty cylinders, which weighed only 7 kilograms less than the full ones, had to be taken back down to the beach and loaded into the workboat. By the end of 1946, each of the three lighthouse steamers had been issued with a DUKW.

Although motor trucks were used at Bustard Head during construction of the two new cottages and alterations to the lighthouse, they had been removed at the completion of both jobs. But at the end of 1946 an ex-American Army jeep and trailer were delivered to the station to replace the horse and cart. The Head Lightkeeper at the time, Stan Goldsmith, noted in the station logbook that he was "Instructing Lightkeeper Smith in driving jeep". Either Stan Goldsmith was an inept instructor or the Lightkeeper was a slow learner, because eleven months later the same comment was being made in the logbook.

The relationship between Head Lightkeeper Stan Goldsmith and Light-keeper William Smith was not good. Until Stan Goldsmith's arrival at Bustard Head towards the end of the war, William Smith had been the Acting Head Lightkeeper for two years. So it was understandable if William Smith felt some resentment in now being ordered around by a man who had the reputation for not being particularly considerate to his lightkeepers. Every two

The beautifully proportioned Bustard Head lighthouse in pristine condition.

A huge Chance Brothers Second Order eight-sided lens, of exact design to the one used at Bustard Head from 1868 until 1935.

The first sight of the lightstation for visitors in the 1970s after walking up the 'main road' from the boatshed.

Little more than a metre in height, but still a magnificent piece of craftsmanship. The AGA Fourth Order lens replaced the original Chance Brothers Second Order lens when the light was electrified in 1935.

In the early 1970s, the light source — a 500 watt incandescent bulb (called the 'lamp') — was replaced by a 1,000 watt tungsten halogen lamp.

The Head Lightkeeper's cottage built in 1935. The author and his wife Shirley lived there from 1974–79, and again in 1981.

Gentle waves spill onto Aircraft Beach, with Clews Point in the background.

No job for the faint-hearted. Lightkeeper Kev Wright paints the dome of the tower.

Photograph provided by Jean Wright.

Jeep and trailer replaced the horse and cart during 1946. Head Lightkeeper James 'Lofty' Hayes prepares to take the lighthouse children for a drive.

Photograph provided by James 'Lofty' Hayes.

The 'main road' winds its way through the bush from the boatshed at Pancake Creek to the station. Aircraft Beach is to the left; Jenny Lind Creek at the top right.

Photograph provided by Malcolm Muir.

Lightkeeper's wife Jill Muir visits hermit Laurie 'The Admiral' Thomson at his Pancake Creek shack.

Photograph provided by Malcolm Muir.

All the mod cons — an electrified lighthouse and a station vehicle. The engine room is beside the tower. To the left is the workshop.

Photograph provided by Jean Wright.

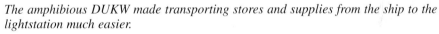

The amphibious DUKW made transporting stores and supplies from the ship to the lightstation much easier.

Photograph provided by Kevin Urban.

months or so, the simmering animosity between the two men would come to a head — Lightkeeper Smith would refuse to carry out an order given by Goldsmith, who would then report him to the Deputy Director in Brisbane. The Deputy Director must have felt some sympathy for the Lightkeeper's situation, as no reprimand ever appeared to be given. This melodrama continued for two years until Lightkeeper Smith was promoted and transferred to Dent Island as Head Lightkeeper.

It was decided in June 1947 that the station's horse and cart were no longer needed. They were sold to Bertha Bowton from Middle Island who, for some time, had expressed an interest in them. No sooner had Bertha left the station with her new purchase, when the jeep experienced a number of mechanical failures. On 1 January 1948, following another jeep breakdown, Bertha was requested to bring the horse and cart back to Bustard Head on loan, so the lightkeepers could transport their stores up from the boatshed. She returned to Middle Island next day, but a week later was asked to bring the horse and cart back again, this time for a week. After delivering them and arranging the date on which she would return to collect them, she set off on foot for the 12 kilometre journey home. On her return to Bustard Head, she found that two mechanics had arrived on the stores boat to repair the jeep. But to get it going again, spare parts were needed; these had been ordered and were to be delivered by special launch the following day. Again Bertha set off on foot to Middle Island, agreeing to leave the horse and cart for a further week. The repairs to the jeep proved successful, allowing Bertha to stay at home for a while.

To the great delight of the lightkeepers' wives, kerosene refrigerators were installed in the cottages during 1947. The tiny freezer compartments were designed to hold just two iceblock trays, but it was enough to freeze some meat each stores day so the families did not have to wholly rely on salted or tinned meat. Shortly after the war, the time between stores days was reduced from four to three weeks. The stores service was mostly done by charter launch from Gladstone, while the lighthouse steamer visited the station four times a year, mainly to offload fuel and maintenance materials.

Twelve years previously, when the main light was converted from kerosene operation to electric, two red sector lights were installed in the lantern room, one of which shone a fixed arc of red light to cover the outlying rocks. At the same time, when the automatic light at Clews Point was established, it was fitted with a red sector to cover Outer Rock. Unlike the two old kerosene auxiliary lights, which were decommissioned when these changes were made, the new red sector lights didn't have an accompanying series of cut-off screens to indicate to mariners how close their vessels were to the rocks. Although Outer Rock was only 3 nautical miles offshore, the main light's red sector could now be seen from a distance of 20 nautical miles offshore, and Clews Point light's red sector from 11 nautical miles. This now meant that the red light, when seen by mariners, indicated the direction of the rocks but not how far away they were.

This set of circumstances was a major factor in the disaster that awaited the 12 metre fishing launch *Edith* during February 1948. On Tuesday 3 February at 5.00 p.m., *Edith*, with a crew of six, slipped her moorings at Bundaberg and headed for Pancake Creek 70 miles away. *Edith*, built for the State Government in 1910 as the Maryborough fisheries patrol boat, was now privately owned by two of those on board — skipper Ray Rasmussen and Alex Jealous, both in their early thirties. The crew were in high spirits, looking forward to a few days fishing in the Bustard Head area.

During the evening, the fresh south-easterly wind gradually increased in strength, helping to push *Edith* along at a good rate of knots. At about 1.00 a.m. the vessel was abeam of Bustard Head lighthouse. The wind, now gusting at over 30 knots, heaped the sea into steep, foam-capped crests. Alex Jealous was at the wheel, while crewman Ben Betts stood just outside the wheelhouse door. The other four men were asleep in their bunks. Like the rest of the crew, Ben Betts was wearing only swimming togs. It was Ben Betts' first visit to Bustard Head, and he was thoroughly enjoying the adventure, relishing the salt spray that had him soaking with water as he watched the Bustard Head light flash its message through the darkness. As *Edith* entered the main light's southernmost red sector, Ben Betts commented to Alex Jealous:

"I can see the red sector light. Aren't we too close to the rocks?"

"We're all right," Alex Jealous replied curtly. "You can see the red sector light from miles out to sea. Look, I know what I'm doing. I've been up here dozens of times before. This is only your first time."

He had hardly finished speaking when, with a violent splintering crash, *Edith's* bow reared high out of the sea as she smashed headlong into Outer Rock. The vessel holed and immediately began to founder. The four men in their bunks below, abruptly awakened by the impact, quickly joined Betts and Jealous on deck. They all climbed over the gunwale onto the rock, which was awash with water that surged well over their knees. Crewman Gordon Cantrell, knowing that his mate Vince Allendorff couldn't swim, thrust a loose hatch-cover at him to use as buoyancy. Hanging on to this, Vince was swept into the blackness. The launch's timber dinghy, which was attached to *Edith's* stern by a long line, was driven towards the rock. With the idea of using the dinghy as a life raft, Ben Betts upturned it to provide more buoyancy. Three of the men rushed to untie the line from the dinghy's bow, but appeared to be having difficulty in doing so.

"Who tied this bloody knot!" someone shouted out in frustration.

A large wave swept the dinghy into deep water, taking Ray Rasmussen, Alex Jealous and Harry O'Brien with it. Gordon Cantrell saw the three men hanging on for their lives as the dinghy was buffeted by foaming waves. Only Gordon Cantrell and Ben Betts remained on the rock now. An overturned drum of tar from *Edith* had emptied its contents into the sea. Ben Betts and Gordon Cantrell, still wearing only swimming togs, became covered with this black goo as the waves broke over them. Ben Betts grabbed two empty 2 gallon demijohns to use as flotation, and with one in each hand let himself be swept off the rock. Gordon Cantrell picked up the empty tar drum that was swirling in the debris nearby and followed him. Ben Betts heard a bloodcurdling scream from the direction of the three men clinging to the dinghy. In horror, he immediately thought that someone had been taken by one of the large sharks that he had been told inhabited the area. In less than eight minutes from hitting Outer Rock, *Edith* had disappeared from sight.

Throughout the night as the beams from the lighthouse swept overhead, Gordon Cantrell, pummeled by waves and clinging to his tar drum, attempted to make some headway through the unabating seas towards shore, constantly aware of the imminence of shark attack. As dawn eventually broke after a seemingly endless night, Gordon Cantrell sighted Ben Betts about 200 metres away. They shouted and managed to swim over to each other. Ben gave one of his demijohns to Gordon to use, but no sooner had he done so, when a wave separated the men and they lost sight of each other. Gordon made his way towards the shore at Clews Point. Ben tried to do the same, but no matter how hard he tried, the tide seemed to be taking him in the opposite direction.

At about 6.30 a.m., Gordon saw a large barge leaving Pancake Creek. He waved frantically, but was unsuccessful in attracting the crew's attention. As the hot summer sun rose in the morning sky, Ben and Gordon's skin began to burn and blister from the tar. Three hours later, Gordon managed to make his way inshore, thankfully landing on the beach below Clews Point. Almost naked, bleeding, burnt and covered in tar, Gordon staggered along the beach and up through the bush towards the lighthouse. Head Lightkeeper Stan Goldsmith saw Gordon coming and went to meet him. Gordon's tongue was so swollen he could barely gasp out what had happened. Goldsmith helped the injured man into his cottage, applied first aid and made him as comfortable as possible before telephoning the Gladstone police. Goldsmith and Lightkeeper William Smith then set off in the jeep to search for other survivors, trying to attract their attention by blowing the vehicle's horn as they went.

In the meantime, the tide had taken Ben Betts south-east towards Jenny Lind Creek, where he managed to swim ashore on the crest of a wave, unfortunately being cast onto razor sharp oyster-covered rocks, which badly injured his knee and deeply lacerated his body and limbs. After resting for a while, Ben began to climb up the headland. He had only gone a short distance when he heard a car horn. Before long he was in the jeep, heading for the station and first aid. For the remainder of the afternoon, the lightkeepers continued to search for other survivors without success.

Earlier that afternoon, police and an ambulance bearer left Gladstone on board the motor launch *Jessalia* for Bustard Head. Despite battling heavy seas and gale force winds, *Jessalia* anchored in Pancake Creek just on dark. Head Lightkeeper Goldsmith met the party and took them up to the station in the jeep. The ambulance bearer praised the lightkeepers and their wives for the standard of care and first aid they had provided for Gordon and Ben.

Early next morning the injured men left on *Jessalia* for Gladstone Hospital. The lightkeepers and police continued to search the shoreline of Bustard Head and Rodd's Peninsula, while aircraft flew low along the coast from Bundaberg to Gladstone, hoping for some sign of the other four men.

The six men on board *Edith* were all returned soldiers and members of the Bundaberg Returned Services League. The branch secretary, Stan White, appealed on radio for volunteers to join the search for the missing men. The response was so great that, shortly afterwards, he had to go on air again to say no more volunteers were required. Small groups were formed to search 180 kilometres of isolated coastline from Bundaberg to the northern end of Curtis Island. Planes were chartered by the Bundaberg and Gladstone Returned Services Leagues. Parties of men were dropped off by launch at places that were difficult to access by land. In all, hundreds of men were involved in the search.

After five days, only a hatch cover and a drum of fuel from *Edith* had been found. The search parties still held hope that the missing men may have reached shore and then made their way inland to find civilisation. But as the days passed without word, it became obvious that the men had died at sea.

Ben Betts, who had received more injuries than Gordon Cantrell, remained in hospital for a week. Ben firmly believed that sharks had taken the other four men, and that he and Gordon had been spared only because the smell of tar on their bodies had acted as a repellent.[2]

The tragedy may never have happened if the two auxiliary lights at Bustard Head had not been removed in 1935. However, then as always, safe navigation remains the sole responsibility of the skipper. A simple running fix (a method of plotting the vessel's position when only one object — in this case the Bustard Lighthouse — is in sight) would have shown that *Edith* was heading for disaster.

At 10.00 a.m. on Good Friday 15 April 1949, seven yachts crossed the starting line for the inaugural 300 nautical mile Brisbane to Gladstone Ocean Yacht Race. As the yachts were not equipped with radios, their positions were reported each day by Barrier Reef Airways Catalina flying boats and the light-keepers at Double Island Point, Sandy Cape, Lady Elliot Island and Bustard Head. Carrier pigeons released from the yachts were used as well, but not with much success. The winner of that first race was John Bourne's *Sea Prince* with an elapsed time of 56 hours 48 minutes and 45 seconds. On the more relaxed return journey to Brisbane, some of the yachts anchored in Pancake Creek for a few days, and their crews visited the lightstation. As the number of yachts in the race increased year by year, it became a tradition to visit the lighthouse at Bustard Head. Over the years many friendships were formed between the yachties and the lightkeepers.

A cyclone in March 1949 had caused extensive damage to the ageing Bustard Head telephone line. Although the Commonwealth Lighthouse Service still owned the line, and was responsible for its maintenance, the Postmaster-General's Department charged an annual fee of £114 for removal of faults and line inspections. So, in December 1950, it must have been a pleasant surprise for the Lighthouse Service to receive a letter from the Postmaster-General advising that plans were in hand to do major repairs to the line, including the replacement of one hundred wooden poles with galvanised iron ones and the replacement of the single galvanised wire line with two copper wires.

Because heavy rain had made vehicle access from the Middle Creek end of the line impossible, the Postmaster-General's Department requested that some poles, wire and camping gear be sent out on the fortnightly stores boat (towards the end of 1950, the period between stores days was reduced from three to two weeks) and transported to the site with the help of the lightkeepers and the station jeep. The Lighthouse Service readily agreed.

During January and February 1951, Head Lightkeeper Stan Goldsmith and Lightkeeper James 'Lofty' Hayes spent twenty-eight hours of their own time manhandling and transporting the extremely heavy equipment. As the result of a claim made by the lightkeepers for payment regarding this extra work, the Lighthouse Service paid each man £2.10. 0.

The "pleasant surprise" of an almost new telephone line, which the Lighthouse Service assumed it was getting at no cost, backfired when they received a bill from the Postmaster-General's Department for £4,300. Much correspondence followed; but although the Postmaster-General "regretted that the work was carried out without the Lighthouse Service's prior authority" it still demanded the full amount. Negotiations continued well into 1952, when it was finally agreed that the Lighthouse Service pay only £792. However, at the same time, the Postmaster-General increased the annual fee for removal of faults and line inspections from £114 to £203.[3]

It was hate at first sight between Head Lightkeeper Stan Goldsmith and sixty-one year-old Laurie Thomson. Laurie was no stranger to Pancake Creek. Trained as an engineer, but tiring of city life, Laurie forsook his profession to try his luck at fishing. He bought an 18 metre fishing boat called *Duckwing* and put to sea. Maintenance on the planked vessel was not high on Laurie's list of priorities, and year by year as the caulking disintegrated, the volume of water that had to be regularly pumped out of the bilge increased. *Duckwing* came to its end on Tryon Island in the Capricorn Group of islands 47 miles north-east of Gladstone, when Laurie intentionally put her aground to do some urgent caulking. As the tide rose, the water entered between the planks quicker than it could be pumped out, and the vessel filled. Laurie and his crew were rescued from the island, abandoning the boat, which eventually broke up.

After acquiring another vessel in 1951, Laurie began building his 'retirement home' on a small point of land in Pancake Creek, halfway between the boatshed and Clews Point. The materials he used — timber framing and corrugated galvanised iron — looked suspiciously similar to those used at Lady Musgrave Island in the construction of the Big Game Fishing Club of Queensland's huts, which had recently begun to disappear.

Because Laurie was illegally building the shack on the Bustard Head lighthouse reserve, it didn't take long for Head Lightkeeper Stan Goldsmith to tell him to move off. Laurie refused. Stan informed the Department, which decided that, because of Laurie's age and the fact that he was a wounded First World War veteran, he could stay. Laurie and Stan settled down to an uneasy truce, but as time went by, and Head Lightkeepers came and went, Laurie was accepted as a part of Bustard Head. As the years passed, he visited Gladstone less and less, and became known as the hermit of Pancake Creek. He welcomed visitors, more so if they brought a bottle of rum with them. Owing to the number of Laurie's old dinghies lying in various states of disrepair on the foreshore beside his shack, local fishermen nicknamed him The Admiral. On Christmas Day, the Head Lightkeeper of the time would usually invite Laurie up to the station for lunch. For that occasion, Laurie would go to the unusual lengths of washing, shaving and putting on a clean shirt. Despite those formalities, The Admiral, who was always accompanied by his black and tan mongrel dog Pete, which everyone except his master detested, readily joined into the day's festivities.[4]

At the end of July 1953, Head Lightkeeper Stan Goldsmith was replaced by Vivian Rooke. In July of the following year, Rooke wrote to the Department requesting that electric lighting be installed in the cottages. The Department replied that this couldn't be done, as "no one particular station can be selected for preferential treatment". However, Rooke was advised "that the existing petrol engines on stations are to be replaced by diesel units in the near future and no doubt the question of house lighting will be raised then". For two more years the Aladdin kerosene lamps illuminated the lightkeepers' cottages at night.

Eventually, in June 1956, Mechanic Gidney from the New Farm Depot arrived at the station to replace the motors and electrify the cottages. The two Ronaldson and Tippett petrol motors were replaced by two, single cylinder Armstrong-Siddeley air-cooled diesels coupled to 2.5 kW generators. A new 110 volt DC switchboard was installed, and the alarm circuit connected to two 12 volt batteries. The cottages were wired and each provided with ten lights and two power points. Not before time, the residents of Bustard Head could now feel part of the twentieth century.

Chapter 12

FIGHT FOR LIFE

Well-known professional fisherman from Bundaberg, seventy year-old Alex 'Sharky' Smith and his fifteen year-old grandson John Dahms were hoping for another successful day's fishing to add to the 200 kilograms of mackerel they already had in the icebox of their 8 metre launch. The weather looked promising — there was only a slight swell, and a gentle breeze formed a few whitecaps on the crests of the small waves. It was just after first light on Sunday 3 June 1956, and the two were trolling around the rocks off Bustard Head. Sharky Smith had spent most of his life on fishing boats, first in Scotland before immigrating to Australia, where he had joined the Australian Imperial Force to fight in the First World War. He lost a leg during the conflict and returned to Bundaberg, out of which port he had fished ever since. Sharky had only recently installed a new diesel motor in his launch, and had fitted it out for prawn trawling. Throughout his whole fishing career he had never experienced a serious mishap.

As the launch motored slowly past Outer Rock, without the slightest warning, something lifted the vessel high out of the water, then tipped it side-ways, catapulting Sharky and his grandson into the sea. The launch plunged back into the water, narrowly missing the man and the boy, before resurfacing keel up. Young John scrambled on top of the upturned hull and managed to pull Sharky up beside him. In an attempt to stop the launch drifting rapidly out to sea, John dived under the boat to try and release the anchor that was inside a fastened deck locker. It took him six dives before he succeeded. The anchor line wasn't long enough to reach bottom, but the weight of the anchor slowed the boat's drift. It was a cold winter's morning, so it wasn't long before Sharky and John were shivering in their wet clothes; nevertheless, Sharky removed his shirt and rigged it as a signal in an effort to attract the attention of the light-keepers at Bustard Head. The chance of the signal being seen from the light-station — a distance of over 3 miles —was extremely slim; with the naked eye it would have appeared no more than a speck in the ocean.

The upturned launch drifted throughout the morning. Sharky and John had not seen what 'thing' had caused the heavy vessel to suddenly rise out of the sea. They could only surmise that a whale had surfaced underneath them. Then, just before midday, the signal was seen by two Gladstone fishermen, Laurie Brunke and Jack Thompson, who had come out to fish at Outer Rock. After rescuing the couple, an attempt was made to tow the launch into Pancake Creek, but in doing so it filled with water and sank. Although devastated by the loss of his boat, Sharky was grateful that he and his young grandson were still alive.[1]

Yet again, the white ants had been active on the station, this time in the timber framing of the fuel store and boatshed. In March 1957, Head Lightkeeper Vivian Rooke requested a further supply of black arsenic and castor oil for treating the affected timber. The fuel shed was saved, but the boatshed required major renovations. So, in October of the same year the asbestos cement wall and roof sheeting were removed, more than half the timber framing renewed, and the old sheeting refitted.

By 1957 the Blue Flame kerosene stoves had been replaced by Aladdin kerosene stoves. The new stoves, although more expensive, were cheaper to operate with a saving of 8 gallons of kerosene per stove each month. At that time, a lightkeeper was allowed a monthly ration of 18¾ gallons of kerosene for the refrigerator and stove. If more than that amount was used, the light-keeper had to pay the Department 2/1d per gallon excess, plus 6d cheque exchange. A lightkeeper was also allowed ½ gallon of methylated spirits each month for priming the Aladdin pressure stove.

When James 'Lofty' Hayes returned to Bustard Head as Head Lightkeeper in January 1958, he was appointed Telephone Office Keeper of the Non-Official Bustard Head Post Office at the annual rate of £27.10. 0. Faults were still occurring to the telephone, and at one stage it was out of order for twelve days in a row. The lightkeepers often walked up to 30 kilometres in a day looking for a break in the line, only to discover later that the fault lay in the equipment at the Gladstone end.

The thought of a medical emergency arising on the station at a time when the telephone was out of order, must have been a constant concern for parents. Even when the telephone was working, it was impossible to receive medical help quickly, as Head Lightkeeper Lofty Hayes experienced in October 1958. At that time, Lofty and his wife Jeannie had four children on the station — Robin, their seventeen year-old daughter; Olwyn, seven years; Christopher, five; and Linley, three. Jeannie was three months pregnant. The other man on the station was Relief Lightkeeper Arthur Renton. The following story, told in Lofty's words, is taken from his manuscript titled "A Goat around Capricorn":

Arthur and I had been trying to stop an oil leak in one of the diesels that supplied power to the lighthouse. We were unsuccessful and

159

decided to run the plant on the alternate system (the power setup was duplicated for just such an emergency). When I returned to the cottage, I found my wife Jeannie lying down.

"Have you got a migraine headache?" I asked.

"No," she answered, "I think I've had a miscarriage."

"Why didn't you send one of the kids to get me?"

"I didn't want to worry you while you were trying to get the light working."

The poor little devil had been lying there frightened and worried, but wouldn't tell me because she thought I was worried about the oil leak.

The amount of blood she had lost convinced me that she had to go in to Gladstone immediately. Our only way was by sea, a thirty mile journey. There had been a fishing boat in the vicinity that day — Weona, *owned by the Leach brothers, good friends of mine. I took the jeep and drove the two miles to the boatshed at Pancake Creek, from where I could see the various anchorages. Nothing. I returned to the station desperately worried. We were connected by telephone to Gladstone, but by the time a launch could be arranged from there, then get to Bustard and return, nine to ten hours at least would have elapsed.*

As I gave one more despairing glance around from the top of the station hill, I glimpsed a light about five miles up Middle Creek. The Leach brothers! They must have gone up Middle Creek to get away from the 20 knot northerly. By this time it was getting late, and the light, glimmering faintly, could be put out at any time, so I fixed in my mind exactly where they were.

Luckily, I had built an eight foot dinghy some months previously. Arthur helped me tie this onto the jeep, and I quickly returned to the boatshed. The tide was right out, so I carried the dinghy on my back across 200 yards of sand, dead coral and rock to the water's edge. A hard northerly was blowing, putting up a fair chop, and as I rowed it was hard to avoid being blown sideways onto the shore. Luckily, the dinghy was a beauty, with a V bottom and a large spring to the keel, very good in a sea and easy to row. However, a certain amount of water came inboard; in my haste I had forgotten to take a bailer, and eventually she became loggy with the water inside. I headed for the Middle Bank, a large sandbank in the centre of Pancake Creek. Before I got there, I took one over the stern, and the dinghy sank, but I was only in four feet of water. I struggled the dinghy onto the bank, tipped the water out, and started off again. By this time the tide had begun to run in with the wind, lessening the sea, and I was getting shelter from the shore. The only difficulty now was to avoid being blown or running ashore on the sand and mud banks that abounded at this stage of the tide.

Eventually, I got alongside Weona, *— forty-eight feet long and capable of ten knots — and banged on the hull. Frank Leach put his head out of the wheelhouse. I told him of my trouble.*

"Well, Lofty," he said, "I don't know if we can get down to the boatshed at this stage of the tide, but it is making, and we'll give it a go."

Frank started the engine while Ian and Boyd got the anchor up. With consummate seamanship and local knowledge, they threaded their way back along the channel I had laboriously traversed, Ian and Boyd thrusting long sticks ahead and down to gauge the depths of water. After touching lightly a few times, Weona *was at last abreast of the boatshed where she anchored.*

"We'll come ashore in the net dinghy, while you're up getting Jeannie," said Frank.

I rowed ashore and drove back to the cottage. Jeannie had packed a few clothes, and we rushed back to the beach, where the Leach boys were waiting. I watched, heart in mouth as they came alongside Weona, *the dinghy plunging heavily, but Jeannie got on board without difficulty. The big launch rolled heavily as she cleared the headland, and I thanked God that it was* Weona, *as a smaller vessel would not have been able to go.*

About five o'clock in the morning I got a phone call from Ian.

"Jeannie is safely in hospital," he said.

"I can't begin to thank you, Ian," I answered. "What sort of trip did you have?"

"It was pretty bad," he replied. "We had to take it in turns to hold Jeannie in the bunk. There was a big sea running."

Later that morning, I rang the Gladstone Hospital.

"Your wife is resting comfortably. She is in no danger, and we have managed to save the baby," the reassuring voice of the ward sister came across the wire.

Six months later, little Mike was born, quite well and healthy. The Leach family still call Mike the "Leach baby" and consider they have a stake in him, something that I would in no way dispute.[2]

But Lofty and Jeannie's troubles with baby Michael weren't yet over. As each of Jeannie's pregnancies had become a little more complicated, it was decided that, after her recent emergency trip on *Weona*, she and the children would stay in Gladstone. This would also be an advantage for their daughter Robin, who was about to enter her final year at high school. Lofty's story continues:

Next leave, which we always took in the summer holidays, we bought a War Services Home. Jeannie and the children settled in, while I returned to Bustard alone.

But life became one long worry for my wife. The children, previously shielded from civilisation's illnesses by isolation, now caught every complaint that was going. Chicken pox, scarlet fever and measles followed in swift succession. In the midst of all this, Michael James was born and Jeannie brought him down during the May holidays. Poor Robin, she didn't get much time to study, but, great kid that she is, helped her mother with the invalids. Then Chris got pneumonia, while the three girls had heavy colds. Through it all, the little fellow appeared to thrive. Then Jeannie rang me. I knew there was something very wrong by her voice.

"It's baby Michael, Jim," she said with a catch in her voice. "He's terribly ill, can you come in?"

After trying to reassure her, I rang the children's ward of the Gladstone Hospital.

"Can you tell me how Michael Hayes is?" I asked.

"He's a very sick little boy, Mr Hayes," the Sister answered. "I do think you should come in straight away."

The little fellow was ten weeks old.

Ringing the Regional Lighthouse Engineer in Brisbane, I was given permission to leave the lightstation by any method I could. My assistant, Keith Window, would carry on while I was away. Luckily, the stores launch Tuscana, *operated by my good friend Phil Robson and his brother Geoff, was at the Town Wharf and they immediately got underway. I handed over to Keith, and then came the long wait until the launch arrived. The sea was calm, and by dusk we were alongside the Gladstone wharf. A taxi ride, and minutes later I held Jeannie in my arms, while the tears, held in check all this time, fell freely.*

I was allowed to look at my infant son, a tiny restless figure beneath the oxygen tent, fighting to get each choking, gasping breath.

Matron Smith spoke to us compassionately:

"The little fellow's putting up a wonderful fight."

Jeannie and I sat huddled together on the verandah of the children's ward throughout that endless night, expecting every moment to be called. Earlier, a clergyman had baptised the wee boy, a sad little rite. In the small hours, Dr Farmer, the resident doctor, wheeled another oxygen cylinder into the ward, where the Matron herself kept watch over the child.

"He's still holding his own," the doctor said. "We thought he had the usual virus pneumonia at first, but when the penicillin didn't help, we realised he had a massive pneumonic infection. After trying other drugs, we've given him Atromycin as a last resort and there is a chance. Now I suggest that Mrs Hayes sleeps here in the women's ward, and you go home and have some sleep."

I had hardly touched the pillow it seemed, when my friend Charlie Bycroft woke me.

"Come on Lofty," he said. "The little fellow is worse."

As we drove up to the hospital, grey skies and rain matched my greyness of spirit. Dr Farmer met me.

"He's at the crisis, Mr Hayes."

Numbly, Jeannie and I sat miserably together, while rain dripped off the guttering and eaves, and a cold wind blew as if the whole day were a part of our misery. Charlie and Mrs Bycroft brought us a meal at midday. Still the little fellow fought on.

Matron Smith came out to comfort us.

"It's amazing the stamina that baby has. I've never seen such a sick little child fight so hard."

We both thanked God for the fact that Jeannie had been able to breastfeed Michael; the strength it had given was helping now. I thought to myself also, how little possessions really mattered. I would have given all I owned to know Michael James was well.

Towards evening, the doctor came to us and we could tell before he spoke that the news was good.

"I think he may live, now go home and have a good sleep. Come back early tomorrow."

Next day was gloriously sunny. As Charlie drove us to the hospital, the blue sky seemed to say "He'll be okay". And he was; over the crisis, a sick little boy still, but he was going to live. Going to live! Thank you God, and thank you all the great-hearted people who helped. Thank you all the people, dozens of them, who came up to Jeannie and me in the street to say how pleased they were at the good news.

A few days later, I took the three older children, who Robin had looked after all this time, back to Bustard Head aboard Roy Perry's boat. Not for them the town life, until it became absolutely necessary, but school by correspondence and the happy, open-air life that hardly knows illness and disease. Jeannie and Michael joined us later.

Michael had a terrible rattle for many months, but good food and sunshine worked wonders. He grew to be a normal, healthy teenager, and though I love all my children dearly, his walk through the valley of the shadow gives him a special place in my heart.[2]

Washed, shaved and wearing a clean shirt, Laurie 'The Admiral' Thomson — the hermit of Pancake Creek — joins the lightkeepers for Christmas lunch 1963. Front row from left to right: The Admiral, Robin Hayes, Head Lightkeeper James 'Lofty' Hayes holding his son Michael, and Jeannie Hayes with Pipsi the dog. Second row from left to right: Jean Wright, Olwyn Hayes, Chris Hayes, and Lightkeeper Kev Wright. Back row: Linley Hayes.

Photograph provided by James 'Lofty' Hayes.

Ian Leach and his 14.5 metre fishing boat Weona. *In darkness and battling huge seas, Ian made an emergency dash from Bustard Head to Gladstone with Jeannie Hayes, in an attempt to save her unborn baby. The seas were so big that Jeannie had to be held in her bunk throughout the trip.*

Photographs provided by Elma Leach.

Bustard Head overlooks Bustard Bay and Round Hill Head, where Lieutenant James Cook landed in 1770. Bustard Head Cemetery is at the bottom right-hand side of the photograph, just to the right of the 'main road'.

The dangerous entrance to Jenny Lind Creek has claimed many a life. Nevertheless, in 1867 the 48 ton paddle-wheel steamer Gneering *crossed the bar on a number of occasions to offload the lighthouse building materials.*

Like an ethereal apparition, Bustard Head lighthouse casts its warning light into the darkness.

Until 1978, the boatshed at Pancake Creek marked the start of the 'main road' to the station.

The panels of the lighthouse are bolted together like a gigantic prefabricated toy. In 1935 the internal steel sheet lining was removed and the external stairs repositioned inside the tower. The centre column at the right, called the weight tube, contained the heavy weights used to revolve the lens, prior to the light being electrified. The automatic emergency alarm radios sit on the table.

The AGA Fourth Order lens inside the lantern room. The black curtains suspended from a frame that revolves with the lens are positioned between the beams of light to reduce minor flashes of light that may be seen at sea between the main flashes. Above the lens, a suspended platform carries the two red sector lights.

As the sun drops below the horizon, the lighthouse beams out its message to those at sea.

COMMONWEALTH OF AUSTRALIA.

POSTMASTER-GENERAL'S DEPARTMENT.

AGREEMENT TO ACT AS TELEPHONE OFFICE KEEPER

The Deputy Director,

Post and Telegraphs,

Brisbane

I, *James Sherbourne Hayes.*
(Name in full)
of *Bustard Hds, C/o Customs, Gladstone, Q.* hereby agree

to act as Telephone Office Keeper at *Bustard Heads*

and to provide the necessary accommodation and perform the duties for the departmental scale rates of payment ; such payment to be subject to periodical adjustment either by way of increase or reduction in conformity with the increase or reduction in the volume of business transacted or variation in the nature of the services rendered. I am also willing to perform such additional duties as may be necessary by the connexion of telephone subscribers.

I also agree to conduct the Telephone Office for a term of not less than three years, or in the event of my relinquishing the conduct of the Telephone Office within that period, to nominate another resident ready and willing to undertake the duties without extra cost to the Postmaster-General's Department.

Witness *H.C. Bailey*

Signature *J. S. Hayes.*

Occupation *Lightkeeper.*

Date *21/5/58*

Head Lightkeeper James 'Lofty' Hayes' Agreement to act as Telephone Office Keeper, stamped with the Bustard Head postmark.

Chapter 13

THE PITILESS SEA

There was standing room only for most of the thirty yachtsmen packed into Head Lightkeeper Lofty Hayes' cottage at Bustard Head. It was the week after the 1963 Brisbane to Gladstone Ocean Yacht Race, and the crews from a number of participating yachts, on their way back to Brisbane, were enjoying a few leisurely days anchored in Pancake Creek. The group of thirty had walked up the road to make the traditional visit to the lightstation. One of those yachtsmen was the renowned boat designer and builder Norm Wright Jnr. In his yacht *Mouse of Malham*, Norm had won that year's race.

"Where're all these famous Bustard Head mud crabs you're always telling us about, Lofty?" Norm Wright asked.

"All right, Norm," Lofty replied, taking up the challenge, "the tide's just right, let's go and get some."

Lofty, accompanied by the lighthouse children, led the men down to Jenny Lind Creek, where they soon collected sixty mud crabs from the creek bed. Back at the station the crabs were cooked in an old wood-fired copper boiler, then, complemented by slices of fresh bread baked by Jeannie Hayes, they were quickly devoured.

Norm must have enjoyed his mud crab lunch, because the following year after the race he arrived at the station with a carton of large chocolate Easter eggs for the lighthouse children, a ritual he continued for many years.

The participants in the Brisbane to Gladstone Yacht Race were appreciative of the lightkeepers for keeping watch and reporting yacht positions during the race, and were quick to reciprocate whenever they could. Following the 1962 race, while Mechanic Irwin Freye was on the station overhauling No.1 engine, it was found that some spare parts were urgently required. Vic Meyer, skipper and owner of the famous racing yacht *Solo*, delivered the parts from Gladstone on his way back to Brisbane, rendezvousing with the lightkeepers outside the entrance to Pancake Creek.

Although tragedy had affected some Bustard Head families, the lifestyle for most was a sojourn in paradise. The creeks abounded with mud crabs, fish and oysters; and walking the pristine headlands and long golden beaches with their magnificent vistas was living with nature at its purest. For the children it was a huge adventure. There were sheltered coves, coral reefs, caves and forests to explore, where they could pretend to be pirates, shipwrecked sailors, smugglers and anything else they fancied, limited only by the bounds of their imagination. The children had their own names for the places where they played: 'The Garden' — the lightkeepers' vegetable garden, which was hidden in the bush beside a well, and surrounded by lush mango and lemon trees to protect the crops from the salty atmosphere; 'The Jungle' — a thick patch of dark green shadowy rainforest down beside the banks of Jenny Lind Creek; 'The Bog' — a marshy area halfway down the headland, where the children once rescued a hopelessly entrapped calf; and many others.

Lofty and Jeannie Hayes' children, Robin, Olwyn, Christopher, Linley and Michael had a pony named Mandy. Along with Jean Wright, the young daughter of Lightkeeper Kev Wright, they often set off with Mandy to visit Bertha and Elsie Bowton at their Middle Island property. They followed the telegraph line on the 24 kilometre round trip, each child taking turns to ride Mandy for a distance of six telegraph poles. It was a happy, healthy lifestyle for the youngsters who, now in adulthood, all remember Bustard Head with passionate fondness.

The 1960s were a time of great change and improvement for Bustard Head as well as the Commonwealth Lighthouse Service. In 1960 the lightkeepers were provided with a Victa motor mower. Up until then, cattle had kept patches of the 3 acre grassy lighthouse precinct reasonably short, while hand clippers were used to trim around the cottages. Now, the whole station area could be made to look neat and tidy. So impressed with the new mower's results on the first day it was used, Lofty Hayes wrote in the station logbook: "Converting grass into lawn".

The following year, the jeep was replaced by a Land Rover and the kerosene fuelled stoves replaced by LP gas stoves. In 1963 Bustard Head Telephone Office was declared a "Pastoral Office". Because of this, Telephone Office Keeper Lofty Hayes' allowance for this position was reduced from £50 per annum to £1. In a letter of objection to the Postmaster-General, Lofty explained that despite the decrease in payment, he was still expected to do the same amount of work and therefore requested that the matter be reconsidered. Lofty's request was refused.

The ageing lighthouse steamers, *Cape Otway*, *Cape Leeuwin* and *Cape York*, were replaced by three new sister ships, *Cape Don*, *Cape Moreton* and *Cape Pillar* respectively during 1963-4. Built at the State Dockyards at Newcastle, each ship was 74.2 metres in length with a loaded displacement of almost 2,500 tonnes. Equipped with an electric crane and helicopter landing pad, each vessel carried a complement of thirty-eight officers and crew in individual air-conditioned cabins. There was also accommodation for an additional twelve passengers, to cater for official visitors and lightkeeping families on transfer between stations.

On her first visit to Bustard Head on 11 February 1964, *Cape Moreton* anchored for a few days, while the crew replaced the automatic light structure at Clews Point. During the same year, kerosene fuelled coppers were installed in each cottage's laundry, and the bathrooms were extended to take a full size bath. But owing to the limited capacity of the few rainwater tanks on the station, the precious water was rarely wasted in a bath. Instead, a 4 gallon metal container with a shower nozzle fitted to its base was filled with hot water and suspended over the bath. Often, three or four children would shower at the one time; the importance of conserving water was instilled into them from a very early age. Even so, during the dry winter months, it was not uncommon for the lightkeepers to cart water every day from a spring at Pancake Creek.

To ease this situation, two 5,000 gallon spherical fibreglass rainwater tanks were delivered to the station — one for each cottage — during 1965; but it wasn't until later the following year that they were assembled and connected to the cottages. At the same time, because of the increased water capacity on the station, septic tanks were installed and the earth closets demolished. As well, kerosene fuelled water heaters were fitted in the bathrooms.

But the greatest change to the station during the decade occurred in November 1965, when mechanics Dickson, Wilson and Sardie from the New Farm Lighthouse Depot arrived to remove the 110 volt DC Armstrong-Siddeley plant and replace it with a 240 volt AC plant. One of the old generating sets was moved from the engine room and temporarily set up in the base of the lighthouse, while the old concrete engine beds were broken up and new ones poured. Then two, new, twin cylinder Petter PJ2 diesels connected to 7.5 KVA generators were installed together with a new switchboard. The lighthouse and cottages were completely rewired, as was the alarm system to the light. The new diesels were run at night to power the light and then usually switched off during the day. However, exceptions were made to run washing machines and other household appliances.

A week before the mechanics arrived on the station, Head Lightkeeper Lofty Hayes cut a walking track through the bush from the 'main road' to Doboy Beach, the long flat beach that lay between the lighthouse headland and Clews Point. He was preparing for the arrival of the Regional Lighthouse Engineer Mr Fulton, who had arranged to land on the beach at low tide in a light aircraft. As far back as 1930, the occasional light plane had landed on Doboy Beach, but Mr Fulton was so impressed by the twenty minute flight from Gladstone compared to the five or six hour trip by boat that, from then on, an aircraft was used to transport lightkeepers and mechanics whenever an emergency arose. The beach soon became known as Aircraft Beach. However, it wasn't until 1976 that a proper vehicle track from the 'main road' to the beach was built.

Further improvements were made to the station in April 1967, when a Commonwealth Department of Works team arrived to build a new engine room. The new brick structure with aluminium roof sheeting was built around the original timber framed engine room. On completion, the old building was demolished. Total cost of the works was $5,467.13.[1]

Shortly after midnight on 11 January 1968, lightning struck the lighthouse with such a force that it blew every light on the station. Acting Head Lightkeeper Don Swanson and Lightkeeper Malcolm Muir immediately ran to the engine room. They found the main switchboard blown and the operating engine sheared off its mountings. Realising it was impossible to use the spare motor, the men quickly replaced the bulbs from the main light and red sector with the emergency Tilley lamps and began to turn the lens by hand, sharing shifts throughout the remainder of the night. By the following evening, lighthouse mechanics flown to the station by light aircraft had temporarily restored power. Shortly afterwards a lightning conductor was fitted to the lighthouse.

For the benefit of the lightkeepers and the efficiency of the motors, it was decided to run a diesel motor twenty-four hours a day, thereby increasing fuel consumption to 20,000 litres per year. To provide for this, in June 1968, three 6,800 litre cylindrical steel storage tanks were installed beside the fuel shed at a cost of $6,833.[2] Each day, by means of an electric pump, diesel was transferred from the bulk fuel tanks to the header tanks in the engine room.

During 1967, the *Cape Moreton's* amphibious DUKW was replaced by a heavier and more powerful amphibian called a LARC (Lighter Amphibious Resupply Cargo). The LARC weighed 10 tonnes and could carry a load of half its weight. Diesel fuel was transported from ship to the lightstation in a rubber fuel bladder of 4,500 litre capacity, which was lashed to the deck of the LARC. The fuel was then pumped straight from the bladder into the bulk fuel tanks. No longer did the lightkeepers have to manhandle the dozens of heavy, 200 litre fuel drums. *Cape Moreton* usually delivered fuel twice a year to the station, while lighthouse mechanics visited every three months to overhaul the motors. The mechanics boarded with the lightkeepers, who were paid by the mechanics a daily amount for their food and accommodation.

The semi-rotary hand-pumps used over the past thirty-five years to pump rainwater from the main tanks to the concrete header tanks were discontinued in 1970, when a new 2,250 litre fibreglass header tank and a 6 metre high steel framed stand was erected at each cottage. The fibreglass tanks and stands were delivered to the station in kit form and assembled by the lightkeepers. Electric pumps were installed to lift the water to the header tanks. And in 1971, the kerosene fuelled water heaters in the bathrooms were superseded by electric hot water systems, which provided hot water not only to the bathrooms, but to the kitchens and laundries as well.

The continual breakdowns with the telephone and the kilometres of walking by the lightkeepers to find breaks in the line came to an end on 13 September

The lighthouse children made many a trip on Mandy the pony to the Bowtons' property on Middle Island. Here, Jean Wright leads Mandy while her stepbrother John (forward) and Michael Hayes (aft) enjoy the ride.

Photograph provided by Jean Wright.

The Bowtons' Middle Island homestead photographed in 1965. Two years later it was discovered the building was riddled with termites. Bertha and Elsie demolished the structure to floor level, refitted the roof sheeting, and moved in under the house.

Photograph provided by Kathy Mian and Boyd Rich.

Loading the fortnightly stores into the trailer at Pancake Creek. The stores boat Aquamaid lies at anchor in the background. The jeep was replaced by a Land Rover in 1961.

Photograph provided by Malcolm Muir.

Replacing the ageing Cape Leeuwin, *the* Cape Moreton *anchors off Clews Point.*

The LARC lumbers out of Pancake Creek, carrying a new vehicle for the lightstation.

Unloading a new Lightkeeper's personal effects is effortlessly done with the LARC's crane.

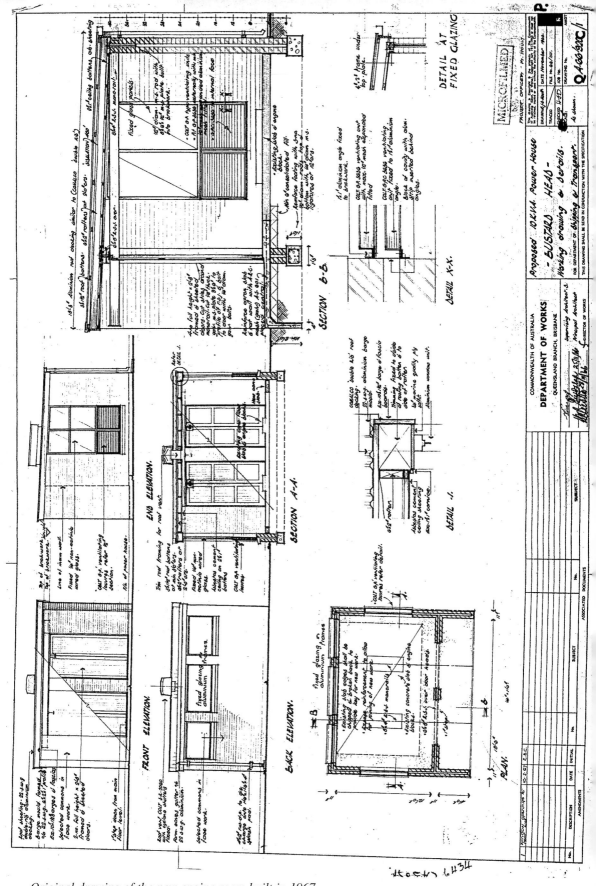

Original drawing of the new engine room built in 1967.

Provided by Australian Maritime Safety Authority.

The new brick engine room was built around the old structure. On its completion, the old building was demolished. The workshop is to the left of the engine room.

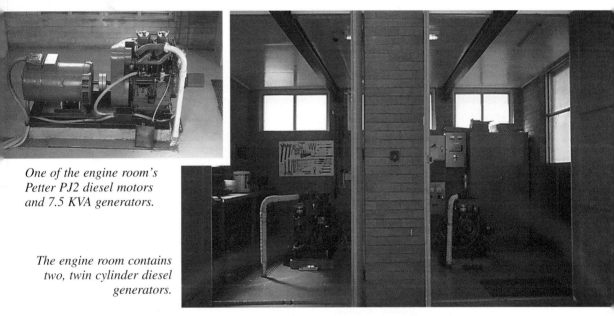

One of the engine room's Petter PJ2 diesel motors and 7.5 KVA generators.

The engine room contains two, twin cylinder diesel generators.

Diesel fuel is pumped from a 4,500 litre rubber bladder strapped to the LARC's deck into the station's bulk fuel tanks.

1971 when two radio telephones were installed in the lighthouse with extensions to each cottage. The antennas for the phones were fitted to the balcony handrail.

During February 1972, Laurie 'The Admiral' Thomson — the hermit of Pancake Creek — became ill. Head Lightkeeper Jack Atherton arranged for him to be flown in to Gladstone by light aircraft. The Admiral was taken to hospital, but died shortly afterwards. His ashes were taken to Bustard Head and buried on the small headland where he had lived his lonely life for the past twenty-one years. In July of the same year, under the supervision of Senior Lighthouse Engineer Mr Fulton, The Admiral's shack was burnt down by the lightkeepers.

In near calm conditions at 11.00 a.m. on Easter Friday 31 March 1972, a fleet of twenty-five yachts crossed the start line for the twenty-fourth Brisbane to Gladstone Ocean Yacht Race. Thirty minutes later, three trimarans, in a separate race organised by the Multihull Yacht Club of Queensland, set off for the same destination. At the time, a severe tropical storm lay about 750 nautical miles off the coast east of Cooktown. Brisbane's Bureau of Meteorology expected it to form into a cyclone, but believed it would curve to the south-east and stay away from the coast.

At 9.00 p.m. the Bureau of Meteorology issued a cyclone warning for Queensland waters. Cyclone Emily was on the move towards the coast. Many of the competitors heard the warning broadcast on commercial radio stations, and decided to return to Brisbane or retire into Mooloolaba harbour. But a number of the yachts remained unaware of cyclone Emily until the race radio schedule at 6.03 a.m. on Saturday morning, when the Bureau of Meteorology predicted winds of up to 120 knots, and suggested to the race organisers that the race be cancelled. But as was normal in such a situation, the organising club — Queensland Cruising Yacht Club — stated it was up to the individual skippers to decide whether they should retire or not.

The nine leading yachts, two of them trimarans, remained in the race, not for bravado but because they had passed the point of no return; they were so far up the coast from the nearest safe harbour at Mooloolaba, that to go about and bash into the 35 knot south-easter, which was all the time increasing, would be more damaging and dangerous for boat and crew than running downwind to Gladstone. The leading yacht, trimaran *Captain Bligh*, was already past Breaksea Spit and managed to arrive safely in Gladstone at 8.45 on Saturday evening. Shortly before one o'clock on Saturday afternoon, when *Onya of Gosford* was halfway along Breaksea Spit, her crew sighted the cruising yacht *Istria* travelling in the same direction. There were four men on board *Istria*, and it was noticed by *Onya of Gosford's* skipper Peter Rysdyk that *Istria* did not have her storm boards in place. At the time, Rysdyk described the sea as "wild". *Istria* and her crew were never heard of again.

178

As cyclone Emily approached the coast, 60 to 70 knot winds whipped the seas into 10 metre high, foaming mountains of water. The yacht *Pilgrim* headed out to sea, far away from reef and coastline; the other yachts rounded Breaksea Spit and headed for the next mark of the course — Lady Elliot Island. As the monohull race leaders, *Onya of Gosford* and *Makaretu*, approached the island at 6.25 p.m., the crew from both yachts reported on the radio they had sighted red distress flares. These were from the trawler *Kotoku*, which had been driven onto the reef at Lady Musgrave Island, 35 miles east of Bustard Head. The four men on board were safe, but next morning huge seas overturned the stranded vessel. Three of the men, including skipper Lionel Moss, were washed overboard, but one man, Peter Gaddes, managed to hang onto the wreckage for twenty-six hours until he was rescued by helicopter. Lionel Moss and crew member Bob Stockwell clung to a white plank from the wreckage and were swept away from the island. Crew member Ken Owens had disappeared. At about 8.30 p.m. Bob Stockwell slipped from the plank and drifted out of sight. Throughout Sunday night and next day, Lionel Moss, although exhausted, continued to cling to his plank. During the afternoon he was sighted by an RAAF Neptune aircraft, and at 5.30 p.m. was rescued by the patrol boat HMAS *Barricade* 5 nautical miles west of Lady Elliot Island. Moss had spent thirty-three hours in the water, and was sighted only because of the white plank. Ken Owens and Bob Stockwell were never found.

On Sunday morning, as cyclone Emily closed on Bustard Head, the wind and rain increased, reducing visibility to less than 200 metres. The strongly built station cottages and outbuildings were defying the fierce onslaught of the wind, and had suffered only minor damage. The lightkeepers and their families knew that if the situation worsened they could always find safety inside the lighthouse. At 6.00 a.m., Head Lightkeeper Jack Atherton reported a wind speed of 112 knots. Two hours earlier the racing yacht *Kintama*, under storm jib alone, missed Outer Rock by only a few metres. At about 7.00 a.m. the crew of the trimaran *Australian Maid* suddenly found themselves perilously close to Bustard Head, just outside the treacherous bar of Jenny Lind Creek. The helmsman immediately rounded the vessel up; the jib flogged and blew out, rendering the trimaran helpless. The engine was started, but proved ineffectual against the mountainous seas. Part owner and co-skipper Charlie Stewart, and crew member Normie Sidoti tried to set another jib, but were washed off the foredeck while doing so. One of the three remaining men on board, Ken Mackay, went below to get some lifejackets. As the vessel neared the bar, a huge wave rolled *Australian Maid* over; water flooded through the open companionway hatch. Ken Mackay was thrown around inside the yacht. Disorientated and scrambling for his life, he eventually found his way through the hatch. He pulled his way to the surface on the yacht's safety lines and began swimming for shore.

Australian Maid was dismasted when she capsized, and the two men on deck — co-owner Bob Brown and Maurie Sweeney — were thrown into the water. Brown surfaced 30 metres from the yacht. As he tried to swim back to it, a huge wave threw him on top of the boat, entangling him in a mass of loose rigging. Like a helpless insect caught in a spider's web he was dragged under the swirling cauldron of white water. In a burst of herculean strength, he fought his way to the surface. Suddenly he felt himself free, and before long the huge waves cast him like flotsam onto the beach.

Ken Mackay and Bob Brown had been washed ashore on the northern bank of Jenny Lind Creek. Exhausted and in shocked disbelief, they watched as the upturned *Australian Maid* was swept along in the frothing turmoil to the western side of the lagoon; they could see no sign of the other three crew. Knowing that the manned lighthouse was above them, but unaware that a track led from the creek to the station, they crashed through the thick scrub up the steep headland in a frantic bid for help.

Visibility was still below 200 metres, even so, in the tradition of light-keeping, Head Lightkeeper Jack Atherton had kept the light lit throughout the morning in the off-chance that its powerful beam would be seen by those unfortunate enough to be at sea. At midday, through his kitchen window, Jack saw the two distraught men stagger from the bush and head towards the cottage. Jack went to meet them and ushered them inside. Hearing their story, Jack telephoned the Gladstone police, then sent Lightkeeper Ron Davies down to Jenny Lind Creek to try to find any survivors. Jack's wife, Babs, tried to calm the shocked men, who were shaking so uncontrollably they could barely drink the cups of tea she made for them. Jack insisted the men took hot showers and provided them with dry clothes.

At Jenny Lind Creek, Lightkeeper Davies found Maurie Sweeney exhausted but safe. Charlie Stewart's body was found washed up on the beach nearby; there was no sign of Normie Sidoti.

By mid-afternoon, cyclone Emily had moved inland and weakened enough for the police to reach Bustard Head by helicopter. Accompanied by Ken Mackay, Charlie Stewart's body was flown in to Gladstone. Early next morning, the body of Normie Sidoti was found in the mangroves close to the capsized trimaran.

Apart from the yacht *Rival*, which was capsized and dismasted, and later towed into Gladstone by HMAS *Barricade*, the few other yachts left in the race reached Gladstone safely.

The following week, Bob Brown, Ken Mackay and a group of helpers returned to Jenny Lind Creek, where they righted *Australian Maid* and sailed her in to Gladstone for repairs. Before leaving Bustard Head, Bob and Ken presented Head Lightkeeper Jack Atherton and Babs with a bottle of wine, one of the few items to survive the capsize.[3]

It wasn't routine procedure for the Harbours and Marine boating and fisheries inspectors from Bundaberg to visit the Bustard Head district by themselves. The area was controlled from Gladstone, but for safety reasons any patrol in that isolated region was done by two officers, one from each district. However, because the Gladstone inspector was on leave during June 1972, Bundaberg inspectors Ron Kelley and Ken Murchison decided to patrol Pancake and Middle Creeks. There was another reason for their visit — Ken was taking Ron on a familiarisation trip. Although Ken Murchison knew the labyrinth of creeks near Bustard Head, Ron Kelley was new to the area. Three weeks previously, Ron, with his wife and thirteen month old daughter, had been transferred from Kurumba in the Gulf of Carpentaria to Bundaberg to replace Ken, who had submitted his resignation from the service to take effect the following week.

The two men left Bundaberg at about 8.00 a.m. on Thursday 22 June towing a 3.5 metre long aluminium dinghy behind their Land Rover; they were expected back in Bundaberg the next day. After visiting a crabber's camp on the mainland side of Middle Creek, Ken and Ron drove along the rough bush track to Pancake Point on Rodd's Peninsula, where they camped for the night. The following morning, shortly before first light, they launched their dinghy in Pancake Creek and set off upstream towards Middle Creek Crossing, the 9.8 horsepower outboard pushing their craft along at a good speed. There was little breeze, and it looked as though it was going to be another balmy winter's day.

The inspectors were mainly interested in the activities of some of the professional crabbers who lived in shacks on the banks of Middle Creek, 2 kilometres upstream from Bertha and Elsie Bowton's homestead. It was well known that some of the crabbers were involved in illegal fish netting and the taking of undersized and female mud crabs. Although a few had been charged and fined, most attempts by the Department of Harbours and Marine to convict these men had failed due to lack of conclusive evidence. On the surface, the relationship between the inspectors and the crabbers was amicable enough, but in reality the crabbers were a thorn in the side of the fisheries inspectors. The crabbers' feelings for the inspectors were mutual.

Before Kelley and Murchison reached Middle Creek Crossing, they saw a dinghy approaching from the opposite direction. In it were professional crabbers Desmond Allen and his wife. The two dinghies pulled alongside each other. The Allens knew Ken Murchison but not Ron Kelley. After a short chat, the Allens went to check their crab pots, while the inspectors continued along the creek, past the Bowtons' homestead towards the crabbers' camps.

At about 7.30 a.m., the inspectors landed at the camp of Duncan Dorron, near the mouth of Middle Creek. Six men were living there, all just awakening after a heavy night of drinking. The inspectors accepted the men's invitation to join them for a beer. Ken Murchison sat down at the table with the crabbers who were drinking beer and rum, while Ron Kelley went outside to check a bag of crabs. He found all the crabs were of legal size. Two hours later, as the Allens were returning to their camp further up the creek from Dorron's, one of Dorron's friends beckoned them ashore. The Allens declined to stay for a drink, but advised the inspectors that if they intended to return to Pancake Creek the way they had come, they would have to leave immediately; any later and the tide height would be too low to negotiate Middle Creek Crossing.

Ron Kelley appeared anxious to leave, but Ken Murchison said:

"It'll be all right. The sea's calm. We'll cross the Middle Creek bar into Bustard Bay and go up the outside into Pancake Creek. We might as well have a look at Jenny Lind Creek on the way."

"Have we got enough fuel?" Ron replied.

"I'll give you some of ours just to be on the safe side," Duncan Dorron offered.

Ron went off with Duncan to top up the fuel tank, while Ken Murchison continued drinking with the others.

"When Ken gets around the grog you can't get him away," Ron said facetiously to Duncan.

Shortly after 10.00 a.m., Ken Murchison, holding a stubby, walked down to the dinghy and climbed in. With Ron Kelley at the controls, the two inspectors headed for the Middle Creek bar.

Desmond Allen and his wife, whose camp was at the mouth of Middle Creek, heard the outboard motor and watched to see if the men crossed the bar safely. The Allens observed that Ken Murchison was now at the controls. It was nearing low tide and the interior of the dinghy was easily seen as its bow lifted to climb each of the steep waves formed by the shallow water. The Allens continued to watch until the inspectors cleared the bar and disappeared from sight.

At 12.30 p.m., Duncan Dorron's brother Edsil and two of his mates motored over to Middle Island and rode their motor bike and trailer along the ocean beach towards Jenny Lind Creek, where Edsil was going to show the men where to set a fishing net that night. Nearly 2 kilometres from the mouth of Jenny Lind Creek the men found a felt hat and a green oar washed up on the beach. Edsil Dorron didn't recognise the hat, but suspected that the oar was from the fisheries inspectors' dinghy. The men continued on to the mouth of the creek. As the men rode slowly back along the beach towards Middle Creek they kept a lookout for the inspectors' dinghy, but saw nothing.

Duncan and Edsil Dorron drove back to their homes in Bundaberg later that Friday afternoon. They knew that the inspectors were expected to return the same day, so that night about eight o'clock Edsil went to see if Ron Kelley was home. Ron's wife Maureen said he wasn't, but was expecting him home some time that night or early next day at the latest, as he had to attend a sale of confiscated fishing nets during the morning. Not wanting to alarm Maureen unnecessarily, Edsil didn't mention the hat and oar. But on Saturday morning when Ron wasn't at the net sale, Edsil told Maureen what he had found. The police were immediately notified and plans for a search arranged.

The police telephoned the lightkeepers at Bustard Head to ask if they had seen the inspectors or their dinghy. Lightkeeper Bennett's wife, who had been fishing at the mouth of Jenny Lind Creek between 10.00 a.m. and 4.00 p.m. the previous day when the inspectors crossed the Middle Creek bar, said she had seen the three crabbers on their motor bike stop at Jenny Lind Creek. They left the bike and walked along the southern bank and entered a grove of oaks. Some time later they returned and rode back along the beach. She hadn't seen a dinghy enter Jenny Lind Creek or pass the headland.

Boats in the Bustard Head area were asked by radio to keep a lookout for the inspectors. About 5.00 p.m. the crew from the trawler *Laurel-May* found the inspectors' dinghy floating upside down 3 miles offshore north-east from Middle Creek. The outboard motor was still attached, its throttle at the three-quarter open position. The crew lifted the dinghy on board, marking the position where they had found it with a buoy.

That evening around six o'clock, police and civilians in two Land Rovers towing dinghies arrived at Duncan Dorron's camp at Middle Creek. After setting up a base camp on Middle Island, at high tide they motored past Middle Creek Crossing into Pancake Creek, where they found the fisheries inspectors' Land Rover at Pancake Point, but no sign of Kelley or Murchison.

At first light on Sunday morning, ground and sea search parties equipped with two-way radios set off to comb the beaches north and south of Middle Creek. Eight other trawlers apart from *Laurel-May* had joined the search and were trawling in grid pattern 800 metres offshore. At 7.30 a.m., 1.5 kilometres south of Jenny Lind Creek, one of the search parties found a suede boot with the laces done up. Six hundred metres further north they found a pair of khaki shorts and a wallet type notebook. Radio contact was made with the trawler *Kasanet* which, along with the other trawlers, converged on the area offshore from where the clothes were found. In 3 metres of water the crew from *Kasanet* saw some dark objects on the seabed. One of the deckhands made a number of dives, recovering a shirt with the singlet still inside it, and other pieces of clothing — all badly torn. At about the same time, the shore party found a second pair of shorts with the right leg and crutch torn out, but with the belt still buckled.

Divers who were called in, recovered other pieces of clothing, including a pair of torn overalls. During the early afternoon, two RAAF helicopters from Amberley Air Force Base joined the search. From the air, about 100 metres off the beach from where the clothing was found, three schools of sharks were sighted. Each school consisted of thirty to forty sharks about 1.5 metres long. Fifty metres further out, six 4 metre long sharks were seen. The search

Ripped by sharks. Some of the fisheries inspectors' clothing found on the seabed.

Photograph provided by Coroner's Section, Department of Justice.

The first indication of trouble: this hat and oar were found washed up on the beach by crabbers.

Photograph provided by Coroner's Section, Department of Justice.

The belt was still buckled, but the right leg and crutch were torn out of the shorts. No blood or human remains were found on the clothing.

Photograph provided by Coroner's Section, Department of Justice.

continued throughout the afternoon, but nothing else was found. As darkness fell it was decided to call off the search.

The clothing was identified as belonging to the inspectors. Although no traces of blood or human remains were found on the clothing, forensic tests showed that the rents were consistent with having been torn, possibly caused by bites from moderately large sharks while the clothes were being worn. One shirt had cuts that could have been made by the propeller of the outboard motor when the boat capsized. A shark expert stated that if one of the men had been bleeding, it would have greatly increased the likelihood of shark attack.

From the time of the inspectors' disappearance, rumours of foul play were rife. Newspapers and the public questioned how two experienced boatmen, both good swimmers, could disappear on a day when the sea was slight with a barely discernible swell. But at the inquest that followed, the Coroner found beyond all doubt that the missing inspectors had died at sea in the area between the mouth of Middle Creek and Bustard Head, their deaths due to misadventure. He said: "Exactly how their boat came to be overturned is still a matter of mere conjecture . . . It may be that they tried to enter Jenny Lind Creek from the sea, in which case they could have experienced real difficulty in crossing its bars. All the evidence . . . points to the bodies having been taken by sharks". The Coroner went on to say that although both men had consumed some intoxicating liquor before crossing Middle Creek bar, "the quantity was not such, in the case of either person, to have played any real part in the tragedy in which each lost their lives". In regard to the rumours of foul play, the Coroner stated: " . . . I find there is no evidence whatsoever to suggest this; I repeat, none whatsoever."

To this day, those rumours still persist.[4]

For the safety of lives at sea, it was a lightkeeper's first priority to keep his light illuminated throughout the night. However, on the evening of Saturday 8 July 1972, Head Lightkeeper Jack Atherton was asked to assist in saving the lives of four people by putting the Bustard Head light *out* for a short period. Earlier that afternoon, the Bundaberg police were advised of a Mayday distress signal received from the 9 metre motor launch *Alambra*. Four boats put to sea but failed to find the distressed craft. At about 7.00 p.m. the search boat *Susan* made radio contact with *Alambra*. The crew of four advised that their engine had failed, the boat was taking water and in danger of sinking. They could see the flash from a lighthouse, but didn't know if it was Bustard Head or Sandy Cape.

Working in conjunction with Head Lightkeeper Jack Atherton, the police received permission from the relevant authorities for the Bustard Head light to be extinguished for one minute. However, when the police tried to contact Bustard Head to arrange a time, they found the line continuously engaged. Inadvertently, the handset in the Head Lightkeeper's cottage hadn't been replaced properly. The telephone technician, who was trying to attract the attention of someone at the lightstation, could just hear a well-known television program in the background. It was decided to try to attract Jack's attention by flashing a message on the television screen:

WOULD THE BUSTARD HEAD LIGHTHOUSE KEEPER
PLEASE ANSWER HIS TELEPHONE

Jack's attention was certainly attracted, and within seconds it was arranged that he would extinguish the light at precisely 11.25 p.m. for one minute. At 11.26 p.m. the crew of *Alambra* radioed to advise they had witnessed the blackout. With the search area narrowed, the rescue vessel *Susan* picked up *Alambra* on radar just after midnight and soon had her under tow heading for Bundaberg.[5]

Conditions for the lightkeepers continued to improve. In September 1972, an additional 5,000 gallon spherical fibreglass rainwater tank was installed at each cottage. The same year, one large electric chest freezer was sent to the station to be shared between the two families. The following year a group of men and heavy earth moving equipment from the Commonwealth Department of Works landed by barge to improve the 'main road' from Pancake Creek to the station. The sandy road was widened and topped with a red chalky clay mixture quarried from the headland near the Jenny Lind Creek track. At some of the steeper sections, timber corduroy ramps were installed to provide good traction for the Land Rover and to minimise ruts and wash-outs during periods of heavy rain. And in July 1974 both cottages' timber framed double hung windows were replaced by aluminium framed hoppers and flyscreens. At the same time, the asbestos cement guttering was replaced by stainless steel. During 1975 an electric two-door refrigerator/freezer and a large chest freezer were supplied to each cottage.

Until the 1960s it had been the Department's preference to employ men as lightkeepers who had experience as seamen or been in the services. This now changed. The new criteria stated that lightkeepers must be able to climb and work from a bosun's chair at 100 feet, paint and do carpentry, handle stores to 60 pounds, do heavy repair work to roads, walk over loose sand and rocks, and stand night watches up to six hours alone. Lightkeepers were now employed from many walks of life, their final suitability being judged during an interview with the Regional Lighthouse Engineer and the Personnel Officer.

Substantial increases were made to lightkeepers' salaries during the early 1970s, the gap between Head Lightkeeper and Lightkeeper being narrowed. As well, lightkeepers were paid by the Bureau of Meteorology for submitting weather reports. Until the late 1960s this amount had been a pittance, but now it became a major part of the yearly salary. The weather reports were shared equally between the Head Lightkeeper and Lightkeeper. During the cyclone season from December to April inclusive, a weather report was submitted

Using a hydraulic pump, Senior Radio Technical Officer Barrie Ellis raises the "delta" radio antenna for the first time, as Head Lightkeeper Jack Atherton looks on. Senior Mechanic Ron Eddolls is in the background.

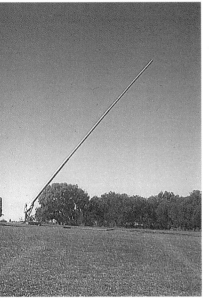

Halfway there; the "delta" radio antenna.

Many a distressed mariner was helped by Jack Atherton, Head Lightkeeper of Bustard Head 1971–76.

It was all part of the job for lightkeepers to show visitors over the station. One group to visit in the mid-seventies was the Westlakes, a musically talented family cruising on their yacht Kermandie. *From left to right: Nigel, Heather, Kathy and Donald Westlake, and the author's wife Shirley. Donald later became concertmaster of the Sydney Symphony Orchestra; Nigel went on to compose the theme music for the famous movie "Babe".*

NAVIGATIONAL AID STATION LOG

NA 36
(Rev. 2/74)

Station *BUSTARD HEAD* Week Ending 22 | 2 | 1976

Day and Date	On Duty and Attention to Light				Remarks	Meteorological Reports	
	From	To	Light	Signature of Lightkeeper		Time of Obs.	Initials
MON.	0530	0730	E.L	M. Buchanan	Routine Engine Inspection Oil and oil filter change to No 1 motor.	0300	X
						0600	M.B
16TH	1810	1855	L.U.	M. Bradley	Washing out engine room. Cleaning external and	0900	M.B
						1200	M.B
	2100	2115	C.L	M. Bradley	internal ports to tower Polishing brasswork.	1500	M.B.
						1800	M.B.
						2100	M.B.
TUE.	''	''	''	M. Buchanan	Routine Engine Inspection Cleaning lens.	''	M.B.
	''	''	''	M. Bradley	Washing down internal walls of tower	''	M.B
17TH	''	''	''	M. Bradley		''	M.B.
						''	M.B.
WED.	''	''	''	M. Buchanan	Routine Engine Inspection HK. returned from leave by air 1615.	''	M.B
	''	''	''	M. Bradley	Stores launch arrived 1830. Land Rover stalled whilst out on sandbank. Urgent attempts were made	''	M.B
18TH	''	''	''	J. Atherton	by staff & fishermen to extricate vehicle but it was eventually submerged as the tide rose. U.S. Starter & only one battery caused this.	''	M.B.
						''	X
THU.	''	''	''	M. Buchanan	Routine Eng. Insp. Informed RLE re L/R mishap.	''	M.B
	''	''	''	J. Atherton	Carrying fresh stores up by hand!	''	M.B
19TH	''	''	''	J. Atherton		''	JA
						''	JA
FRI.	''	''	''	M. Buchanan	Routine Eng. Insp. Met Helicopter at 0800 & transferred remainder of Stores & Personal effects up	''	JA
	''	''	''	J. Atherton	to Station. Canopy cover salvaged from L/R & a "Comm. Property" notice affixed -	''	M.B
20TH	''	''	''	J. Atherton	pending salvage.	''	M.B
						''	JA
						''	JA
SAT.	''	''	''	J. Atherton	Routine Eng. Insp.	''	JA
	''	''	''	J. Atherton	Work on own Qtrs - weeding etc. & essential duties.	''	JA
21ST	''	''	''	J. Atherton		''	JA
						''	JA
SUN.	''	''	''	M. Buchanan	Routine Eng. Insp.	''	M.B
	''	''	''	M. Buchanan	Essential Duties only.	''	M.B
22ND	''	''	''	M. Buchanan		''	M.B
	''	''	''	M. Buchanan		''	M.B

John Atherton
Head Lightkeeper

22 | 2 | 1976.

Lightstation daily logbook 1976. Entry for 18 February notes that the station Land Rover stalled at the low water mark in Pancake Creek and was submerged by the incoming tide.

Provided by Australian Maritime Safety Authority.

every three hours with the exception of midnight. For the remainder of the year, three daily reports — 3.00 a.m., 9.00 a.m. and 3.00 p.m. — were sent. When a cyclone was in the area, the Bureau often requested hourly reports.

Time had taken its toll on Bertha and Elsie Bowton from Middle Island. Over the years Bertha had been a frequent visitor to the lightstation, arriving on horseback to collect her mail sent in the Bustard Head mailbag. In 1974, at the age of eighty-two, Bertha made her last trip to the station. From then on, the lightkeepers delivered her mail by dinghy. Bertha had fared better than her eighty year-old sister Elsie, who was now crippled from arthritis and totally blind. Since their arrival on Middle Island in 1907, Elsie had left the island twice, each time for only a few days. Bertha suffered the emotional and physical strain of looking after Elsie stoically, but realised that in case of a medical emergency some form of communication to obtain help was now essential.

In this regard she purchased two walkie-talkies from Gladstone, one for herself and the other for Head Lightkeeper Jack Atherton. She was assured by the seller that the range of these transceivers would easily cover the 10 kilometres between Bustard Head and her homestead. The transceivers proved so useless that, in Jack Atherton's words: "Bertha would have more luck trying to contact us by leaning out her window and shouting than using the walkie-talkie".

When the plight of the two maids became known, a group of volunteers from Bundaberg offered to install a two-way radio link between the sisters' homestead and Bustard Head. Bertha accepted and agreed to pay for the equipment. With no electricity at the homestead, the 12 volt battery that powered the radio was kept charged by an automotive alternator driven by a two-stroke motor mower engine, which Bertha needed to run for only a few hours each week. The radios were installed during July 1975, and a daily radio sked arranged between Bertha and the Head Lightkeeper.

The first stage of a plan to transfer the base radio station for the lighthouse network from Cape Capricorn to Bustard Head got underway in January 1976, when the *Cape Moreton* anchored off the lightstation for two days while ten of her crew, assisted by the lightkeepers, poured a massive 8 cubic metre concrete footing for an 18 metre high "delta" radio antenna mast. The second stage was not to begin for a further year.

In the meantime, Head Lightkeeper Jack Atherton and his wife Babs went on extended leave beginning from July 1976. Due to Departmental financial restrictions, the unusual step of not providing a relief lightkeeper for such a lengthy period, resulted in the author and his wife Shirley, who were there at the time as lightkeepers, spending six months alone on Bustard Head — the longest time in the station's history that one man tended the light.

It was the calm before the storm, because the following year, due to modern technology, changes began that turned Bustard Head into the most advanced lightstation on the Queensland coast, but which ultimately led to its demise.

Chapter 14

BEGINNING OF THE END

The second stage of technological change at Bustard Head began in March 1977, when Senior Radio Technical Officer Barrie Ellis arrived to rig the "delta" radio antenna and connect it to the new radio equipment on the ground floor of the lighthouse. At the same time, he installed a separate automatic emergency alarm and single-sideband two-way radio. This unit was connected to the cottages' alarm system and linked to the International Marine Radio-telephone Distress frequency (2182 kHz), enabling those on board a distressed vessel, fitted with the reciprocal equipment, to summons the lightkeepers to the radio at any time of the day or night by setting off their alarms.

The major change occurred in September 1977, when computer equipment was installed on the first floor of the tower to monitor the operation of North Reef lighthouse 50 miles north of Bustard Head. It was the Department's plan to automate and deman North Reef lighthouse later that year; already, the huge Second Order lens and kerosene lamp had been replaced by revolving panels of sealed beams. These were powered by a bank of batteries kept charged by a diesel generator programmed to switch on and off automatically as required. All functions of the new light were recorded on the computer print-out at Bustard Head, so the lightkeepers would know its status at all times. The computer was also linked to the cottages' alarm system, which would activate if any serious malfunction occurred to the North Reef light or its associated equipment.

The Bustard Head computer was designed to monitor many more light-houses that were listed for demanning. Demanning of the coastal lights was not new policy. In 1915, when the coastal lights were transferred from State to Commonwealth Government control, there were twenty-eight manned lights in Queensland. By 1977 only twelve remained manned. However, it was expected that the majority of those would always be staffed by lightkeepers.

The computer link between North Reef and Bustard Head was completed on 2 October 1977. And on 18 December, after ninety-nine years of continuous occupation, the last lightkeepers were withdrawn from their tiny coral island.

Bertha and Elsie Bowton also left their island during 1977. Bertha had come to realise she could no longer cope with caring for Elsie, who was in need of proper medical attention. The sisters moved into a nursing home at Calliope, west of Gladstone. After seventy years on Middle Island, their unique and lengthy association with Bustard Head had come to an end.

The exposed wiring on the new "delta" radio antenna was capable of giving a severe shock to anyone who touched it while the radio was transmitting, so in February 1978 a long, timber paling fence was built around its base. To further protect the complex equipment now installed in the lighthouse, a new lightning conductor was fitted to the tower during March.

Time had not lessened the voracious appetite of Bustard Head's white ants. Although the boatshed at Pancake Creek was freshly painted and looked sound externally, much of its timber framing was paper-thin. It was now rarely used. For years the station dinghy had been kept at the lighthouse precinct and taken by trailer to the creek whenever required. Under instructions from the Senior Regional Lighthouse Engineer Mr Fulton, the boatshed was demolished by the lightkeepers in 1978. For many years the white walls and dark green roof of the boatshed had been a landmark indicating the boat anchorage and the start of the 'main road' to the station. With it gone, Pancake Creek had lost a part of its identity.

At the end of November 1978, following a message from the pilot of a commercial airliner that he had seen a crashed aircraft on a beach south of Bustard Head lighthouse, the Department of Civil Aviation asked the lightkeepers to investigate the sighting and report back to them. Halfway along Middle Island, Head Lightkeeper Davies and the author found a 10 metre motor launch stranded on the beach; nearby was an overturned Cessna aircraft. The pilot, who was only slightly injured, explained he had tried to land near the vessel in the hope of claiming salvage rights. The plane had flipped when its nose-wheel hit a patch of soft sand.

A helicopter took the pilot to Gladstone Hospital, while a larger Alouette helicopter lifted the Cessna in an attempt to take it to the mainland, safe from the incoming tide. On the way, the rope slings began to unravel, and it was only just in time that the helicopter pilot managed to put the Cessna down on a tiny sand island near the mouth of Middle Creek.

Two weeks later, after difficult on-site repairs, the Cessna pilot floated his plane on a raft of dinghies to the mainland beach, where he made a successful take off and headed back to civilisation. The motor launch was refloated at the top of the spring tides.

The plan to move the base radio station for the lighthouse network from Cape Capricorn to Bustard Head eventuated on Monday 18 December 1978, when Head Lightkeeper Harold Simpson, who had been in charge of Cape Capricorn for the past sixteen years, was transferred to Bustard Head to continue his role there. With the radio call sign VL4OY, the Bustard Head

To prevent anyone receiving a severe shock from the wiring of the "delta" antenna, a long timber fence was built around its base.

Timber corduroy ramps were installed at some of the steeper sections of the 'main road' to prevent wash-outs and provide good traction for the Land Rover. At the right, Aircraft Beach curves round towards Clews Point.

A unique and lengthy era came to an end in 1977, when Bertha and Elsie Bowton decided to leave Middle Island. During the sisters' seventy years on the island, Elsie (right) made only two brief visits to the mainland. The photograph was taken on the day of their departure.

Photograph provided by Kathy Mian and Boyd Rich.

The comfortable 19 metre stores boat Reef Lady *waits in Pancake Creek while the lightkeepers answer urgent mail. It was a condition of contract that the stores boat waited a maximum of two hours.*

The station Land Rover was replaced by Land Cruiser in 1978.

Senior Radio Technical Officer Barrie Ellis enjoyed his official visits to Bustard Head so much, he returned with his family for a camping holiday in 1978. Farewells are said as they prepare to depart from Aircraft Beach. From left to right: Pilot Renato Piccolo, Barrie Ellis, his daughters Justine and Joanne, Marianne Ellis, and the author's wife Shirley.

The powerful Alouette helicopter lifts the damaged Cessna off the beach. It wasn't long before the rope slings began to give way.

Photograph provided by Nev Loxton.

lightkeepers held radio skeds every three hours — except at midnight and 3.00 a.m. — with three other lightstations that were still without telephone — Dent Island, Pine Islet and Lady Elliot Island. The main skeds were 9.00 a.m., noon and 3.00 p.m., when lightkeepers on the outlying stations could forward messages and stores orders, and receive any messages sent to Bustard Head by telephone. Weather reports from Pine Islet were forwarded direct to the Lady Elliot Island lightkeepers who, along with their own report, radioed them to Brisbane. Bustard Head's weather reports were telephoned direct to Brisbane.

During October 1979, the two old Petter diesel generating sets in the Bustard Head engine room were replaced by two, twin cylinder Lister HR2 diesel motors and 10KVA generators. And in June 1980, additional timber corduroy ramps were installed at some steep sections of the 'main road'.

A bombshell exploded within the lighthouse service during 1980, when the Federal Government announced it intended to deman fourteen of Australia's forty-two manned lightstations within the next five years. Seven of the stations to be demanned were in Queensland. But Bustard Head was one of five in the State to remain manned. A massive public outcry resulted from the demanning decision. Air Sea Rescue organisations, Coastguard, yacht and boat clubs, commercial fishermen, yachtsmen and small-craft owners, and thousands of private individuals protested to the Federal Government, stating how safety standards would be drastically lowered by converting manned lights to automatic operation. Unlike manned lights which, if they failed, would be out for no more than twenty minutes, a failed automatic light could be out for days.

A group based in Melbourne, consisting of marine historians, master mariners, architects and a former lighthouse engineer formed an organisation to fight the government's proposal. Named the Australian Lighthouse Association it soon had representatives and members in all States. The Association stated that by demanning a light, not only would its reliability be reduced, but other advantages of human presence would be lost too, such as weather reporting, aiding distressed mariners, assisting search and rescue operations, Customs, Fisheries, coastal surveillance, and prevention of damage and vandalism to flora, fauna, archaeological sites, and the lighthouse itself.

The Federal Government rejected those arguments, saying that the coastal lights were there solely for the benefit of the large shipping companies, which paid light-dues to the Federal Government. Large ships, with their advanced navigational equipment, no longer had a need for the 100 percent reliability of a manned light, and the companies hoped that the government through cost saving from automation would reduce the present light-dues.

It was stated by the Federal Government that although commercial fishermen, yachtsmen and small-craft owners paid boat registration fees to the various State Governments, the revenue obtained was put towards boating and navigational facilities *within* harbours; and as that section of the boating community did not pay light-dues, although they could make use of the coastal lights, they had no say in the demanning policy. The Australian Lighthouse Association found this unacceptable and, through the media and other avenues, kept pressure on the Federal Government with the hope of an inquiry being instigated.

During January 1981, Head Lightkeeper Harold Simpson suffered a serious heart attack on the station and was taken in to Gladstone by helicopter. He recovered, but nevertheless decided to retire. Although only two years at Bustard Head, Harold and his wife Betty had spent thirty-two years in the lighthouse service. Later that year he was replaced by Head Lightkeeper Kevin Urban and his wife Irene.

With the knowledge that Bustard Head was to remain manned, two men from the New Farm Lighthouse Depot were sent to the station in February to install new plumbing, drainage, and absorption trenches to both cottages; and in May, vinyl tiles were laid in every room.

Eventually, enough pressure was brought to bear by the Australian Lighthouse Association that, in 1983, two months after a federal election had resulted in a change of government, the new Minister for Transport Peter Morris (the man responsible for controlling coastal lighthouses), announced that an inquiry into the demanning of Australian lighthouses would be conducted by the House of Representatives Standing Committee on Expenditure. In December of the same year the Committee's findings were published in a 238 page report titled *Lighthouses: Do we keep the keepers?*

The report recommended that thirty-three of the forty-one manned lights in Australia should continue to have a manned presence. However, it was stated that a "manned presence" meant having only a caretaker on a station after its light had been converted to automatic operation. The Inquiry concluded that only four lightstations in Australia should remain manned in the traditional sense. Bustard Head was *not* one of those four. It was estimated that by demanning Bustard Head, there would be an annual saving of $69,000.[1]

Despite unceasing protestation from the Australian Lighthouse Association, the Inquiry's recommendations were accepted by the government and tabled in parliament. But there might as well not have been an Inquiry, because the government went on to do as it pleased. At some lights, after they had been converted, the caretaker was withdrawn after a few months, leaving them susceptible to decay and vandalism.

Most of the major lights along the Queensland coast were converted to automatic operation by replacing their large crystal lenses with revolving plastic lenses no bigger than a football and lit by bulbs the size of a fingernail, all powered by battery banks kept charged by solar panels. Consequently, the range and brilliance of the lights were greatly reduced.

But Bustard Head was spared this reduction in power. In 1985, a 25 kilometre long mains power line (single wire earth return) was built from the road near "Turkey" cattle station to the lighthouse, the new line basically following the path of the old telephone line. This meant that the Fourth Order AGA lens and 1000 watt tungsten halogen lamp would be retained.

In January 1986, mechanics Spearritt and Walpole arrived at the station to convert the light to automatic operation. In case of mains power failure, one of the Lister diesel generating sets in the engine room was programmed to cut in and run until the mains power was restored, unless the motor ran out of diesel fuel first. The second diesel generating set was removed. Since the establishment of the light in 1868, each morning at sunrise, when the lightkeeper 'put out' the light, calico curtains were hung on the inside of the lantern room against the glass panes. This was to prevent the sun's rays becoming magnified through the now motionless lens and creating a hot spot that could damage the filament of the lamp, or cause severe temperature differences between the crystal prisms and the brass frames in which they were held, thereby fracturing the prisms. To compensate for having no lightkeepers to put up the curtains, the lens would now have to revolve twenty-four hours per day, the lamp programmed to light at night by means of an electronic light sensor.[2]

Twenty minutes before sunset on 21 January 1986, Head Lightkeeper Kevin Urban climbed the stairs of the tower for the station's last manual 'light up'. No man could have been more suited for this final historic event. Like Bustard Head's first Head Lightkeeper, Thomas Rooksby, Kevin had sailed to all parts of the world as a merchant seaman. In 1955 Kevin joined the Commonwealth Lighthouse Service as a Lightkeeper. It was a lifestyle he and his wife Irene grew to love passionately. Although Kevin could have accepted a transfer to another station after the demanning of Bustard Head, he and Irene had decided to retire. For them, 'the lights' had come to an end. Some of Kevin's thoughts on his last two days at Bustard Head are expressed in part of a letter he wrote after his retirement:

> On the evening of my last 'light up', Irene and I felt that the end of our world had come. Thirty-one years in 'the lights', and the fact that we enjoyed every one of them, made the thought of leaving all the more heart wrenching.
>
> The end of an era had come for the lighthouse too. From now on no man would be there to check the apparatus and 'put up' the curtains. An automatic sensor would switch on the light; and in the event of failure there would be no-one on hand to rectify the fault. This possibility was uppermost in our thoughts, but obviously not in the minds of those in authority. As an ex-seaman I knew the value of lighthouses. As a conscientious lightkeeper I could not imagine a lightstation without a keeper.
>
> It didn't seem possible that this would be our last evening on a lightstation. How many nights had Irene and I sat down together with the children, accepting it as just another day with many more

to follow? The children had grown up and gone on with lives of their own. It had been just Irene and me for years now, and I knew how fortunate it was that Irene loved the life as much as me, because no man will stay a lightkeeper unless his wife is prepared to share that life.

At sunrise next morning I was overwhelmed by a sense of loss as I 'put out' the light and returned to the cottage to help Irene pack our few remaining things, while the mechanics made the final alterations to convert the light to automatic operation.

Early in the afternoon, we climbed onto the LARC with the last load of our belongings and made our way down the 'main road' and out through the mouth of Pancake Creek where the lighthouse ship Cape Don *was anchored, waiting to take us back to Brisbane and retirement. As she steamed away, Irene and I couldn't force ourselves to look astern at what we were leaving behind. We had many plans for the future, some of those already underway. But somehow we knew that nothing would replace the life we had at Bustard Head. It was best not to look back at what was no longer a true lighthouse. After all, we still had our memories.[3]*

Chapter 15

WHAT NOW?

After Kevin and Irene Urban's departure from Bustard Head, former Light-keeper Peter Harrison remained on the station as caretaker. At that time, the Department of Transport (the Commonwealth Government department then in control of coastal lighthouses) was implementing a policy of "economic rationalisation". As a result, the cost of keeping a caretaker at Bustard Head was considered to be unacceptable, and a decision was made to remove him. In July 1986, Lighthouse Engineer Mizen and a team of mechanics arrived at Bustard Head on board the lighthouse steamer to dismantle the station equipment. The three bulk fuel tanks, flagpole and Stevenson weather-screen were loaded onto the ship. Furniture and appliances were removed from the cottages and, presumably to prevent squatters from reconnecting the electricity, all light switches and power points were smashed out of the walls. Security bars were fitted to the ground floor windows of the lighthouse, and a chain wire security fence built around the tower and engine room. An emergency telephone inside a metal container was attached to the fence. Caretaker Harrison was with-drawn from the station on 14 July 1986. That night for the first time since the light was established 118 years earlier, Bustard Head lightstation was devoid of human presence.

When charter boat proprietor Des Mergard from the Town of Seventeen Seventy heard that the station was to be demanned, he applied to the Depart-ment of Transport to use the cottages for tourist accommodation in return for maintaining the buildings. His offer was refused.

During 1986 the automatic light on Clews Point was taken over by the State Government. Their Harbours and Marine section replaced the old steel structure with an aluminium one, and at the same time laid buoys and beacons in Pancake Creek to improve access to the more protected anchorage further up the creek.

Wanting to rid itself of the responsibility for all but the lighthouse and engine room, the Department of Transport declared the Bustard Head light-house reserve as "surplus to requirements" and passed the property to the

BUSTARD HEAD CEMETERY

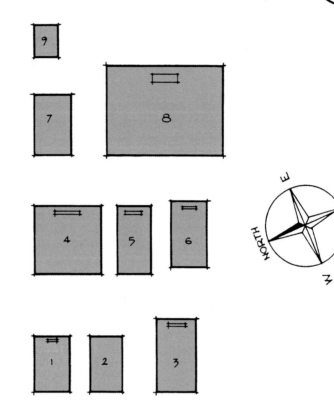

Nº	NAME	DATE OF DEATH
1	PHILLIPS, HENRY POPE ROBERT	14 OCTOBER 1879
2	UNNAMED	
3	POWER, ALFRED	15 MAY 1889
4	GIBSON, KATE	5 MAY 1887
	GIBSON, MARY	15 MAY 1889
	GIBSON, NILS	25 FEBRUARY 1896
5	WILKINSON, ELIZABETH ANNIE	15 MAY 1889
6	WAYE, MILLY CHARLOTTE ANNIE	6 JANUARY 1898
7	UNNAMED	
8	BOWTON, FREDERICK JAMES	17 OCTOBER 1905
	BOWTON, KATHERINE	5 MARCH 1940
9	HOVELL, FREDERICK	5 JANUARY 1911

UNMARKED GRAVES

	ANDERSON, MARY EMILY MAUDE	3 FEBRUARY 1908
	ANDERSON, ETHEL ELIZABETH	31 MARCH 1912

METRES

0   5   10

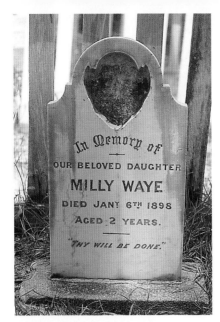

In Memory of
OUR BELOVED DAUGHTER
MILLY WAYE
DIED JANY 6TH 1898
AGED 2 YEARS.

"THY WILL BE DONE."

In Loving Memory
OF
CAPTAIN
F. J. BOWTON,
DIED 5TH OCTOBER 1905.
KATHERINE E. BOWTON.
DIED 5TH MARCH 1940.
"AT REST."

In loving memory
of
OUR DEAR FATHER
NILS GIBSON
WHO DIED 23RD FEB 1898, AGED 58 YEARS
AND OUR DEAR MOTHER
WHO DIED 4TH MAY 1897
AGED 49 YEARS.
ALSO OUR DEAR SISTER MARY
WHO WAS ACCIDENTALLY DROWNED
11TH MAY 1893, AGED 20 YEARS.

IN LOVING MEMORY
OF
ELIZABETH ANNE
WILKINSON
DROWNED IN PANCAKE
CREEK
MAY 15TH 1889
AGED 39 YEARS.
A GOOD WIFE AND LOVING
MOTHER.

BUSTARD HEAD
CEMETERY HEADSTONES

BABY FREDERICK HOVELL
SON OF ELIZABETH AND HENRY HOVELL
DIED 1911

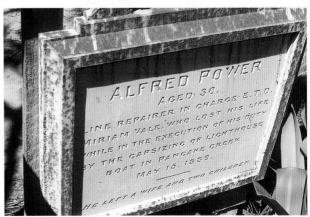

ALFRED POWER
AGED 30.
LINE REPAIRER IN CHARGE E.T.O.
MIRIAM VALE, WHO LOST HIS LIFE
WHILE IN THE EXECUTION OF HIS DUTY
BY THE CAPSIZING OF LIGHTHOUSE
BOAT IN PANCAKE CREEK
MAY 15, 1889.
HE LEFT A WIFE AND TWO CHILDREN

"Bustard Head Lightstation — After the Fire". A painting by Cheryl Nugent. Cheryl's father, Allan Nugent, was a Lightkeeper at Bustard Head from 1934–35.

Many a tragic story lies buried in the Bustard Head Cemetery.

Generations of lightkeepers have painted the tower, protecting it from the ravages of the sea air.

The last Head Lightkeeper of Bustard Head, Kevin Urban with his wife Irene. They enjoyed thirty-one years in 'the lights'.

Emblem of the Commonwealth Lighthouse Service.

Glenn Barkley, 1770 Environmental Tours' guide, relates the history of the Bustard Head graves to a party of tourists.

Des and Betty Mergard, proprietors of 1770 Environmental Tours. They keep the history of Bustard Head alive.

The shady bank of Jenny Lind Creek provides an ideal lunch spot for tourists on a day trip to Bustard Head with 1770 Environmental Tours. Proprietor Des Mergard stands beside the amphibian Sir Joseph Banks.

Automated and demanned in 1986, the lightstation was left in perfect condition by Head Lightkeeper Kevin Urban. A chain wire security fence was built around the tower and engine room — then the deterioration began.

Year by year, damage to the buildings increased.

With no lightkeepers to do maintenance, the 'main road' developed deep wash-outs from the heavy summer rain.

A pack of mindless morons went on a frenzied rampage of destruction — but who was really to blame?

Department of Administrative Services Property Section. Some months later, that Department advertised for expressions of interest in the station from the public. But the offer had to be withdrawn when it was discovered that a Certificate of Title for Bustard Head did not exist, and in consequence a lease couldn't be issued. While attempts were being made to resolve this issue, control of the reserve was handed over to the Great Barrier Reef Marine Park Authority.

Not unexpectedly, the Department of Transport's decision in 1986 to remove the caretaker proved inept. For two years the station lay empty but undamaged. However, with no-one to repair the steeper sections of the 'main road', the heavy summer rains washed away much of the road topping, scouring out thousands of tonnes of sand below it, leaving wide crevices up to 6 metres deep. Then, year by year, damage to the buildings increased. First, the doors to the cottages were kicked open and some of the internal joinery ripped out. The emergency telephone was torn from its box, its innards hanging loose like some disembowelled animal. Bullet holes made by a large calibre weapon peppered both cottages. A few windows and wall panels were smashed.

Vandals turned off the mains power at the power pole nearest the lighthouse, and the light remained out for a night. In 1990 there were three power failures, one of which resulted in the light being out for three nights.

During 1994, control of the lighthouse reserve changed hands yet again. This time to the Australian Maritime Safety Authority, which was formed in 1991 to replace the Department of Transport and Communications — formerly known as the Department of Transport. In the eight years since the demanning of Bustard Head, through a maze of bureaucratic ambivalence, the lighthouse reserve was back with its original management.

The same year, the Australian Heritage Commission decided that Bustard Head lightstation — consisting of the lighthouse, cottages, associated buildings and cemetery — was of such historical significance that it should be listed on the Register of the National Estate. This was done on 5 September 1994.

That year also saw the beginning of tourism at the lightstation. Des and Betty Mergard, using the name 1770 Environmental Tours, bought a LARC — similar to the ones used on the lighthouse supply ships — and fitted it out to carry tourists on day trips from the Town of Seventeen Seventy to Bustard Head. Appropriately named *Sir Joseph Banks*, the thirty-two seat amphibian follows the coastline of Bustard Bay, past the spot where Lieutenant James Cook and his party landed, across four tidal creeks to Bustard Head. The LARC stops on the shady northern bank of Jenny Lind Creek near the beach where, in 1867, the *Gneering* landed the materials to build the lighthouse. Later, the guide leads the passengers up the headland to the lightstation, where the history of the lighthouse and cemetery is explained.

Saddened by the sorry state of the lightstation and aware of the bad impression it was making on visitors, Des and Betty Mergard, backed by the Lighthouse Historical Society of Queensland, made numerous offers to the Australian Maritime Safety Authority to provide a caretaker and refurbish the buildings. But at the time, negotiations were underway to transfer the major lighthouse reserves from Federal to State control, and the Mergards' proposal couldn't be considered.

It was proposed that the Queensland Department of Environment and Heritage would eventually control the lighthouse reserve. And so, in 1995, that Department requested the Australian Maritime Safety Authority to prepare a conservation management plan for Bustard Head lightstation. While that was being done, at the end of December 1995, within a period of twenty-four hours, a pack of mindless morons went on a frenzied rampage of destruction, smashing every window and wall panel of both cottages. They ripped out window frames, holed the fibreglass rainwater tanks, shattered porcelain bathroom fittings, and pulled awnings and guttering from their brackets. The workshop, fuel shed and garage fared no better. It is openly said by all who have seen this wanton destruction, that whoever in the Department of Transport made the decision to remove the caretaker in 1986 is as guilty of this vandalism as those who did it.

The conservation management plan was completed in November 1996. It recommended that the lighthouse, all associated buildings and the cemetery be maintained and preserved; and that a caretaker be installed on site to provide maintenance and protection. As at the beginning of 1999, none of those recommendations have been implemented.

The transfer of all Queensland's lighthouse properties from Federal to State Government was finalised on 30 June 1996. Bustard Head then became the responsibility of the Department of Environment and Heritage.

The LARC trip to Bustard Head proved so popular that Des and Betty Mergard bought a second amphibian in 1997. *Sir Joseph Banks* was joined by *Dr D.C. Solander.* Although the Mergards were refused permission to refurbish the buildings and maintain the cemetery, relatives of those buried there commissioned Des Mergard and the Lighthouse Historical Society to care for the graves. At least that part of the station's heritage is being well looked after.

A survey of the lightstation precinct, including the cemetery and access corridors, was done for the Department of Environment and Heritage in 1998. Later that year, on 9 November, the historic and cultural importance of Bustard Head was recognised by the State Government when the precinct was granted permanent listing on the Queensland Heritage Register.

There appears little doubt that the 445 hectare lighthouse reserve will eventually become National Park, but what will happen to the lighthouse precinct is anyone's guess. The Department of Environment and Heritage could refurbish the buildings and install a ranger in one of the cottages, or the buildings could be leased to private enterprise for tourist accommodation.

The fate of Bustard Head now rests in the hands of the State Government. Hopefully, wisdom and an appreciation of the need to protect our cultural heritage will guide those in authority to make the correct decisions. Whatever happens, Bustard Head lightstation should be retained and maintained; not only because it was the first coastal lighthouse built in Queensland, but for 118 years it was the home to generations of lightkeepers and their families, whose first priority was to keep the light burning, providing safety to those aboard the frailest of early sailing ships to the most massive modern bulk carriers. It is an important part of our maritime history; it was a unique life-style that has now gone forever, but one that must never be forgotten.

EPILOGUE

To celebrate the launch of this book, Bustard Head lighthouse was opened to the public for three days in July 1999. In conjunction with the launch, the ABC's *7.30 Report* did a hard-hitting segment on the plight of the heritage-listed site. On that program the then State government Minister for Environment Rod Welford stated that he would be "giving very clear directions (to his department) to get on and look after the lighthouse properties, especially Bustard Head."

True to his word, he put a bomb under his department, and on 30 October 1999 Queensland Parks and Wildlife Service (QPWS) advertised for Expressions of Interest from the public in regard to four Queensland lightstations. Bustard Head was one of them. The author and his wife Shirley, along with Des Mergard of 1770 Environmental Tours, formed the Bustard Head Lighthouse Association Inc and submitted a proposal.

While waiting for a decision from QPWS, on 5 May 2000 the 445 hectare Bustard Head lighthouse reserve was gazetted as National Park. On the same date, the lightstation complex, an area of 3.14 hectares, was gazetted as Bustard Head Conservation Park.

Eventually, after two years of submissions, letters, phone calls and meetings the Bustard Head Lighthouse Association Inc was granted a twenty year lease of the Conservation Park, beginning on 1 February 2002.

Assisted by a Commonwealth government heritage grant, private donations and loans, the Association has restored the buildings to pristine condition. One cottage houses a full-time site-manager, while the other cottage — set up as a display home with lighthouse artifacts — provides visitors with the opportunity to walk through a typical Queensland lighthouse cottage. Visitors pay a Heritage Management Charge, which covers running costs, maintenance of the light-station, and repayment of loans.

Bustard Head lightstation has been given another chance of survival.

January 2006

HEAD LIGHTKEEPERS
OF
BUSTARD HEAD LIGHTHOUSE 1868–1986

Researched and Compiled by Shirley Buchanan
© Copyright Shirley Buchanan

ATHERTON, John (Jack)
BOWTON, Frederick James
BUCHANAN, Stuart M.
BUTLER, Archibald E.
CASEY, Valentine
COLLINS, James
CRAWFORD, Jack R.
DANIELS, Lloyd C.
DAVIES, Ronald
FOSTER, Samuel
GOLDSMITH, Stanley C.
HAYES, James S. (Lofty)
HENDERSON, Archibald
KELLY, Arthur J.
KENT, John A.
KIDD, John A.
KING, Harold R.
NASH, Henry
O'MEARA, Michael V.
POWELL, Walter G.V.
RASMUS, Charles
ROOKE, Vivian M.
ROOKSBY, Thomas
SIMPSON, Harold
SMITH, William E.
SWANSON, Donald
URBAN, Kevin
WOODHEAD, Charles F.

LIGHTKEEPERS
OF
BUSTARD HEAD LIGHTHOUSE 1868–1986

Researched and Compiled by Shirley Buchanan
© Shirley Buchanan

Abbott, J.C.
Allison, J.E.
Anderson, Frederick
Ashby, James

Bailey, H.C.
Barton, Francis
Bennett, Alan
Benson, Dennis J.
Birnie, James
Birrell, Edward E.
Boulton, Raymond
Bowton, Frederick Kendall
Boys, Joshua T.
Bradley, Malcolm
Bridge, Leonard
Brown, Kenneth
Bull, S.

Chapman, William F.
Christmas, Thomas
Christophers, O.J.
Cleaver, William
Cochrane, W.D.
Compton, E.
Coultard, F.G.
Cousins, J.W.
Crouch, N.
Curtis, Charles

Davis, Kevin
Deasey, Harold

Doney, P.E.
Dore, T.H.G.

Edwards, Steven
Elliott, A.J.
Elkington, L.
Everett, A.B.

Finch, T.
Foale, L.R.
Fulton, R. Dudley

Gerber, D.A.
Gerber, H.S.
Gibson, Nils
Goodfellow, George H.
Gorman, Daniel
Gowley, Ken C.
Gunton, G.W.

Haack, Laurie
Haack, Roy A.
Harrison, Peter
Harvey, R.W.
Heasman, George
Hersom, Mervyn B.
Hoffman, A.
Holly, L.
Hopper, J.P.
Hovell, Henry
Howes, P.

Jackson, J.
Jerram, H.

Kay, Lewis A.
Kennedy, M.J.
Kernovski, E.

Leather, George
Lee, Charles D.
Lee, John
Lemon, Arthur T.
Linquist, Charles
Linquist, E.
Linton, Robert
Longland, Robert H.

McArthur, J.E.
McCarthy, Dennis
McKeown, David
Marshall, W.
Matheson, Charles C.
Mitchell, A. Jack
Moore, R.C.
Morrison, M.
Muir, Malcolm J.
Murray, Geoffrey

Nugent, Allan

O'Connor, J.
O'Dea, T.
O'Sullivan, J.
Oxborough, George

Page, Gary
Pern, H.
Perry, J.T.
Phillips, James D.
Plumb, John R.

Ramsay, James
Rapkins, Eric H.
Rasmus, Ernest
Reed, F.
Renton, A.C.
Riley, Arthur F.

Roche, Darrel
Roggenkamp, K.E.
Rollo, A.
Ross, George W.
Ross, I.T.
Rouse, J.

Shanahan, Thomas J.
Sellwood, John H.
Shephard, W.
Shepherd, Thomas
Sherlock, James
Shield, M.C.
Shield, William
Silver, Joseph N.
Simpson, R. Norman
Sinclair, E.
Smith, Mrs
Smith, K.C.
Sofin, J.
Spencer, W.W.

Tandy, W.A.E.
Thomlinson, A.
Thomson, J.
Thomson-Jones, Rick
Todd, C.S.
Toon, S.J.

Vidler, C.

Watson, B.R.
Waye, Ernest
Webb, Lewis P.
Weightman, M.J.
Welsh, H.D.
Whalley, R.J.
Wilce, William H.
Wilken, U.
Wilkinson, John
Window, Keith
Wise, S.
Wright, K.

Young, P.

STAFF LIST
BUSTARD HEAD LIGHTHOUSE 1868–1986

Researched and Compiled by Shirley Buchanan
© Shirley Buchanan

YEAR	HEAD LIGHTKEEPER	LIGHTKEEPER	YEAR	HEAD LIGHTKEEPER	LIGHTKEEPER
1868	Rooksby, T.	Morrison, M. Gorman, D.	1880	Rooksby, T.	Gibson, N. Phillips, J.D.
1869	Rooksby, T.	Morrison, M. Gorman, D. McCarthy, D.	1881	Rooksby, T.	Gibson, N. Phillips, J.D.
1870	Rooksby, T.	Morrison, M. McCarthy, D.	1882	Rooksby, T.	Gibson, N. Phillips, J.D.
1871	Rooksby, T.	Morrison, M. McCarthy, D.	1883	Rooksby, T.	Gibson, N. Christmas, T.
1872	Rooksby, T.	Morrison, M. McCarthy, D.	1884	Rooksby, T.	Gibson, N. Christmas, T.
1873	Rooksby, T.	Lee, J. Gibson, N.	1885	Rooksby, T.	Gibson, N. Christmas, T.
1874	Rooksby, T.	Lee, J. Gibson, N.	1886	Rooksby, T.	Gibson, N. Christmas, T. Goodfellow, G.H.
1875	Rooksby, T.	Lee, J. Gibson, N. Lee, C.	1887	Rooksby, T.	Gibson, N. Goodfellow, G.H.
1876	Rooksby, T.	Gibson, N. Lee, C.	1888	Rooksby, T.	Gibson, N. Goodfellow, G.H.
1877	Rooksby, T.	Gibson, N. Lee, C. Phillips, J.D.	1889	Rooksby, T.	Gibson, N. Goodfellow, G.H. Wilkinson, J.
1878	Rooksby, T.	Gibson, N. Phillips, J.D.	1890	Rooksby, T.	Gibson, N. Wilkinson, J.
1879	Rooksby, T.	Gibson, N. Phillips, J.D.	1891	Rooksby, T.	Gibson, N. Wilkinson, J.
			1892	Rooksby, T.	Gibson, N. Wilkinson, J.

Year	Head Lightkeeper	Lightkeeper	Year	Head Lightkeeper	Lightkeeper
1893	Rooksby, T.	Gibson, N. Rasmus, C.	1910	Rasmus, C.	Anderson, F. Dore, T.H.G. Hovell, H.
1894	Rooksby, T.	Gibson, N. Rasmus, C.	1911	Rasmus, C.	Anderson, F. Hovell, H.
1895	Rooksby, T.	Gibson, N. Rasmus, C.	1912	Rasmus, C.	Anderson, F. Hovell, H. O'Meara, M.V. Heasman, G.
1896	Rooksby, T.	Gibson, N. Rasmus, C. Waye, E.	1913	Rasmus, C.	O'Meara, M.V. Heasman, G.
1897	Rooksby, T.	Rasmus, C. Waye, E.	1914	Rasmus, C.	O'Meara, M.V. Heasman, G.
1898	Rooksby, T.	Rasmus, C. Waye, E. Boys, J.T.	1915	Rasmus, C.	O'Meara, M.V. Heasman, G. Sherlock, J.
1899	Rooksby, T.	Rasmus, C. Linquist, C.	1916	Rasmus, C. Kent, J.A.	Heasman, G. Sherlock, J. Rasmus, E. Shield, W.
1900	Rooksby, T.	Rasmus, C. Linquist, C. Boys, J.T.	1917	Kent, J.A.	Heasman, G. Sherlock, J. O'Sullivan, J. Finch, T. Bowton, F.K. Sofin, J. Simpson, R.N.
1901	Rooksby, T.	Rasmus, C. Boys, J.T.			
1902	Rooksby, T. Bowton, F.J.	Rasmus, C. Linton, R.			
1903	Bowton, F.J.	Rasmus, C. Kent, J.A.	1918	Kent, J.A.	Heasman, G. Simpson, R.N. Nash, H. Shepherd, T. O'Sullivan, J. Bowton, F.K. Perry, J.T.
1904	Bowton, F.J.	Rasmus, C. Kent, J.A.			
1905	Bowton, F.J. Rasmus, C.	Kent, J.A. Bowton, F.K.			
1906	Rasmus, C.	Bowton, F.K. Anderson, F.	1919	Kent, J.A.	Nash, H. Simpson, R.N. Shepherd, T. Gunton, G.W.
1907	Rasmus, C.	Anderson, F. McArthur, J.E.			
1908	Rasmus, C.	Anderson, F. McArthur, J.E. Dore, T.H.G.	1920	Kent, J.A. Kidd, J.A.	Nash, H. Simpson, R.N. Pern, H. Gunton, G.W.
1909	Rasmus, C.	Anderson, F. Dore, T.H.G.			

Year	Head Lightkeeper	Lightkeeper	Year	Head Lightkeeper	Lightkeeper
1921	Kidd, J.A.	Nash, H. Simpson, R.N. Hoffman, A.	1929	Henderson, A.	Woodhead, C.F. Rapkins, E.H. Plumb, J.R. Toon, S.J. Shephard, W.
1922	Kidd, J.A.	Simpson, R.N. Birrell, E.E. Hoffman, A. Riley, A.F.	1930	Henderson, A.	Woodhead, C.F. Rapkins, E.H. Shanahan, T.J. Barton, F. Curtis, C. Bridge, L.
1923	Kidd, J.A.	Birrell, E.E. Foster, S. Coulthard, F.G. Riley, A.F. Pern, H.	1931	Henderson, A.	Shanahan, T.J. Barton, F. Curtis, C.
1924	Kidd, J.A.	Birrell, E.E. Foster, S. Reed, F. Cochrane, W.D. Riley, A.F.	1932	Henderson, A. O'Meara, M.V.	Shanahan, T.J. Barton, F. Deasey, H. Elkington, L. Kay, L.A. King, H.R.
1925	O'Meara, M.V.	Birrell, E.E. Foster, S. Todd, C.S. Cochrane, W.D. Wilce, W.H.	1933	O'Meara, M.V. Powell, W.G.V.	Kay, L.A. King, H.R. Spencer, W.W.
1926	O'Meara, M.V. Nash, H.	Birrell, E.E. Foster, S. Woodhead, C.F. Todd, C.S. Ashby, J.G. Rouse, J. Kennedy, M.J. Shield, W.	1934	Powell, W.G.V.	King, H.R. Spencer, W.W. Elkington, L. Nugent, A.
			1935	Powell, W.G.V. Woodhead, C.F.	Nugent, A. King, H.R. Hopper, J.P.
1927	Nash, H.	Birrell, E.E. Woodhead, C.F. O'Dea, T. Everett, A.B. Kennedy, M.J.	1936	Woodhead, C.F.	King, H.R. Cleaver, W.
			1937	Woodhead, C.F. Casey, V.	Cleaver, W. Lemon, A.T.
1928	Nash, H.	Birrell, E.E. Woodhead, C.F. Rapkins, E.H. Everett, A.B. Kennedy, M.J. Thomlinson, A. Plumb, J.R. Shephard, W.	1938	Casey, V. King, H.R.	Cleaver, W. Cousins, J.W. Kernovski, E.
			1939	King, H.R. Foster, S.	Cleaver, W. Welsh, H.D. Kernovski, E. Vidler, C. Webb, L.P.

Year	Head Lightkeeper	Lightkeeper	Year	Head Lightkeeper	Lightkeeper
1940	Foster, S.	Welsh, H.D. Vidler, C. Abbott, J.C.	1949	Butler, A.E. Goldsmith, S.C.	Doney, P.E. Wright, K. Mitchell, A.J.
1941	Foster, S.	Abbott, J.C. Kernovski, E.	1950	Goldsmith, S.C.	Wright, K. Allison, J.E. Mitchell, A.J.
1942	Foster, S.	Abbott, J.C. Allison, J.E. Bowton, F.K.	1951	Goldsmith, S.C.	Hayes, J.S. Ross, I.T. Allison, J.E.
1943	Foster, S. Kelly, A.J.	Abbott, J.C. Bowton, F.K. Marshall, W. Howes, P. Smith, W.E. Roggenkamp, K.E. Harvey, R.W. Moore, R.C.	1952	Goldsmith, S.C.	Hayes, J.S. Sinclair, E. Jerram, H.
			1953	Goldsmith, S.C. Rooke, M.V.	Jerram, H. Watson, B.R. Wise, S. Rollo, A.
1944	Kelly, A.J. Smith, W.E.	Harvey, R.W. Moore, R.C. Gerber, H.S. Linquist, E. Smith, Mrs Chapman, W.F. Roggenkamp, K.E. Longland, R.H. Allison, J.E.	1954	Rooke, M.V.	Rollo, A. Bailey, H.C. Mitchell, A.J.
			1955	Rooke, M.V.	Bailey, H.C. Crouch, N.
			1956	Rooke, M.V.	Bailey, H.C. Oxborough, G.
1945	Smith, W.E. Goldsmith, S.C.	Moore, R.C. Chapman, W.F. Smith, Mrs Matheson, C.C. Allison, J.E. Linquist, E.	1957	Rooke, M.V.	Bailey, H.C. Haack, R.A.
			1958	Rooke, M.V. Hayes, J.S.	Bailey, H.C. Haack, R.A. Renton, A.C. Window, K.
1946	Goldsmith, S.C.	Smith, W.E. Bull, S. Moore, R.C.	1959	Hayes, J.S.	Window, K. Urban, K.
1947	Goldsmith, S.C.	Smith, W.E. Silver, J.N. Moore, R.C.	1960	Hayes, J.S.	Window, K. Renton, A.C.
1948	Goldsmith, S.C. Butler, A.E.	Smith, W.E. Hayes, J.S. Tandy, W.A.E. Doney, P.E. Weightman, M.J. Silver, J.N.	1961	Hayes, J.S.	Window, K. Renton, A.C. Sellwood, J.H.
			1962	Hayes, J.S.	Renton, A.C. Foale, L.R. Wright, K.

Year	Head Lightkeeper	Lightkeeper	Year	Head Lightkeeper	Lightkeeper
1963	Hayes, J.S.	Wright, K. Thomson, J. Whalley, R.J.	1974	Atherton, J.	Haack, L. Davis, K. Fulton, R.D. Buchanan, S.M.
1964	Hayes, J.S.	Wright, K. Jackson, J. Birnie, J. Smith, K.C.	1975	Atherton, J.	Buchanan, S.M. Bradley, M. Leather, G.
1965	Hayes, J.S.	Jackson, J. Birnie, J. Elliott, A.J. Thomson, J.	1976	Atherton, J. Buchanan, S.M.	Bradley, M.
1966	Hayes, J.S. Crawford, J.R.	Elliott, A.J. Thomson, J. Holly, L. Gerber, D.A. Christophers, O.J. O'Connor, J.	1977	Davies, R.	Buchanan, S.M. Young, P. Gowley, K.C. Bradley, M. Murray, G. Davis, K.
1967	Crawford, J.R. Daniels, L.C.	O'Connor, J. Compton, E. Swanson, D. Muir, M.J.	1978	Davies, R. Simpson, H.	Buchanan, S.M. Brown, K. McKeown, D. Murray, G.
1968	Daniels, L.C.	Swanson, D. Muir, M.J. Ross, G.W. Haack, L.	1979	Simpson, H.	Buchanan, S.M. Boulton, R. Davis, K. Murray, G.
1969	Daniels, L.C. Swanson, D.	Ross, G.W. Haack, L. Thomson-Jones, R.	1980	Simpson, H.	Boulton, R. Davis, K.
1970	Swanson, D. Collins, J.	Haack, L. Davis, K. Hersom, M.B. Wilken, U.	1981	Simpson, H. Urban, K.	Boulton, R. Benson, D.J. Buchanan, S.M.
1971	Collins, J. Atherton, J.	Hersom, M.B. Thomson-Jones, R. Davies, R.	1982	Urban, K.	Boulton, R. Page, G. Benson, D.J.
1972	Atherton, J.	Davies, R. Ramsay, J. Hersom, M.B. Bennett, A.	1983	Urban, K.	Page, G. Edwards, S. Benson, D.J.
1973	Atherton, J.	Bennett, A. Shield, M.C. Haack, L. Ramsay, J.	1984	Urban, K.	Page, G. Roche, D.
			1985	Urban, K.	Page, G. Thomson-Jones, R. Harrison, P.
			1986	Urban, K.	Harrison, P.

SCHOOLTEACHERS
BUSTARD HEAD PROVISIONAL SCHOOL
1882–1917

1882–84	JACKSON, William
1884–88	KENNY, Margaret
1888–89	HENSLEY, Marianne
1889–93	TURICH, Edith May
1893–95	ALS, Mary V.
1895–96	KAYS, Isabella
1896–98	BARRON, Marie Louise
1898–01	THOM, Harriet L.
1901	JOYNER, Amy B.
1901–03	CONNOR, Harriet
1903	ALS, Mary V.
1903–04	MYLES, Kate
1904–06	SUMMERS, Lavinia Anna
1906–09	CRAWFORD, Margaret Annie Matilda
1909–10	ROWE, Eva Mary
1910–12	SEDGMAN, Irene
1912–15	CAIN, Frances May
1915	HEANEY, Gladys
1915–16	WILLMOTT, Margaret
1916–17	CRONIN, Edith Veronica

ENDNOTES

Chapter 1

1. *The Journals of Captain James Cook*, p.326, edited by J.C. Beaglehole.
2. *Captain James Cook*, p.521, Australian Publishing Company.
3. *A Voyage to Terra Australis*, p.12, by Matthew Flinders.
4. *A Voyage to Terra Australis*, pp.12–13, by Matthew Flinders.
5. *A Voyage to Terra Australis*, p.15, by Matthew Flinders.
6. *The Marine Board Act of 1862*, Supplement to the *Queensland Government Gazette*, 5 July 1862. No.58, pp.329–334. Queensland State Archives.
7. *Minutes of Proceedings of the Legislative Council*, Minutes No.16, 26 August 1863. Queensland State Archives.
8. The main British manufacturer of lighthouse equipment at that time, Chance Brothers of Birmingham, developed a method of classifying their various lenses. Each lens size was called an 'order', the size being dependent on the focal distance, i.e., the distance from the light source to the lens, or half the diameter of the apparatus measured at the focal plane. The greater the focal distance, the more powerful the resulting beam of light. Chance Brothers' orders were:

First Order	920 millimetres
Second Order	700 millimetres
Third Order	500 millimetres
Third Order (small type)	375 millimetres
Fourth Order	250 millimetres
Fifth Order	187.5 millimetres
Sixth Order	150 millimetres

    In later times, two larger lenses were manufactured:

Hyper-radial	1330 millimetres
Meso-radial	1125 millimetres

9. *Report from The Select Committee on the Rivers and Harbors [sic] of the Colony.* 31 August 1864. Queensland Legislative Assembly, First Session of 1864 Parliament. Votes and Proceedings, pp.1199–1202. Queensland State Archives.

10. Tender descriptions of Bustard Head and Sandy Cape lighthouses. Heath to Colonial Treasurer. Queensland State Archives COL/A77.

11. A dioptric system is one in which the light is refracted or bent by a glass agent, such as a prism or lens, in the direction required, as opposed to a catoptric system in which the light is reflected from a polished surface. Holophotal refers to an apparatus that collects all the light from a luminous source — the burner or lamp — and emits it in one direction.

12. *Report from the Engineer of Harbors [sic] and Rivers*, 10 June 1865. Queensland Legislative Assembly. Votes and Proceedings pp.1296–7. Queensland State Archives.

13. *Report from the Engineer of Harbors [sic] and Rivers*, 25 April 1866. Queensland Legislative Assembly. Votes and Proceedings p.1575. Queensland State Archives.

14. *Report from the Engineer of Harbors [sic] and Rivers*, 18 May 1867. Queensland Legislative Assembly. Votes and Proceedings p.754. Queensland State Archives.

Chapter 2

1. Heath to Port Curtis Harbour Master, 6 August 1867. Queensland State Archives HAR/G1, 221/67.

2. Wreck of the *Jenny Lind*, *Moreton Bay Courier*, 28 March 1857. State Library of Queensland.

3. Ferguson to the Colonial Architect, 4 November 1867. Queensland State Archives ARC4.

4. *The Story of the Port of Mackay, Queensland*, by Ling Roth. John Oxley Library.

5. Ferguson to the Colonial Architect, 22 December 1867. Queensland State Archives ARC4.

6. Ferguson to the Colonial Architect, January 1868. Queensland State Archives ARC4.

7. Ferguson to the Colonial Architect, 23 March 1868. Queensland State Archives ARC4.

8. Ferguson to the Colonial Architect, 24 May 1868. Queensland State Archives ARC4.

9. Ferguson to the Colonial Architect, 22 June 1868. Queensland State Archives ARC4.

10. A compilation of two reports: (a) Heath to the Colonial Treasurer, 29 June 1868. Queensland State Archives HAR/G1, 199/68. (b) *Report of the Portmaster upon the Ports and Harbors [sic] of the Colony*, 2 December 1868. Queensland Legislative Assembly. Votes and Proceedings pp.595–6. Queensland State Archives.

11. Colonial Architect to Heath, 14 July 1870. Queensland State Archives.

Chapter 3

1. Blue Book of Queensland 1869. Queensland State Archives.
2. General Instructions to Keepers. Queensland State Archives HAR/79(e). For full description see Appendix 1.
3. Heath to Port Curtis Harbour Master, 31 August 1868. Queensland State Archives HAR/G1, 246/68.
4. *A Record For The Civil Service* by D. Eglinton. *The Queenslander*, 14 June 1902, pp.1310–2. State Library of Queensland.
5. *The Brisbane Courier*, 9 May 1870. State Library of Queensland.
6. *Report upon the Ports and Harbors [sic] of the Colony*, 28 December 1871. Queensland Legislative Assembly. Votes and Proceedings p.765. Queensland State Archives.
7. Notice To Mariners, 4 December 1872. *Queensland Government Gazette*, July–December 1872, p.2040. Queensland State Archives. For full description see Appendix 2.
8. *The Brisbane Courier*, 30 July & 5 August 1873. *The Queenslander*, 12 July 1873. *The Bulletin, Rockhampton*, 11 & 25 July 1873. State Library of Queensland.
9. *Report by the Portmaster upon the Harbor [sic] Departments of the Colony, for the Year 1873*, 26 April 1874. Votes and Proceedings, VOL 2, p.848. Queensland State Archives.
10. *Report by the Portmaster upon the Harbor [sic] Departments of the Colony, for the Year 1873*, 26 April 1874. Votes and Proceedings, VOL 2, p.846. Queensland State Archives.
11. Notice To Mariners, 28 March 1876. *Queensland Government Gazette*, January–June 1876, p.745. Queensland State Archives. For full description see Appendix 3.
12. *Report from the Superintendent of Electric Telegraphs on the Working of his Department during the Year 1877*, 11 March 1878. Votes and Proceedings, p.542. Queensland State Archives.
13. From an account of the voyage of *Scottish Knight* from Keppel Bay 7 January 1880, by Thomas Archer. Mitchell Library of N.S.W.
14. *Report of the Department of Ports and Harbours*, 26 March 1879. Votes and Proceedings, p.911. Queensland State Archives.
15. Sailing Directions from *Pugh's Almanac*, 1882, pp.202–3. State Library of Queensland. For full description see Appendix 4.
16. Correspondence from Bustard Head School file. Queensland State Archives EDU/Z 435.
17. Sailing Directions from *Pugh's Almanac*, 1883, p.212. State Library of Queensland.
18. *Report on Harbours and Lighthouses*, 10 September 1889. Votes and Proceedings, VOL 3, p.834. Queensland State Archives.

19. *A Record For The Civil Service* by D. Eglinton. *The Queenslander*, 14 June 1902, pp.1310–2. State Library of Queensland.

20. *Report on Harbours and Lighthouses*, 1886. Votes and Proceedings, p.605. Queensland State Archives.

Chapter 4

1. Facts taken from the Inquest Report, death of Kate Gibson at Bustard Head 5 May 1887. Queensland State Archives JUS/N143, 209/1887.

2. Epitaph provided by Rochelle Starr-Thomas, great grand-daughter of Thomas and Annie Rooksby.

3. Facts taken from the Inquest Report, death of Elizabeth Wilkinson, Mary Gibson and Alfred Power at Bustard Head 15 May 1889. Queensland State Archives JUS/N167, 248/1889.

4. Extract from the diary of Grace Rooksby provided by her grand-daughter, Rochelle Starr-Thomas.

5. *Report on Harbours and Lighthouses*, 10 September 1889. Votes and Proceedings, VOL 3, p.834. Queensland State Archives.

6. *A Record For The Civil Service* by D. Eglinton. *The Queenslander*, 14 June 1902, pp.1310–2. State Library of Queensland.

Chapter 5

1. *Lands Department Annual Report 1891*, p.10. para.54. Queensland State Archives.

2. *Meteorological Report for 1887*. Votes and Proceedings, VOL 4, p.1075. Queensland State Archives.

3. *Preliminary Report of the Government Meteorologist for the Year 1887*. Votes and Proceedings, VOL 3, p.1016; and *Meteorological Report for 1892*. Votes and Proceedings, p.948. Queensland State Archives.

4. *Preliminary Report of the Government Meteorologist for the Year 1887*. Votes and Proceedings, VOL 3, p.1015.

5. Notice To Mariners, 22 December 1892, *Queensland Government Gazette*, 1892, p.1238. Queensland State Archives. For full description see Appendix 5.

6. *Report on the Marine Department for Years 1893–94*. Votes and Proceedings, VOL 3, p.1100. Queensland State Archives.

7. *Harbours in Europe and the United States*. (Report on visit to, by E.A. Cullen, Engineer), 13 August 1900. Votes and Proceedings, p.1021. Queensland State Archives.

8. *Report on the Marine Department for the Year 1901–1902*. Votes and Proceedings, p.959. Queensland State Archives.

9. *Report on the Marine Department for the Year 1906–7*. Votes and Proceedings, p.706. Queensland State Archives.

10. *The Brisbane Courier*, 12 October 1907. "Round the Lighthouses — 1. A Trip with the Portmaster" by John Munro.

11. Department of Public Instruction internal memo. No.03858, 14 March 1904. Queensland State Archives EDU/Z 435.

12. Hensley to Department of Public Instruction. No.04487, 22 March 1904. Queensland State Archives EDU/Z 435.

13. Joyner to Department of Public Instruction, 25 November 1901. Queensland State Archives EDU/Z 435.

14. Department of Public Instruction to Summers. No.05.5530, 29 March 1905. Queensland State Archives EDU/Z 435.

15. Summers to Department of Public Instruction. No.06715, 11 April 1905. Queensland State Archives EDU/Z 435.

16. Department of Public Instruction to Summers. No.05.6715, 15 April 1905. Queensland State Archives EDU/Z 435.

17. Summers to Department of Public Instruction. No.08950, 5 May 1905. Queensland State Archives EDU/Z 435.

18. Department of Public Instruction to Summers. No.05.8950, 15 May 1905. Queensland State Archives EDU/Z 435.

19. Crawford to Department of Public Instruction. No.14633, 14 August 1908. Queensland State Archives EDU/Z 435.

20. Crawford to Department of Public Instruction. No.8398, 1 May 1909. Queensland State Archives EDU/Z 435.

21. Fox to Department of Public Instruction. No.12414, 31 May 1910. Queensland State Archives EDU/Z 435.

22. Rowe to Department of Public Instruction. No.14570, 27 June 1910. Queensland State Archives EDU/Z 435.

Chapter 6

1. *The Bedsors of Tinana Queensland*, a family history by Bill Bedser [sic]. And an interview with a relative of the family, Roger Eason, who kindly provided the photograph of Thomas and Margaret Kettlewell.

2. *Australia Pilot Volume 1V.* For full description see Appendix 6.

3. *Report on the Marine Department for the Year 1907–8*. Votes and Proceedings, p.897. Queensland State Archives.

4. Information on the death of Arthur Cogzell and the abduction of Edith Anderson was supplied by Desmond Gibney from his manuscript "The Turkey Station Tragedy". Desmond, the co-author with his brother James of the best-seller *The Gatton Mystery*, kindly gave me his permission to precis his manuscript for use in this book. Desmond's research was taken from numerous newspapers, published works and:

Murder Files — Arthur Cogzell. Queensland State Archives File No.72N. A/49724–6. February 1912 to May 1963., and:

Inquest of Death — Arthur Cogzell. Queensland State Archives JUS/ N505, 491/1912.

Chapter 7

1. *Report on the Lighting of the North-East Coast (Torres Strait to Cape Moreton)* by Commander Brewis, R.N. June 1912, p.26.

2. Inspector of Works to The Under Secretary and Government Architect, 14 February 1914. No.01692. Queensland State Archives A/64939.

3. *Report of the Marine Department for the Year 1914–15*, 23 September 1915. Votes and Proceedings, p.1654. Queensland State Archives.

4. Nagle to Hardacre, 15 December 1915. Queensland State Archives EDU/Z 435.

5. Queensland State Archives EDU/Z 435.

6. Notice to Mariners, 13 February 1917, *Queensland Government Gazette*, 1917, No.94, VOL 108, p.850. Queensland State Archives. For full description see Appendix 7.

7. Assistant Surveyor-General to Acting Director of Lighthouses, 16 July 1926. National Archives, Brisbane, Queensland J56/11, QL 4870.

8. Kent to District Officer, 18 March 1918. No.18/942. National Archives, Brisbane, Queensland BP250/1/0, 11C.

9. McDonald to District Officer, 3 January 1923. National Archives, Brisbane, Queensland J2826/2, A35/2.

10. The fragile Collodion mantle was pre-shrunk and stiffened with collodion at the manufacturers, making it expensive to freight and liable to damage during delivery to the lightstation. The Autoform mantle was sent to the lightstation in a soft, pliable form, and stiffened into a bulbous shape when lit for the first time on the vapour burner; and together with its much greater candlepower per unit of area than the Collodion, made it a superior mantle. The Autoform mantle was first introduced into the British Lighthouse Service by Mr D.W. Hood, Engineer-in-Chief to Trinity House. No Notice to Mariners was issued for the increase of power to the Bustard Head light in 1923, but the 1924 Admiralty Light List shows the new candlepower as 31,000 for the fixed light and 191,000 for the flashing light. The date of the increase in power was obtained from Lighthouse Mechanic Potter's notes.

Chapter 8

1. *The Gladstone Observer*, 23, 24 & 28 May 1930, and 11 June 1930. *Bundaberg Daily News And Mail*, 23 & 24 May 1930. State Library of Queensland.

2. Taken from "Reminiscences of the Shanahan Family". Compiled in 1998 by Philip Shanahan, who kindly gave me his permission to use part of his manuscript in this book.

Chapter 9

1. Taken from the diary and letters of Neville Murphy, who was astute enough to record not only the lifestyle of the lightkeepers but the details of the lighthouse during his visit to Bustard Head in 1934. Neville generously gave me *carte blanche* to publish those writings in this book.

Chapter 10

1. Notice to Mariners, Commonwealth of Australia. Lighthouse Service. 1935, No.8. (1) Main Light. For full description see Appendices 8 & 9.
2. Notice to Mariners. Commonwealth of Australia. Lighthouse Service. 1935, No.8. (2) Auxiliary Light (U). For full description see Appendices 8 & 9.
3. Bowton to Deputy Director Marine Branch, 22 March 1938. National Archives, Brisbane, Queensland BP250/1, 11A.
4. Acting Secretary McCarthy, Department of Commerce, to Deputy Director Marine Branch, 27 June 1938. M.C.38/651/1. National Archives, Brisbane, Queensland BP250/1, 11A.
5. Engineer and Ship Surveyor A.H. Miller to Deputy Director, Navigation and Lighthouses, Queensland, 4 May 1939. National Archives, Brisbane, Queensland J2826/2, L28.
6. Deputy Director I.J. Burch, Navigation and Lighthouses, Queensland, to Director of Navigation, Melbourne, 12 April 1939. National Archives, Brisbane, Queensland J2826/2, L28.
7. Secretary J.F. Murphy, Department of Commerce, to Attorney-General's Department, 31 August 1939. National Archives, Brisbane, Queensland J2826/2, NQ800D.
8. Secretary J.F. Murphy, Department of Commerce, to Deputy Director Marine Branch, 9 March 1942. National Archives, Brisbane, Queensland J2826/2, NQ800D.

Chapter 11

1. The DUKW, manufactured by General Motors Corporation in America, was named from the company's model description system:
   D referred to the mass production model date 1942.
   U referred to the vehicle being an amphibian.
   K referred to the vehicle being an all-wheel drive model.
   W referred to the vehicle having twin rear axles.
   Information provided by Bob Todkill, retired Senior Carpenter from Australian Maritime Safety Authority.

2. *The Courier-Mail*, 5, 6, 7 & 9 February 1948. *Bundaberg News-Mail*, 6 & 9 February 1948. State Library of Queensland. And an interview by the author with Ben Betts, one of the two survivors from the wreck of *Edith*. The interview was held in 1998, when Ben was eighty years of age.
3. Director, Posts and Telegraphs to Deputy Director, Marine Branch, 28 September 1951. Director-General, Postmaster-General's Department to The Secretary, Department of Shipping and Transport, April 1952. National Archives, Brisbane, Queensland BP250/1, 11A.
4. Information regarding Laurie 'The Admiral' Thomson, was obtained from James 'Lofty' Hayes, Head Lightkeeper of Bustard Head 1958–66 and author of the manuscript "A Goat Around Capricorn", which describes his family's life in the Commonwealth Lighthouse Service.

Chapter 12
1. *Bundaberg News-Mail*, 6 June 1956. State Library of Queensland.
2. Taken from the manuscript "A Goat around Capricorn" written by James 'Lofty' Hayes, Head Lightkeeper of Bustard Head 1958–66. Lofty kindly gave me his permission to use the story in this book.

Chapter 13
1. Correspondence from New Powerhouse files. National Archives, Brisbane, Queensland BP881/1, SM298 and J344/13, QA1966/920C/1.
2. Correspondence from Fuel Storage files. National Archives, Brisbane, Queensland BP881/1, SM309 and J344/13, QA67/1427C.
3. *Australian Sea Spray Annual*, Volume 5, "When Emily Screamed". *The Courier-Mail*, 3 and 4 April 1972. *Telegraph*, 1, 3 and 5 April 1972. *The Observer*, Gladstone, 4 and 7 April 1972. Entries in the Bustard Head lightstation logbook, 1 and 2 April 1972, National Archives, Brisbane, Queensland, J2826/2. Interview with Head Lightkeeper Jack Atherton and his wife Babs, who were stationed at Bustard Head during cyclone Emily in April 1972.
4. Inquest of Ronald Rawson Kelley and Kenneth Stewart Murchison, Coroner's Section, Department of Justice, Brisbane, Queensland. Information kindly supplied by Ron and Betty Kelley, parents of Ronald Rawson Kelley. *Bundaberg News-Mail*, 26 and 27 June 1972. *The Observer*, Gladstone, 27 June 1972. *The Courier-Mail*, 26 June 1972. Information from Head Lightkeeper Jack Atherton and his wife Babs, who were stationed at Bustard Head at the time of the fisheries inspectors' disappearance.
5. *The Courier-Mail*, 10 July 1972. *Australian Post Office News*, No.4, September 1972. Information from Head Lightkeeper Jack Atherton and his wife Babs, who were stationed at Bustard Head at the time of this incident.

Chapter 14

1. The Report from the House of Representatives Standing Committee on Expenditure *Lighthouses: Do we keep the keepers?* December 1983, stated that by demanning Bustard Head lightstation there would be an annual saving of $125,000. However, that estimate was grossly inflated because of the North Reef computer link. If compared to other lightstations in the area such as Cape Capricorn, Sandy Cape and Lady Elliot Island, the annual saving would reduce to $69,000.

2. Information in this chapter from entries in the Bustard Head lightstation logbooks, National Archives, Brisbane, Queensland, J2826/2, and from the author's experience while stationed at Bustard Head.

3. Part of a letter written by Kevin Urban, Bustard Head's last Head Lightkeeper. Kevin kindly gave permission for the letter to be published in this book.

APPENDICES

APPENDIX 1

General Instructions to Keepers
(Circa 1870)

In the use of the lamp belonging to a Lighthouse Apparatus, the Keepers are especially enjoined to bear in mind that, unless its full power and development are obtained, the value of the Apparatus itself is in a large measure lost, and that the latter is entirely dependent on the former to enable it to do its part of their united duties.

To obtain this end, the Lamp should develop a flame as shewn on the annexed full-sized diagram (author's note: Unfortunately, the diagram was not attached to the Instructions); and this can be readily obtained by attention to the principles which regulate its production, and by unceasing watchfulness during the time of its exhibition.

There are two chief components by which the flame is produced, viz., the Wicks and the Oil, but they must be associated with a due supply of atmospheric air, without which there could be no proper combustion; and hence the necessity of sufficient draught.

Of these two components, neither of which could be of use without the other, the Keepers are especially enjoined to observe that the Wicks are simply the medium of conveyance to the Oil, and that the consumption of the former should be as much as possible avoided.

The principal features, therefore, to be observed are —

1st   That the substance to be consumed is not the Wick but the Oil.

2nd   That the Oil, when brought into use, should be pure, free from sediment, and in a state to assist the proper action of the Wick.

3rd   That to do this it should be supplied abundantly to the flame, so as to obviate the charring of the Wicks (the invariable cause of low flames) and constant trimming.

The best way to carry out these requirements with vegetable Oils will be found in adjusting the Wicks to the height of ¼ to ⅜ inch above the edge of the burner-tips and supplying them with Oil, overflowing the burner-tips in the proportion of about six times the consumption. The average temperature of the Oil overflowing should be 70 degrees Fahrenheit, which is to be ascertained by dipping a Thermometer in it. With the single-wick fountain Lamp, in which the Oil does not overflow the burner-tips, the level of the surface of the Oil is to be maintained at about ⅜ inch below the level of the edge of the burner-tips.

In preparing the Wicks, the Keepers are to see that they are dry, and fit perfectly between the tips of their respective Tubes, without crease or fold; — that when already in use, the hard part caused by the charring of the previous night be carefully removed, and that they are cut perfectly smooth and level.

When burning mineral Oils, the Wicks should be adjusted to the height of about ¹⁄₁₆ inch above the edge of the burner-tips; and the level of the surface of the Oil in the burner should be carefully maintained at about 1¼ inch below the level of the burner-tips. After the first burning with Mineral Oil, the Wicks should not be trimmed with scissors; a better flame will be obtained by brushing off the charred part of the Wick with a small brush or a piece of flannel. If in doing so the cross threads of the Wick unravel, the projecting threads may be removed by the scissors. Great care is to be taken to keep the burner-tips, tubes, and air-spaces perfectly clean.

At Lighting time the Wicks should be lit as simultaneously as possible, the Throttle Valve being opened, so that the overflow may commence at a rate commensurate with the flame. The Glass Cylinder should then be placed on its Gallery with its shoulder as nearly as possible in the position shown on the annexed diagram, and connected with the Smoke Tube. They will form together a continuous Chimney and have then an important duty to perform, as by their means the draught is regulated. This is done by the action of the Damper, partially closing which will increase the volume of the flame, but will give it a red tint, and cause it soon to smoke. Partially opening the Damper will reduce the flame, but increase its intensity and render it whiter.

The Flame should be increased carefully during the first half-hour after Lighting, while the Burner is being heated to its proper temperature, and the Wicks, at first very low, are being gradually raised to their proper height above the edge of the Burner. At the end of that time, or when the Wicks and Flame are at their full development, slight adjustments only of the Damper will be required for the remainder of the period of burning. *The Keepers are enjoined to pay the utmost attention to the least alteration of the Flame, which should be met by a corresponding use of the Damper; and it is only by unremitting attention to this point that the Flame can be maintained in its full power, the Wicks kept from charring, and from the consequent necessity of Trimming (which should not be requisite during the longest night).* As a rule, the Wicks should scarcely be touched after attaining their proper height, for, although raising them will for a short time raise the Flame, it will soon decrease again, they will become Carbonized, and the Capillary Action will be lost.

There are some other points which the Keepers must also bear in mind: first, the Lamp and the Apparatus must be in perfect accord. To effect this, and to insure the Light proceeding from the Flame being properly directed, the Lamp itself must be accurately placed — that is, the axis or centre of the Burner must be exactly in the axis or centre of the Apparatus; — secondly, the upper part of the Burner must be perfectly level, and in the position indicated by the cross lines attached to the inside of the lens, whose bisection also marks the true centre.

When out of adjustment the Lamp can be easily re-adjusted by the means at the Keeper's command, and in the use of which they are instructed in the course of their training.

The Keepers are to ascertain carefully the quantity of Oil consumed nightly by measuring the Oil into the Lamp when filling it in the morning; and by drawing off and re-measuring the quantity remaining after the Light is extinguished. By this means the exact quantity consumed will be ascertained: the unconsumed Oil is to be filtered before it is replaced in the Lamp, and the deficiency filled up with fresh Oil.

The Keepers are also to change the Burner of the Lamp on the first day of every month, to ensure that each spare Burner shall be kept in a proper state of efficiency.

The accompanying full-sized Diagram of the Flame, as required to be maintained, together with a copy of these Instructions, are to be hung up in the Light Room.

APPENDIX 2

NOTICE TO MARINERS
4TH DECEMBER, 1872
ALTERATION AND ADDITION TO LIGHT AT BUSTARD HEAD

After this date, the light on Bustard Head will, during the fixed light, shew red through an arc of 5°; the outer Rock, off the Head, lying in the centre of the arc, on a bearing of N.5°E.

The light will also shew red to the westward of W.N.W., until shut in with the high land at the back of Point Richards.

Two additional small white lights, placed to the south-eastward of the Lighthouse, will also be exhibited, which, when in the same plane, and in line, will point to the outer rock.

When vessels, passing the headland, enter the red light, they will know that the outer rock is coming into line with the Lighthouse, — when the back light is seen, just clear of, and over the nearer of the two small lights, that they are outside the rock, — and when they again enter the white light, that they are past the immediate neighborhood of the danger.

Vessels bound to Port Curtis from the southward, or working along the coast between Bustard and Gatcombe Heads, will be clear of the outlying rocks off Rodd's Peninsula, and of the East Banks at the entrance to Port Curtis, while Bustard Head light is seen as a white light. From an E.S.E bearing eastwards, Bustard Head light will be seen as a red light, showing a too near approach to the shore.

In fine weather, when the light can be seen at that distance, vessels entering Port Curtis from the southward by the north channel, should be careful not to open out the Bustard Head fixed light as a red light, until the Gatcombe Head light shows red, and is steered for on a W.S.W. bearing. Similarly, on leaving the port, vessels bound southwards should not keep away until the Bustard Head fixed light is changed from red to white.

G.P. HEATH, Commander R.N.,
Portmaster.

Department of Ports and Harbors,
Brisbane, 4th December, 1872.

APPENDIX 3

NOTICE TO MARINERS
28TH MARCH, 1876
SMALL LIGHT AT BUSTARD HEAD

On and after the 3rd proximo, the two small leading lights which point out the position of the Outer Rock off Bustard Head will cease to be exhibited. On and after that date the too near approach of vessels to the Rock will be shown by a single light exhibited from a square tower, 18 feet high, placed 500 yards S.E. by S. from the principal light, and 280 feet above high water level.

Between the bearings of S. by E. ¾ E. and S.W. ¾ S. the light will be of the 5th order, though the direct flame of the lamp may be also seen as far southwards as a S.W. by W. ½ W. bearing, and also from the westward between the bearings of S.E. and E.S.E.

The light is so shut off by a screen as to be obscured between the bearings of S.S.W. and S. by E. to a distance, at half tide, of 1 mile outside the rock — the northern line of eclipse running in a W. by N. ½ N. direction. If, therefore, a vessel while passing the headland shuts out this light between the bearings of S. by E. ¾ E. and S.W. ¾ S., and before the beam of red light from the principal lighthouse is passed, she will be approaching the danger too closely and should at once haul out and open the light.

As the plane of the eclipsed light passes about 50 feet above the top of the Rock, the greater the height of the eye above the water level, the proportionately nearer will a vessel approach the danger before she shuts out the light.

G.P. HEATH, Commander R.N.,
Portmaster.

Department of Ports and Harbors,
Brisbane, 28th March, 1876.

APPENDIX 4

SAILING DIRECTIONS FROM
PUGH'S ALMANAC 1882

BUSTARD HEAD LIGHT

This light is exhibited from an iron tower 58 feet high, painted stone colour, standing on the south-east headland of Bustard Head, at an elevation of 320 feet above the level of the sea. It is a dioptric white light of the second order — fixed, varied by flashes. It is seen as a fixed light during every alternate minute; and a bright flash, preceded and followed by a short eclipse, occupying the intermediate minutes. The fixed light shows red through an arc of about 5°, the centre of which is in a line with the outer rock, which lies 3 miles N. 5° E. from the lighthouse. It also shows red from W.N.W. westward until shut in with the high land of Rodd's Peninsula. Outside the line of this red light, vessels are clear of the East Banks, Port Curtis, and all dangers off the shore of Rodd's Peninsula. To further protect vessels from the danger of running on the rocks lying off Bustard Head, the too near approach of vessels to the outer rock is shown by a single light exhibited from a square tower, 18 feet high, placed 500 yards S.E. by S. from the principal light, and 280 feet above high water level.

Between the bearings of S. by E. ¾ E. and S.W. ¾ S. the light is of the fifth order, though the light may be also seen as far southwards as a West bearing, and also from the westward between the bearings of S.E. and E.S.E.

The light is so shut off by a screen as to be obscured between the bearings of S.S.W. and S. by E. to a distance, at high tide, of one mile outside the rock — the northern line of the eclipse running in a W. by N. ½ N. direction. If, therefore, a vessel while passing the headland shuts out this light between the bearings of S. by E. ¾ E. and S.W. ¾ S., and before the beam of red light from the principal lighthouse is passed, she will be approaching the danger too closely, and should at once haul out and open the light.

Between the bearings of S. by E. ¾ E. and S.E. where the 5th order light is obscured by the land, the deficiency is made good by a second light placed 160 yards W.N.W. of the main light, and 276 feet above the sea level, and which is shut off by a screen when a vessel approaches the shore too closely in the same way as the 5th order light, with a view to draw a vessel's attention to her approach to the outlying rocks off the Head. Three warning screens are placed beyond the limits of the main screen. The first of these would give a warning when a vessel, approaching from the southward, was within some 1,250 yards of the second or easternmost rock. The other warnings being given at intervals of about 150 yards. The warning screens eclipse the light at short intervals. As the plane of the eclipse light passes about 60 feet above the top of the Rock, the greater the height of the eye above the water level, the proportionately nearer will a vessel approach the danger before she shuts out the light.

When the arc of red light is passed, and the white light again opened, vessels will be past the immediate neighbourhood of the danger. The outer rock is steep-to within a reasonable distance, but three other patches of rock lie between it and the shore. Bustard Head light is visible about 23 miles, so that under ordinary conditions of the atmosphere, vessels will be clear of Masthead Island and its outlying reef while the light is in sight. But as, after warm days, there may be an unusual amount of refraction, vessels when approaching the limits of the range of the light northwards should be careful not to bring it to southward of S.S.E. ¼ E.

APPENDIX 5

NOTICE TO MARINERS

No. 23 OF 1892

STORM SIGNALS — QUEENSLAND COAST

Notice is hereby given that, after the 12th January, 1893, storm signals will be made from the following stations when bad weather is anticipated, viz. :—

Cape Moreton, Sandy Cape, Bustard Head, Cape Capricorn, Flat-top Island, Cape Bowling Green, Cape Cleveland, Port Douglas, Cooktown, Thursday Island and Karumba.

The Cone, with point downwards, means that strong winds are probable from S.S.W. or S., by S.E., to E. or E.N.E.

A ball under the Cone (cone point downwards) means that strong winds are probable from W.N.W. or W., by S.W., to S. or S.S.E.

The Cone, with point upwards, means that strong winds are probable from N.N.W. or N., by N.E., to E. or E.S.E.

A ball under the Cone (cone point upwards) means that strong winds are probable from N.N.E. or N., by N.W., to W. or W.S.W.

Storm signals will be made from the quarters of the yard-arm, and the balls and cones will be of large size, and must not be mistaken for tide signals, which will be made from the yard-arm.

T.M. ALMOND,
Portmaster.

Department of Ports and Harbours,
Brisbane, 22nd December, 1892.

APPENDIX 6

AUSTRALIA PILOT VOLUME 1V
FIRST EDITION 1917

BUSTARD HEAD *(Lat. 24° 01′ S., Long. 151° 47′ E.)* is a double, flat-topped point of moderate height; detached rocks extend 2½ miles northward from the head.

If bound for Port Curtis and requiring a pilot, the signal should be made off this head, as sometimes the pilot is there.

SIGNAL STATION — On Bustard Head is a signal, telegraph, and storm signal station. Vessels can communicate by the Commercial code. Signals are forwarded to any part of the Australian Commonwealth.

OUTER ROCK, 2 feet high, lies 14° true nearly 2½ miles from Bustard Head, and is steep-to. Outer Rock is covered by a *red* sector from Bustard Head light. Middle Rocks are two patches awash at high water 1¼ miles 20° true from the head. Inner Rock is 2 cables off the head, and also awash at high water. Between Outer and Middle Rocks, half a mile apart, there are depths of from 11 to 16 fathoms; and between Middle and Inner Rocks 6 to 9 fathoms will be found.

LIGHTS *(Lat. 24° 01′ S., Long. 151° 47′ E.)* — A light, 320 feet in height above high water, is shown from a white circular tower, 58 feet high, with a red dome, on the south-eastern part of Bustard Head.

Also from a white square tower, 18 feet high, 500 yards south-east from the lighthouse, an auxiliary light is shown at 280 feet above high water.

Where the above light is obscured by the land, the deficiency is made good by a second light 160 yards north-westward of the main light; the light is screened off when approaching the rocks off the head, and the plane of the light passes 60 feet above the top of Outer Rock.

Therefore, when passing Bustard Head, these auxiliary lights must be kept in sight until past the ray of *red* light from the main lighthouse.

TIDAL STREAMS — Off Bustard Head the flood stream runs to the north-westward and the ebb to the south-eastward.

PANCAKE CREEK, immediately westward of the north-western point of Bustard Head, affords good shelter to small vessels from all but north-westerly winds. The entrance is narrow, with a depth of from 2 to 3 fathoms.

The western side of the entrance channel is formed by Shelter Spit, of sand, and the limits can be easily seen. Ledges of rock which cover at two-thirds flood, lie 2 cables off-shore, on the east side.

Two white beacons on Shelter Spit, in line, lead in mid-channel in not less than 10 feet. The anchorage is in 2 to 2½ fathoms, a little eastward of the line of leading beacons, with the boathouse 122° true.

Approaching from westward, Bustard Head lighthouse must be kept open of the north-west point, to clear Shelter Spit and Jansen Rock, until the beacons are in line.

At high spring tides Pancake Creek is connected with Jenny Lind Creek on the south side of Bustard Head. The flood and ebb streams run through Pancake Creek from 1½ to 2 knots.

Fresh water can always be obtained at the back of the beach, abreast the anchorage. There is a good road to the lighthouse from the boathouse.

APPENDIX 7

NOTICE TO MARINERS
COMMONWEALTH OF AUSTRALIA
1917. *No. 8*

The Astronomical positions are only approximate unless seconds are given. The bearings are given both True and Magnetic, and those relating to lights are from seaward. The visibility of lights is that in clear weather. Fog signals are sounded only in thick or foggy weather. The heights given are heights of focal plane above high water.

AUSTRALIA — EAST COAST

BUSTARD HEAD LIGHT — INTENDED ALTERATION IN CHARACTERISTICS

Mariners and others are hereby notified that the power of the Fixed and Flashing Light on Bustard Head will be increased, and that the length of the flash will be reduced to 9 seconds on or about 15th May, 1917.

Position: Lat. 24° 01′ S.; Long. 151° 47′ E.
Character: Fixed and Flashing with White and Red Sectors, thus:—

Fixed	Eclipse	Flash	Eclipse
60 secs.	25½ secs.	9 secs.	25½ secs.

Power: White fixed, 20,000 candles. White flashing, 120,000 candles.
Note: The other details of the Light will remain unchanged.
Remarks: No further notice will be given.
Publications Affected:
　　　　　Admiralty List of Lights and Time Signals, Part VI., 1917.

By Direction:
STEPHEN MILLS, Comptroller-General of Customs.
JOSHUA F. RAMSBOTHAM, Director of Lighthouses.

Department of Trade and Customs,
Melbourne, 13th February, 1917.

APPENDICES 8 & 9

NOTICE TO MARINERS
COMMONWEALTH OF AUSTRALIA
LIGHTHOUSE SERVICE
1935. No.8

Astronomical positions are approximate unless seconds are given. Bearings are True and in degrees from 000° (North) to 359° measured clockwise, and those relating to lights are from seaward. Visibility of lights is that in clear weather. Fog signals are sounded only during thick or foggy weather. Elevation given is the height of focal plane above mean H.W. springs.

AUSTRALIA — EAST COAST — CURTIS CHANNEL

BUSTARD HEAD — ALTERATION IN LIGHTS
NEW LIGHT ESTABLISHED

Mariners and others are hereby notified that the Fixed and Flashing Light with White and Red Sectors was altered on 26th June 1935, and that the two Fixed Lights were replaced by a Flashing Light with White and Red Sectors on 28th June, 1935.

Previous Notice — No.2 of 1935.

(1) MAIN LIGHT

Position — On the south-eastern part of Bustard Head. Lat. 24° 02′ S., Long. 151° 46′ E., on Admiralty Chart No.345.

Alterations —

> *Character* — The fixed and flashing light with white and red sectors is replaced by a *group flashing white light* showing *two flashes every ten seconds*, thus:—

Flash	Eclipse	Flash	Eclipse
0.3 sec.	2.7 secs.	0.3 sec.	6.7 secs.

> A *fixed red* light having two arcs of visibility from the high land near Richards Point to 118° and from 188° to 220° is exhibited from the same lantern as the above group flashing white light.

241

Power — The power of the white light is increased from 31,000 and 191,000 candles to 560,000 candles. The power of the red light is 16,000 candles.

Visibility — The range of the white light remains unaltered, whilst that of the red light is 20 miles.

Note — In other respects the light remains unaltered.

(2) AUXILIARY LIGHT (U)

The auxiliary Fixed White Lights shown near (1) above were discontinued on 28th June, 1935, and an auxiliary Flashing Light with White and Red Sectors was established near the northern extremity of Bustard Head.

Position — Lat. 24° 01′ S., Long. 151° 45′ E., on Admiralty Chart No.345. Near the northern extremity of Bustard Head, 16.6 cables 313° 26′ from (1) above.

Character — *Flashing every second* with *white* and *red* sectors, thus:—

Flash.	Eclipse.
0.2 sec.	0.8 sec.

Sectors — *White* from 118° to 212°, *red* thence to 242°, *white* thence to 320°, obscured elsewhere.

Elevation — 131 feet.

Power — White, 1,000 candles. Red, 400 candles.

Visibility — White, 14 miles. Red, 11 miles.

Structure — Red steel framework tower, 25 feet in height.

Note — The light is unwatched.

Remarks — The coastline shown on Admiralty Chart No.345 at the site of (2) above is approximately 0.4 cable north-east of its charted position.

Charts affected —
Admiralty Chart No.345 — Sandy Cape to Keppel Isles.
Admiralty Chart No.2763 — Coral Sea and Great Barrier Reefs, Sheet 1.
Admiralty Chart No.2759a — Australia, Northern Portion.
Admiralty Chart No.2759b — Australia, Southern Portion.
Admiralty Chart No.780 — Pacific Ocean, South-West Sheet.

Publications affected —
Admiralty List of Lights, Part VI., 1933, Nos.3003, 3004, and 3005.
Australia Pilot, Vol. IV., Second Edition, 1928, page 37.
Sailing Directions and other information for the Ports and Harbors
of Queensland, 1934, page 31.

By direction,
LEWIS F. EAST,
Secretary, Marine Branch.